THE STORY OF JESUS

C.J. LOVIK

www.lighthouse.pub

Visit our website to purchase books and preview upcoming titles.

Contact us at:
feedback@lighthouse.pub

Copyright © 2020, C.J. LOVIK
All rights reserved

Cover Design and Interior Layout by Sergio E. León

Sergio was born and raised in Mexico City, where he studied Design and Arts in the National Autonomous University of Mexico (UNAM). For more than 20 years, Sergio has worked in a variety of positions, primarily acting as Art and Design Director for major brands and publications. Today, Sergio is the Art and Design Director for Lighthouse Gospel Beacon, where he is responsible for all digital and print media. Every day, Sergio is growing in Christ while continuing to produce art and media to help illustrate the love of the Savior. Sergio is married to his wonderful wife, Monica, and they have two amazing children.

TABLE OF CONTENTS

INTRODUCTION .... A

MEET THE BIOGRAPHERS .... B

THE STORY OF JESUS

CHAPTER ONE
CHRIST'S LIFE PRIOR TO HIS MINISTRY 1

CHAPTER TWO
THE MINISTRY OF JOHN THE BAPTIST 33

CHAPTER THREE
BEGINNING OF JESUS' MINISTRY 43

CHAPTER FOUR
FIRST TO THE SECOND PASSOVER 55

CHAPTER FIVE
SECOND PASSOVER TO THE THIRD 79

CHAPTER SIX
THIRD PASSOVER UNTIL JESUS' ARRIVAL AT BETHANY 145

CHAPTER SEVEN
LAST WEEK OF JESUS' MINISTRY 217

CHAPTER EIGHT
RESURRECTION OF JESUS 283

OUR INVITATION 296

INTRODUCTION

◇◇◇

Welcome to the Most Amazing True Story Ever Told

The story of the life of Jesus, as told by four separate biographers, weaves together a harmonized story that accurately portrays the life of Jesus Christ.

The harmonized account verifies the miracle of the four separate accounts, as they each stand without contradiction or discrepancy.

The story combines the richness of the four biographies written by Matthew, Mark, Luke, and John. The harmonized account allows the careful reader to marvel at the truthfulness of the testimonies of the four Gospel writers.

The central personality of the story is, of course, Jesus Christ.

We invite you to read this story with a desire to glimpse the revelation of God as he deliberately and graciously reveals himself in ways that invite you to respond to Him in faith and trust.

We believe that the single most important miracle today is that God actually "contemporizes" Himself as his Word is read. And based on this conviction we would invite you to find a copy of the Holy Bible and read the "miracle" accounts written by Matthew, Mark, Luke and John.

In the meantime - we invite you to read the greatest Story ever told!

THE STORY OF JESUS

MEET THE BIOGRAPHERS

Before you start the story, take a moment as we introduce to you the four biographers whose accounts we are using to tell the harmonized version of the Story of Jesus.

As the first year of Jesus' public ministry came to a close, the time was right for him to choose his final disciple. Jesus had spent much of his time in Judea, by the Jordan River where John the Baptist was preaching the message that people should turn away from their sins and be baptized to show that they had changed their hearts. Soldiers sent from King Herod arrested and imprisoned John. After this had happened, Jesus went to a region in Galilee called Capernaum where he healed the sick and diseased, cast out demons, and performed many other miraculous works. As Jesus was walking along the Galilean seashore and teaching those who kept coming up to be with him, he saw a tax collector sitting in his office. Jesus went up to him and said, "Follow me." The tax collector's name was Matthew (also called Levi), and as soon as Jesus called him, he immediately left all his business behind and followed Jesus.

Later, Matthew celebrated his new friendship by having a large celebration for Jesus at his home. The other disciples joined Jesus along with Matthew's friends and acquaintances, which included a large number of tax collectors and other people of low reputation. When the religious leaders (Pharisees and teachers) saw Jesus eating and drinking with tax collectors and other outcasts of society, they criticized Jesus and his disciples by asking, "Why do you eat and drink with tax collectors and sinners?"

When Jesus heard what they were saying, he replied, "It isn't people who are well who need a doctor, but those who are sick."

Jesus went on to say, "I haven't come to call the righteous; I have come to call sinners to repentance."

This incident in the story of Jesus is recorded in the book that Matthew wrote.

One day Jesus left his hometown of Nazareth and went to the Jordan River where John the Baptist was busy preaching that the Kingdom of Heaven was at hand and that men needed to repent and be baptized. When Jesus asked John to baptize him, John objected, by saying, "I am the one who needs to be baptized by you."

Jesus reassured John that this is something he needed to do as a part of what God had already planned. John then agreed to baptize Jesus. As Jesus came out of the water, the Holy Spirit in the form of a dove came down from heaven and rested on Jesus. At the same time a voice thundered from heaven and said, "This is my beloved Son in whom I am well pleased."

The very next day, Jesus passed by John the Baptist and two of John's disciples. John, seeing Jesus, proclaimed, "Behold the Lamb of God who takes away the sin of the world."

John's two disciples, hearing this, began to follow Jesus. Jesus, seeing them, followed and asked them, "What are you looking for?" "Teacher," they replied, "Where are you staying?" Jesus answered, "Come and see."

Teacher, they replied:

- *Where are you staying?*

Jesus answered:

- *Come and see.*

MEET THE BIOGRAPHERS

The two men followed Jesus and spent the rest of the day with him. One of the men was a fisherman named Andrew. After spending just a short time with Jesus, Andrew became convinced that Jesus was the long-awaited Messiah. He went and found his brother Simon and brought him to Jesus. As soon as Jesus met Simon he looked at him with intensity and spoke, "You are Simon, the son of John? You shall be called Peter."

Peter, whose name means "stone," became one of the most ardent disciples of Jesus and a personal witness to Jesus' miracles and his teachings. Peter became one of the leaders of the first Christian church in Jerusalem after Jesus' death and resurrection. It was during that time that Peter became connected with a man named John Mark (simply known as Mark). Mark became Peter's personal secretary. Mark wrote the story of Jesus that is called the Gospel of Mark. Most biblical scholars agree that Peter was the authoritative source of Mark's account. Mark was not one of the 12 disciples, but he was an eyewitness to many of the events surrounding Jesus' life and was part of the wider circle of Jesus' followers. The Gospel of Mark is the second source that we will use to tell the harmonized story of Jesus.

THE STORY OF JESUS

Luke was a Greek physician. He did not witness the life of Jesus personally, but he did carefully compile everything he could learn about Jesus and his ministry from those who witnessed the life and ministry of Jesus Christ. Luke watched the growth of the Church and the miracles of the Holy Spirit that attended that growth. He was a friend and companion of Paul, the apostle. Each of the four "good news" accounts of Jesus was either written by men who knew and walked with Jesus, or were accounts based on personal, firsthand testimonies of men who heard Jesus teach, witnessed his works and testified to the truthfulness of what they saw.

One day a fisherman named John was mending his nets by the Sea of Galilee when Jesus came by and called John to follow him. John left his fishing nets and for the next three years followed Jesus. During that time, he became one of Jesus' closest companions. He listened to what Jesus said and saw most of the miracles that Jesus made happen. It was during this time that John became convinced that Jesus was not just a man - but God. John is the fourth and final source we will use to tell the "harmonized" story of Jesus.

THE RIVER JORDAN NEAR THE SEA OF GALILEE

CHAPTER ONE

CHRIST'S LIFE PRIOR TO HIS MINISTRY

JOHN'S INTRODUCTION

The story of Jesus begins before he was born.

How can this be, you ask?

The answer to this question is one of the most important and profound disclosures ever made to humanity. John the fisherman, and follower of Jesus put it this way:

In the very beginning, before anything else existed, the Word (Jesus) existed. The Word was with God and the Word was God. All things were made by him. He was the creator of all things.

BIRTH OF JOHN THE BAPTIST

Herod† was king of **Judea**† from around 40 B.C. to 1 B.C. It was during this time that a Jewish **priest**† named Zacharias and his wife, Elizabeth, had a child. What made this birth special was the fact that both Zacharias and Elizabeth were very old. This child was Elizabeth's first.

What made this birth even more extraordinary was the fact that the birth was foretold to Zacharias, by an **angel**† of the Lord, **Gabriel**†.

The angel not only foretold the birth of John the Baptist, he also **prophesied**† that John was going to be the forerunner to the **Messiah**† in the spirit and power of the ancient prophet **Elijah**†.

Excavation site of Herod's desert fortress near Bethlehem

† Further reading available at the end of this chapter.

THE STORY OF JESUS

ANNOUNCEMENT TO MARY

When Elizabeth was six months pregnant with John, the angel Gabriel was sent from God to **Nazareth**†, a city in **Galilee**†.

Gabriel visited a virgin who was engaged to be married to a man named Joseph. The virgin's name was Mary.

Gabriel came to Mary and said:

You are highly favored, the Lord is with you.

But Mary was greatly troubled by this greeting, and wondered what it meant.

The **angel**† told her not to fear and repeated that she had found favor with God.

Then Gabriel told Mary that she would conceive a son and that she was to call his name Jesus.

Gabriel continued:

He shall be great, and shall be called the son of the most high.

*And the Lord God shall give unto him the throne of his father **David**†. And he shall reign over the house of **Jacob**† and of his kingdom there shall be no end.*

Mary asked the angel:

How shall this be, seeing I have never had a physical relationship with a man?

Modern Nazareth

† Further reading available at the end of this chapter.

The angel answered and said to her:

*The **Holy Spirit**† will come upon you, and the power of the most high will overshadow you, and the holy thing which is begotten shall be called the Son of God.*

And take notice: Elizabeth your cousin has also conceived a son in her old age and is now six months pregnant.

No word from God shall be proclaimed without power.

Then Mary said:

Behold, the handmaid of the Lord; let it happen to me according to your word.

The angel left.

MARY VISITS ELIZABETH

A week later, Mary went hurriedly to the hill country, into a city in Judea. She went into the house of Zacharias and greeted Elizabeth. When Elizabeth heard Mary's greeting, the baby inside her leaped in her womb and Elizabeth was filled with the Holy Spirit.

She lifted up her voice with a loud cry and said:

Blessed are you among women, and blessed is the fruit of your womb. Why am I so honored that the mother of my Lord should visit me?

Mary then began to magnify the Lord and to rejoice in God her savior.

Mary stayed with her cousin Elizabeth for three months.

THE BIRTH OF JOHN THE BAPTIST

When Elizabeth's time came, she delivered a boy and they called him John, as the angel had directed.

John's father had been struck dumb by the angel Gabriel because he had doubted the message regarding the birth of John. Once John was born, his tongue was loosed, and he blessed God and was filled with the Holy Spirit.

Zacharias said:

Blessed be the Lord, the God of Israel; for he has come back to redeem his people. And he has raised up a horn of salvation for us in the house of his servant David.

† Further reading available at the end of this chapter.

THE STORY OF JESUS

And this child will be called a prophet of the most high; he will go before the face of the Lord and make ready his ways, to give the knowledge of salvation to his people, to shine upon those that sit in darkness.

John grew up and became strong in spirit. He lived in the desert until the day his ministry began, which was when he began to declare that the Messiah was coming.

ANNOUNCEMENT TO JOSEPH

The birth of Jesus **Christ**† came about in this way. His mother, Mary, was engaged to Joseph. Before their marriage was consummated by having physical relations, Mary was found to be with child from the Holy Spirit.

Joseph, being the kind of man who would not stain his family name, but also not wanting to put Mary to shame in public had decided to divorce her as quietly as he could. While Joseph was thinking about the best way to do this, he was visited by an angel of the Lord in a dream.

Sunset over Bethlehem

The angel said:

Joseph, son of David, don't be afraid to take Mary as your wife, for that which is conceived in her is of the Holy Spirit. Mary will have a son, and you will call his name Jesus, the one we have been waiting for to save his people from their sins.

These are the events that the prophet **Isaiah**† *had spoken about when he said:*

> *Behold, a virgin shall be with child, and she will have a son and they will call him Immanuel, which means, God with us.*

Joseph woke up from his sleep and did as the angel of the Lord commanded him. He took Mary as his wife, but he had no physical relations with her until after Jesus was born.

A valley in Galilee

† Further reading available at the end of this chapter.

THE BIRTH OF JESUS

It was during this time that a decree was sent out from the **Roman**† emperor Caesar Augustus that there should be a census for the entire world. People were told to return to their cities.

Mary and Joseph went up from Galilee out of Nazareth, the city of David's family.

Mary was ready to give birth, which she did in **Bethlehem**†. Mary delivered her first-born son and wrapped the baby Jesus up in swaddling clothes and laid him in a manger because there was no room for them in the inn.

THE SHEPHERDS TOLD OF THE BIRTH OF JESUS

Nearby there were shepherds in the fields who were working the night shift over their flocks.

An angel of the Lord stood by them, and the glory of the Lord shone all around them.

But the shepherds were very afraid, as the angel said to them:

Don't be afraid; for behold, I bring you good tidings of great joy which will be to all the people.

For today, in the city of David, a savior, who is Christ the Lord has been born. And this will be the sign: you will find the babe wrapped in swaddling clothes and lying in a manger.

Shepherd's Field near Bethlehem

Suddenly, there appeared a host of angels, all praising God and saying, Glory to God in the highest, and on earth peace among men in whom he is well pleased.

After the angels had left them and returned to heaven, the shepherds said to each other:

† Further reading available at the end of this chapter.

Let's go to Bethlehem right now and see this thing that has happened, which the Lord has made known to us.

They immediately went and found Mary, Joseph and the baby lying in the manger.

When they saw the baby Jesus, they made known what had been told about the child.

Everyone who heard it wondered about the things the shepherds reported.

But Mary kept all these sayings to herself, pondering them in her heart.

Then the shepherds returned to their fields, glorifying and praising God for all the things that they had heard and seen.

THE NAMING OF JESUS

After eight days, having fulfilled the rite of **circumcising**† the child and officially naming him Jesus, and after all the **ceremonial laws**† concerning purification were complete,

An olive tree near Bethlehem

they brought Jesus to **Jerusalem**† to present him to the Lord. This was all done according to the law of the Lord written by **Moses**†.

There was a man in Jerusalem, whose name was Simeon. He was a righteous and devout man who was looking for the era of the Messiah to be ushered in.

The Holy Spirit was upon him and had revealed to him that he would not die until he had seen the long awaited Messiah, the Lord's Christ.

Simeon had been inspired by the Spirit to go into the **temple**† at the same time Joseph and Mary brought their child into the temple in order to perform all the customs and duties that the law of **Moses**† required.

When Simeon saw Jesus, he took him into his arms and blessed God, and said:

*Now let your servant depart in peace Lord, according to your word. For I have seen with my own eyes your salvation, which you have prepared before the face of all peoples. A light of revelation to the **Gentiles**†, and the glory of your people Israel.*

Joseph and Mary were marveling at the things that Simeon was saying about the child Jesus.

† Further reading available at the end of this chapter.

Then Simeon blessed the parents of Jesus and said to Mary:

Behold, this child is going to cause the falling and the rising of many in Israel and many will resist the truth. Yes, and for a sword that shall pierce through your own soul and the thoughts of many hearts may be revealed.

At the ceremony was an old woman named Anna, a prophet of the tribe of Asher. Anna was devoted to the services of the temple and spent much of her time worshiping with **fasting**†, praying both night and day.

When she saw Jesus, she spoke to him and gave thanks to God. She pointed Jesus out to all who were looking for the redemption of Jerusalem.

After Joseph and Mary had completed all the ceremonies and fulfilled the laws required regarding their firstborn, they returned home.

WISE MEN FROM THE EAST

When Jesus was born in Bethlehem, wise men from the east came to Jerusalem.

As soon as they entered Jerusalem, they began asking:

Where is the one that has been born king of the Jews? We have seen his star in the east and are come to worship him.

When King Herod heard about this, he was troubled, as was all Jerusalem. Herod gathered the chief priests and **scribes**† of the people and asked them where the Christ would be born.

They quoted scripture that said:

And you Bethlehem, land of Judah, are by no means least among the rulers of Judah: For out of you shall come a governor, who shall be the shepherd of my people Israel.

Grotto of the Manger in Bethlehem

Herod privately called the wise men to learn the exact time the star appeared. Then he sent them to Bethlehem to go and find out all they could about the young child. He told them that when they found him they should bring all the information to him so that he could he could worship the child.

† Further reading available at the end of this chapter.

The wise men listened to what Herod said and went their way. The star, which they saw in the east, went before them until it stood over where the young child was. When they saw that the star had guided them to the right spot, they rejoiced.

The wise men came into the house that the star had directed them to, and saw the young child with Mary. They fell down and worshipped him and opened up their treasures and offered him gifts of gold and frankincense and **myrrh**†.

And being warned by God in a dream that they should not return to Herod, they returned to their own country by a different route.

After the wise men had left, an angel appeared to Joseph in a dream, saying:

*Get up and take the young child and his mother, and flee to **Egypt**†. You will stay in Egypt until I tell you to return: Herod is going to search for the child in order to destroy him.*

Desert between Bethlehem and Egypt

FLIGHT INTO EGYPT

Joseph got up and took the child and his mother to Egypt that night. They stayed in Egypt until the death of Herod.

This happened in order to fulfill the word spoken by the Lord through his prophets, saying:

Out of Egypt did I call my son.

When Herod realized that he had been mocked by the wise men, he went into a rage and sent out his soldiers to kill all the male children in Bethlehem and the surrounding area who were two years old or younger.

This fulfilled the prophecy that was spoken through **Jeremiah**†, who said:

A voice was heard in Ramah. Weeping and great mourning, Rachel weeping for her children.

---

† Further reading available at the end of this chapter.

Desert caravan in the Negev

The ones that wanted to take the young child's life are dead.

Joseph did as the Lord commanded, left Egypt and came back into the land of Israel.

And she would not be comforted because they are no more.

OUT OF EGYPT

But when Herod was dead, an angel of the Lord appeared to Joseph in a dream saying:

Get up and take the young child and his mother, and go into the land of Israel.

But when Joseph heard that Archelaus, the son of Herod, was ruling over Judea, he became afraid. And being warned by God in a dream, he withdrew from Judea and went to Galilee where he settled in Nazareth.

This fulfilled the prophecy that said that the Messiah would be called a Nazarene.

The child grew and increased in strength. He was filled with wisdom. The grace of God was upon him.

THE BOY JESUS VISITS JERUSALEM

Every year Joseph and Mary went to Jerusalem to celebrate the feast of the **Passover**†. When Jesus was 12 years old, he went up to Jerusalem with his parents to celebrate the custom of the feast.

† Further reading available at the end of this chapter.

THE STORY OF JESUS

After the celebration, Mary and Joseph went home, thinking Jesus was in the crowd that was returning to Nazareth. But Jesus stayed behind in Jerusalem. One day passed, and Jesus' parents realized, after searching all over for Jesus, that he was not among them. They immediately returned to Jerusalem.

After three days, they found him in the temple sitting in the midst of the teachers. Jesus was listening and asking questions. Everyone who heard Jesus was amazed at his understanding and his answers.

When Mary and Joseph saw Jesus, they were astonished. Mary said to Jesus:

Why have you treated us this way? Your father and I have been worried sick looking for you everywhere.

Jesus said to them:

How is it that you were looking for me? Didn't you know that I must be in my Father's house?

Mary and Joseph did not understand what Jesus was saying to them. But they left together to return to Nazareth, as Jesus was subject to his parents.

Jesus advanced in wisdom and stature, and in favor with God and men.

Not much else is known about the life of Jesus until John the Baptist began his public ministry and Jesus bursts on the scene followed by signs, wonders and miracles.

END OF CHAPTER ONE

CHAPTER ONE
COMPANION

ANGELS (pages 1 and 2)

Angels are created beings who live in heaven and whose purpose is to be messengers of God.

In the story of Jesus, the angel Gabriel came to Mary, the mother of Jesus, to foretell Jesus' birth, and to Zacharias, the father of John the Baptist, to predict John's birth *(Luke 1: 11-39)*.

An angel also came to Joseph while he and Mary were still engaged, to reassure him that her pregnancy was a result of the Holy Spirit, and that Joseph should still marry Mary *(Matthew 1: 18-25)*.

They also appeared to the shepherds when Jesus was born *(Luke 2: 8-15)*, ministered to Jesus after he went through 40 days of being tempted by Satan *(Matthew 4: 11)*, and announced his resurrection *(Matthew 28: 1-8)*.

Some angels chose to follow Satan instead of God and became demons.

Angels are also depicted as adults, usually women, as in this painting by Dutch painter Rembrandt in which an Angel stops Abraham from sacrificing Isaac.

BETHLEHEM (page 5)

Near Jerusalem on the heights overlooking the Rift valley, at 2500 feet above sea level it is not uncommon for it to snow, allowing hot summer days but cool evenings.

Olive trees on top of a barren hill outside of Bethlehem.

CHRIST (page 4)

The Greek word that has the same meaning as the Hebrew word "Messiah." Since the New Testament was written in Greek, which was the common language of the day, the Bible records people saying, "Jesus is the Christ" when they are saying that Jesus is the Messiah.

"Messiah" is a Hebrew word referring to a descendant of King David, who would bring about peace and justice on earth. The word literally means "anointed one."

God mandated that prophets, priests and kings be anointed. Oil being poured on them, which symbolized the Holy Spirit coming on them to give them the ability and wisdom to perform their responsibilities.

When Jesus came as the Messiah, he was God in the flesh and the supreme prophet, priest and king in one person.

The Jews thought the Messiah would be a warrior-king who would establish a political kingdom with Jerusalem as the capital city. They didn't believe Jesus was the Messiah because he didn't establish a political kingdom. The Jews ignored the messianic passages written by the prophets who spoke of a suffering servant. Jesus claimed to be the Messiah but also said that his kingdom is eternal and is in peoples' hearts.

The kingdom that Jesus came to establish is more powerful than any political or military kingdom. Rome and many other political kingdoms have been conquered, but the Kingdom of God was established by Jesus' life, death and resurrection. The miracle of this kingdom is that Jesus is still alive and active in the lives of his disciples.

One day Jesus will come to earth again, but not as a servant. His next coming will be heralded by sound of trumpets announcing that King Jesus has come to rule completely and supremely over all creation.

CIRCUMCISE (page 6)

The word comes from two Greek roots meaning to "cut around," and it refers to cutting the foreskin off of a male.

God instituted circumcision with Abraham. It was to be a physical reminder of the covenant (contract or agreement) between God and

Abraham and his descendants. God's covenant with Abraham was that God would make his descendants a great nation and that God would bless the world through them.

Jesus fulfilled that covenant when he came to earth as both God and a descendant of Abraham. He lived a perfect life, died on the cross, and rose from the dead so he could establish a new covenant.

We don't rely on physical circumcision any more as a sign of God's covenant with us, because when we have faith in Jesus and put our trust in Him, He "circumcises" or changes our hearts as a sign that we belong to Him.

EGYPT (page 8)

The Greeks ruled Egypt from about 330 years before Jesus was born to about 50 years before Jesus was born.

Then the Romans ruled for about the next 400 years. Greek was the main language there because of so many years of Greek influence, and the Romans didn't try to change it to their official language of Latin.

Alexandria, the capital of Egypt, became an important center of learning and culture. Since the whole area was controlled by Rome, it was easy for Mary and Joseph to travel to Egypt from Israel.

Bedouin women cross the Sinai desert, which lies between Egypt and Israel

ELIJAH (pages 1 and 8)

Elijah was a prophet in Israel who lived about 800 years before Christ. He challenged and defeated more than 800 pagan priests in a dramatic contest in front of many people of Israel.

He was also taken to heaven in a fiery chariot, so he never died. Many people thought when they saw John the Baptist, that Elijah had returned to earth.

FASTING (page 7)

Going without food, and sometimes without food and water.

The Bible records people fasting on different occasions, usually for two reasons.

First, it was something that people would do as an act of worship to God. They would go without eating so they could devote themselves to reading scripture and praying, and by doing that, demonstrate by their actions that God was more important to them than their physical comfort.

Secondly, people would fast to help them remember that their relationship to God was even more important than eating, and sometimes also to concentrate on God and focus on knowing what God would want them to do when they had a difficult decision to make.

GABRIEL (page 1)

Gabriel is one of two angels mentioned by name in the Bible.

Angels are created beings whose purpose is to be messengers of God. He appeared to Mary to tell her that she would become pregnant and give birth to Jesus while she was still a virgin *(Luke 1: 26-38)*.

He appeared to Zacharias about 6 months before that to tell him that his wife would have a son who would be John the Baptist *(Luke 1: 11-25)*. Gabriel was also sent to Daniel *(Daniel 8: 16; 9: 21)*.

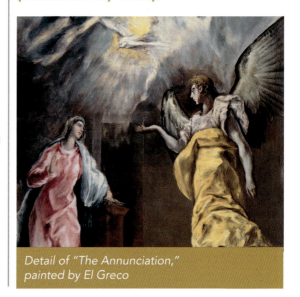

Detail of "The Annunciation," painted by El Greco

GALILEE (page 2)

Then as now, Galilee remains an agricultural region of expansive vistas. The heart of the region, the Sea of Galilee and surrounding towns, was the site of Jesus' first miracles. It was here where Jesus delivered his cornerstone sermon — the Sermon on the Mount — and attracted his following and most of his disciples.

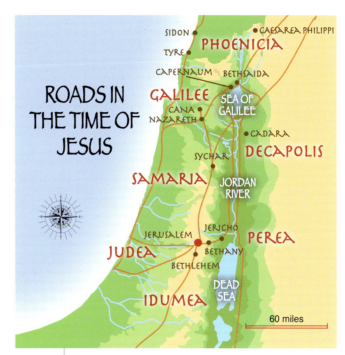

Jesus' home town of Nazareth was here as well as Cana, Nain, Gennesaret, Magdala (of Mary Magdalene), and Capernaum. John the Baptist had much of his ministry in this area, too.

Jesus spent much of his first year of ministry in Judea. When Herod Antipas put John the Baptist in prison, Jesus came back to Galilee.

He went to Nazareth and read a prophecy from the book of Isaiah about the Messiah and told everyone there that he was the fulfillment of that prophecy - God in the flesh. This "blasphemy" so enraged the Jews that they tried to push Jesus over a cliff. They would have killed Jesus had he not miraculously escaped.

Galilee was also a prosperous area, so it wasn't uncommon to see tax collectors.

Hillside near the Mount of Beatitudes

GENTILE (page 6)

Anyone who is not a Jew.

In the time of Jesus, Palestine was almost wholly Jewish, with the exception of the occupying Romans. Mixed Jewish and gentile populations in Decapolis, Phoenicia and Egypt bordered the region.

The Greeks mentioned in **John 12: 20** were probably gentiles who had been worshiping the one God of Israel.

HEROD (page 1)

HEROD was not a personal name, but the family surname. It belonged to all the generations of the Herodian house. Much confusion has arisen because this simple fact has not been understood.

HEROD THE GREAT was born in 72 BC and died in 1 BC. He bore the titles of "Herod the King" and "King of Judea." Herod the Great was greatly stirred when the Magi announced the birth of some great king in his kingdom.

The slaughter of all the children in Bethlehem was not out of character for him, as he had murdered many in his own household in order to make his position secure. Before his death he had all the prominent Jews in his territory arrested and put into the hippodrome at Jericho, with instructions to kill them upon his own death.

Herod ruled from around 37 BC until his death in 1 BC. This is the HEROD who was on the scene at the time of the birth of Jesus.

ARCHELAUS was the eldest son of Herod the Great. This Herod ruled after his father died and is only mentioned once in the biblical account. In the gospel of Matthew, it is recorded that after Joseph had been told that Herod was dead and that he could return home he learned that Archelaus was now ruling over Judea and was afraid. Joseph was warned in a dream not to return to Judea, and so he settled his family in Galilee. So Jesus was born in Bethlehem but grew up in Galilee.

HEROD ANTIPAS was married to the daughter of King Aretas of Arabia. He then took Herodias, his half brothers

Ancient coin with the likeness of Herod.

wife, as his own. John the Baptist called upon Herod Antipas to repent of this sinful act. This resulted in the arrest of John the Baptist, and finally his beheading. Herod Antipas was the one that Pontius Pilot sent Jesus to see when he learned that Jesus was from Nazareth, which was in the region that Herod Antipas ruled. Herod Antipas ruled until around 40 AD.

Philip, the half brother of Herod (Antipas), was ruler of the region of Ituraea. He was the only decent ruler from the line of Herod. He was known for his moderation and his justice. This was the ruler whose wife was stolen by Herod Antipas.

HEROD AGRIPPA or **AGRIPPA 1** dethroned Herod Antipas and ruled for about three years from 41 AD to 44 AD. Herod Agrippa was the king that killed James, the apostle and brother of John. When he saw how this pleased the Jews he had Peter arrested also. An angel delivered Peter from the prison of Herod Agrippa and certain death. You can read about this in the book of the *Acts 12: 1- 3.*

HEROD AGRIPPA or **AGRIPPA 2** was the son of Agrippa 1 and was put in charge of a region north of Judea. This is the Herod that was present during one of the trials of the Apostle Paul. You can read about this in *Acts chapters 25 and 26*. This is the Herod, who told the Apostle Paul "You have almost persuaded me to become a Christian."

Summary of the Herods

Herod the Great - Met with the Wise men from the east. Killed all the babies under two years old in Bethlehem in an attempt to kill Jesus.

Archelaus - Ruled after Herod the Great. This caused Joseph to relocate to Galilee instead of Bethlehem.

Herod Antipas - Beheaded John the Baptist.

Herod Agrippa 1 - Killed the Apostle James and arrested Peter.

Herod Agrippa 2 - Present during one of the trials of the Apostle Paul.

HOLY SPIRIT/ TRINITY (page 3)

Holy Spirit - One of the three persons of the Trinity along with God the Father and God the Son. (There is one God; God is three persons; Each person is fully God.)

One of the first places we see the Holy Spirit in the Gospels is when John the Baptist baptizes Jesus.

The Spirit comes down on him like a dove, and a voice out of the heavens (God the Father) says "This is my beloved Son, in whom I am well pleased." *(Matthew 3: 13-17)*

Before Jesus lived on earth, the Holy Spirit would empower people from time to time to do a specific task or give a certain message.

Jesus told the apostles that he would be leaving the earth and that the Holy Spirit would come.

A few weeks after Jesus ascended into heaven, the Holy Spirit came to earth and lives in the lives of each person who puts their trust in Jesus. *(See John 16: 7-11 and Acts 1: 4-8 and 2; 1-4).*

He is mentioned specifically as having an active role in drawing people to Jesus, and in giving wisdom and empowering people who trust in Jesus to follow Him in the way they live their lives.

Trinity - The Bible teaches that there is one God, and at the same time, three distinct persons.

The word "Trinity" never appears in the Bible, but it is used to represent what the Bible teaches.

There is one God; God is three persons; Each person is fully God. The three distinct persons are the Father, Son, and Holy Spirit.

There is not an example that illustrates this idea exactly. Since we are human, we will never understand this idea completely, but it is clearly affirmed in all parts of the Bible. It is part of the mystery of God.

ISAIAH (page 4)

A prophet who lived about 750 years before Jesus was born.

His prophecies about the Messiah are quoted many times in the gospels as being fulfilled by Jesus.

Isaiah 7: 14 prophesied that a " ... virgin will conceive and bear a son and will call his name Immanuel..." (which means "God with us").

After Jesus had begun his public ministry, he went to the synagogue in Nazareth and read a prophecy from Isaiah about the Messiah and then said that he was fulfilling it (Luke 4: 16-21).

As the apostles looked back at Jesus' life and death, they realized that Isaiah 53: 1-12 was fulfilled by Jesus' life and death. Jesus fulfilled these and other prophecies of Isaiah specifically 750 years after they were written.

JACOB'S 12 TRIBES OF ISRAEL (page. 2)

God promised Abraham that He would make his descendants a great nation. That promise was passed to Abraham's son Isaac, then to Isaac's son Jacob.

Jacob's 12 sons are considered the beginning of the line of each of the twelve tribes of Israel and each tribe is named after the son from whom it descended.

However, there is one slight irregularity in this part of the family tree. Jacob had 12 sons, but two of the twelve tribes are named after his grandsons.

Levi did not get an inheritance of land because his descendants were responsible for assisting the priests and maintaining the temple, so their inheritance was the tithes and offerings of the people.

Jacob made Joseph equal with him as a patriarch because Joseph saved their family from famine when he was second in charge in Egypt and invited them to come and live near him in Egypt.

Jacob made Joseph's two sons Manasseh and Ephraim to each be the head of a tribe.

JEREMIAH (page 8)

A prophet who lived about 600 years before Jesus was born.

When Herod killed all the children near Bethlehem that were two years old or under, it was a fulfillment of Jeremiah 31: 15.

Jeremiah lamenting the destruction of Jerusalem, painted by Rembrandt

JERUSALEM (page 6)

Already more than a thousand years old at the time of Jesus, the city remains venerated as the home of the Temple built by Solomon, son of King David.

At the time of Jesus, Jerusalem was in control of the Roman-backed army of Herod, having been under both Persian and Greek control in previous centuries.

Located on the heights overlooking the Rift Valley, at 2500 feet above sea level, it is not uncommon for it to snow, allowing for hot summer days but cool evenings.

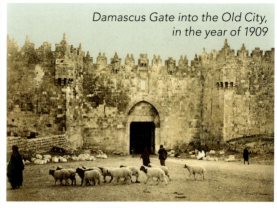

Damascus Gate into the Old City, in the year of 1909

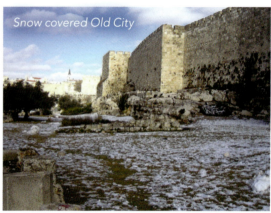

Snow covered Old City

JUDEA (page 1)

Judea is the southern province in Israel. Just north of Judea is Samaria and north of that is Galilee. Jews despised the Samaritans so much that when they were walking to Galilee from Judea, they would go out of their way to cross over to the east side of the Jordan River and go all the way around

Samaria until they were far enough north to cross over into Galilee.

It surprised Jesus' disciples when he went from Judea to Galilee straight through Samaria. It was on one of these trips that Jesus stopped to meet the Samaritan woman at the well.

Judea contained the cities of Jerusalem, Bethlehem, Jericho, Bethany, Bethpage, Emmaus and others. Jerusalem is on a hill, so anytime someone is traveling to Jerusalem, they are going "up to..." and anytime they are going away from Jerusalem they are going "down to ... "

That's why in the story of the Good Samaritan, the traveler was going "down from Jerusalem to Jericho." *(Luke 10:30)* We would usually think that would mean he was traveling south, but Jericho is actually east of Jerusalem.

KING DAVID AND SOLOMON
(page 2)

David was the second king of Israel. He lived about 1,000 years before Christ was born. God promised him that the Messiah would come from his family line.

He was the youngest son of Jesse, and their hometown was Bethlehem. While he was a shepherd, he learned to play the harp and use a slingshot. He was told at a young age by Samuel the prophet that he would eventually be king.

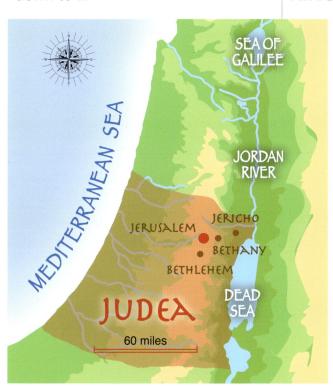

THE STORY OF JESUS

He killed Goliath. He was also a friend of Jonathan, who was the son of King Saul. Saul tried to kill David and failed. After David was king and married to Michal, he got Bathsheba pregnant and then made sure her husband, who was an officer in the army, would get killed in battle.

When God told Nathan the prophet to confront David about it, he repented. Bathsheba's first son died, but her second son, Solomon, later became king.

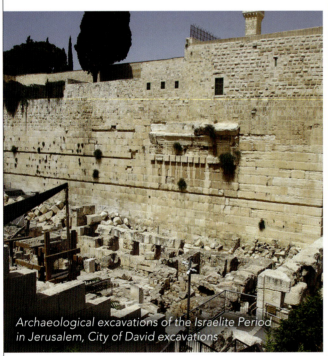
Archaeological excavations of the Israelite Period in Jerusalem, City of David excavations

David also wrote many of the Psalms as songs of confession and praise to God. David also wrote many of the prophesies that were fulfilled when Jesus came to earth.

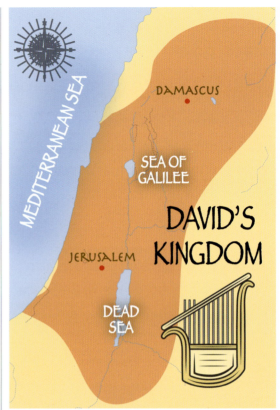

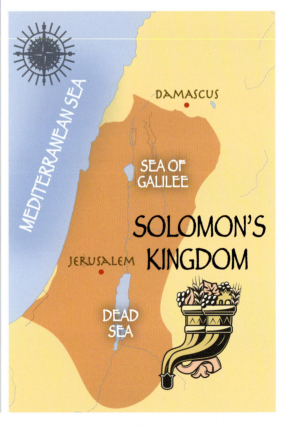

MESSIAH (page 1)

A Hebrew word referring to a descendant of King David, who would bring about peace and justice on earth. The word literally means "anointed one."

God mandated that prophets, priests, and kings be anointed. Oil was poured on them, which symbolized the Holy Spirit coming on them to give them the ability and wisdom to perform their responsibilities.

When Jesus came as the Messiah, He was God in the flesh and the supreme prophet, priest, and king in one person.

The Jews thought the Messiah would be a warrior-king who would establish a political kingdom with Jerusalem as the capital city. They didn't believe Jesus was the Messiah because he didn't establish a political kingdom.

The Jews ignored the messianic passages written by the prophets who spoke of a suffering servant. Jesus claimed to be the Messiah but also said that his kingdom is eternal and is in people's hearts.

The kingdom that Jesus came to establish is more powerful than any political or military kingdom. While Rome and many other political kingdoms have been conquered, the Kingdom of God established by Jesus' life, death and resurrection can never be shaken. The miracle of this kingdom is that Jesus is still alive and active in the lives of his disciples.

One day Jesus will come to earth again, but not as a servant. His next coming will be heralded by the sound of trumpets announcing that King Jesus has come to rule completely and supremely over all creation.

MOSES (page 6)

Moral, ceremonial, and dietary laws were given by God to Moses. They are recorded in the first five books of the Bible.

These books include Genesis, Exodus, Leviticus, Numbers, and Deuteronomy. It was in these books that God gave us the ten commandments and many other detailed rules and regulations.

God gave the law to Moses in order to teach the children of Israel in particular, and mankind, in general, that they were incapable of keeping God's requirements and all fall under God's condemnation.

Moses was born in Egypt during a time when the Egyptians were trying to limit the Jewish population by killing all male newborns.

When Moses was born to a Jewish family, they hid him for three months and then put him in a basket and set him in the reeds near the Nile River. Moses' sister watched from a distance as Pharaoh's daughter came to bathe in the river, found the basket, and recognized him as a Hebrew (Jewish) child.

Moses, by Michaelangelo

The sister then asked Pharaoh's daughter if she needed someone to nurse the child. When she said yes, the daughter went to get her mother.

Pharaoh's daughter paid the mother to nurse Moses until he was weaned. Then Pharaoh's daughter raised him as her son.

When he was a young man, he saw an Egyptian beating a Hebrew slave and got mad and killed the Egyptian. He left the country and lived as a shepherd for forty years.

Then God spoke to him through a burning bush (that didn't burn up) and came back with his brother Aaron to tell Pharaoh to let the Jews leave Egypt.

When they finally left and were on their way to the land God had promised them, God called Moses to climb up Mount Sinai, where He gave Moses the stones with the Ten Commandments engraved on them *(Exodus 20)*.

When they reached the land God had promised them, they didn't really believe that God would give them victory over the people they would battle to take over the land.

Because of unbelief, God said they would wander in the desert for 40 years until the unbelieving generation died off. Moses led them during those years.

Moses also wrote the books of Genesis, Exodus, Leviticus, Numbers and Deuteronomy.

MYRRH, GALL, VINEGAR
(page 8)

Vinegar mixed with myrrh or gall, the vinegar mentioned here was a common sour wine used daily by the Roman soldiers.

Myrrh and gall both refer to a bitter-tasting substance that is a mild analgesic pain reliever.

It was offered to people who were crucified to relieve their pain. Jesus chose to suffer the pain instead.

It is interesting that myrrh is one of the gifts the Magi presented to Jesus when he was a small child.

NAZARETH (page 2)

In Biblical times, Nazareth was a cross-roads village in Galilee, just north of the border of Samaria. Today a modern city is built around the his-

Nazareth's old city

toric core, the center of which is the Catholic Church of Annunciation.

PRIESTS AND HIGH PRIESTS
(page 1)

Priests were descendants of Aaron whose job was to offer sacrifices and represented the people to God.

Since Jesus was the ultimate sacrifice, there are no more sacrifices for sin needed. When we trust in Christ, we have direct access to God, so each of us is a priest *(1 Peter 2: 9; Revelation 1: 6).*

A Priest, a Levite, and an Officer, from the History of Costume

THE STORY OF JESUS

HIGH PRIEST: Aaron, Moses' brother was the first high priest.

Originally, the office was hereditary, and the person held it for life. Their most important duty was to enter the Holy of Holies once a year on the Day of Atonement, to offer sacrifices for the sins of the whole nation.

They were also the head of the Sanhedrin, which was like a Jewish Supreme Court. By the time Jesus was doing his public ministry, Herod or the Roman official in charge appointed the high priest.

It had become a political appointment. They would choose someone they thought would cooperate with them, and appoint someone else whenever they thought it was convenient.

The Jews still had the mindset that this was a lifetime position, so, for instance, even though Caiaphas succeeded Annas as high priest, Luke 3: 2 refers to both Annas and Caiaphas as high priests at Jesus' trial.

PASSOVER (page 9)

This is a feast commemorating the deliverance of the Jews from Egypt.

The Jews were slaves in Egypt when God sent Moses to tell the Pharaoh to let them go. He refused, so God sent nine plagues to persuade him.

When Pharaoh still refused, the Lord sent a tenth and final plague. The Lord sent an angel to kill the firstborn of every house, even of the animals.

However, God warned the Jews and told them that if they killed a lamb and put some of the blood on their doorpost, the angel would "pass over" their house and they would be protected. It happened just that way, and Pharaoh finally relented and let the Jews leave Egypt. Jewish people still celebrate Passover each year.

The feast involves eating a lot of different items that have deep sig-

A typical Passover Seder including unleavened bread and bitter herbs

nificance relating to this event and God's ongoing faithfulness to the Jews. Unleavened bread, bitter herbs, wine, and roasted lamb are just a few.

As we trust our lives to Jesus, he "covers" us from God's wrath by forgiving our sin and bringing us into a new relationship with him. Our salvation is based on what Christ has done, not how many rules we follow.

PROPHET (page 9)

A prophet is a spokesman for God. God would use prophets to give His message to the Israelites. The main purpose of most of the messages was to try and bring the people back to the true worship of God.

The prophets preached against the worship of idols and warned those whose practices were contrary to God's will and character. Sometimes they would also foretell future events. Sometimes a message would have an immediate fulfillment and another fulfillment in the future.

Prophets were very careful about making sure their message was from God, because God had instructed the Israelites to immediately kill any false prophet who claimed that something was from God, and it turned out to be false.

The great prophets of the old testament period before the coming of Christ included men like Ezekiel, Daniel, Jonah, Micah, Isaiah, Jeremiah, and Malachi. Then there was John the Baptist and Jesus, who was the greatest prophet of all.

Prophets like Isaiah and Micah prophesied details about the birth and life of Jesus more than 800 years before he lived. Micah 5:2 said Jesus would be born in Bethlehem, and Isaiah Chapter 53 gives details about the death of Jesus.

There are 60 major prophecies about the Messiah in the Old Testament and Jesus fulfilled all of them. The odds of that happening in one person are staggering. In fact if you just took the probability of eight of them happening in one person, it would be like covering the country of France in silver dollars two feet deep and then getting one chance to pick the correct silver dollar (1 in 100,000,000,000,000,000). Now consider the odds for all 60!

ROME (page 5)

A city in present-day Italy that grew to become an empire and ruled the western world for about 400 years, from about 150 years before Jesus was born.

The empire was still growing in the time of Jesus and would eventually consume far-reaching outposts, including modern day England.

Romans were known for their military that was built on disciplined soldiers and effective tactics. Many countries didn't like being controlled by Rome because the Roman armies maintained order using brutal tactics like public crucifixions, which were not discontinued until the fourth century.

When Rome decreed that a census be taken, Mary and Joseph went to their ancestral home of Bethlehem; otherwise Jesus may have been born in Nazareth where they were living.

Pontius Pilate was a Roman governor in charge of Judea when Jesus was crucified. The Jews did not like being ruled by Rome and objected to their worship of idols and mythological gods.

Zealots were Jews who wanted to overthrow the Roman armies by armed rebellion.

SCRIBES (page 7)

The word "scribe" is the English translation of the Greek word "Grammateis," which means "student of the scriptures." Scribes were men whose primary occupation was writing out copies of the Jewish Scriptures and teaching the people what the law said.

Because they copied the Old Testament books, they were familiar with the Hebrew Scriptures and were respected in society for their literacy and knowledge. The scribes provided teaching that was the religious and moral backbone for the Jewish people during the time of Jesus. Because of their role, there were often addressed as, "Teacher."

They were trusted as professional interpreters and as ones who could judge individual cases as they related to Jewish law. Scribes were, therefore, also trusted as lawyers within Jewish society. As the scribes were the most learned individuals on the fine details of following Jewish law, their duties also consisted of deciding on specific questions of the law in individual cases.

Scribes had no authority in themselves, but rather they continually deferred to the authority of other scribes and traditions to support their positions. The scribes were some of Jesus' most adamant opponents. In their minds, the Messiah who the Old Testament Scriptures spoke about did not seem to match up with who Jesus was.

TEMPLE (page 6)

A building in Jerusalem that was the only place where Jews could offer sacrifices to meet their religious requirements.

Solomon built the first one about 900 years before Jesus was born. It was destroyed by invaders, rebuilt on a smaller scale, and then rebuilt by Herod the Great beginning about 18 years before Jesus was born. Herod's temple was done on such a grand scale that the main part took 10 years to build and the outer courts weren't completed until 65 years after Jesus' birth.

A scribe in modern Israel

Jesus said it would be torn down so that one stone would not remain on top of another. The Romans did just that about 70 years after Jesus was born.

The temple has not been rebuilt since then, and now there is a Muslim holy place, the Dome of the Rock, that is located on the Temple Mount in Jerusalem.

END OF CHAPTER ONE

A model in Jerusalem of the Temple from Jesus' time

CHAPTER TWO

THE MINISTRY OF JOHN THE BAPTIST

JOHN THE BAPTIST

The word of God came to John the Baptist while he was in the wilderness. The message he preached was that men and women should **repent**† because the kingdom of heaven is at hand.

John was the person who Isaiah said would come in the spirit and power of **Elijah**† to make the way ready for the Messiah.

Isaiah said:

Behold I send my messenger, before your face, who will prepare your way.

Judean wilderness

The voice of one crying in the wilderness: Make ready the way of the Lord, Make his paths straight.

Every valley shall be filled and every mountain and hill shall be brought low; and the crooked shall become straight, and the rough ways smooth. And all people will see the salvation of God.

John began **baptizing**† in the wilderness and preaching repentance for the **remission**† of sins. John wore clothing made from camel's hair and wore a leather belt around his waist. He ate locusts and wild honey.

People came from everywhere to hear John preach. They came from the country of Judea and from Jerusalem. They came from the region around the Jordan. He baptized all who came to him confessing their sins.

† Further reading available at the end of this chapter.

THE STORY OF JESUS

JOHN WARNS THE RELIGIOUS LEADERS

When he saw **Pharisees**† and **Sadducees**† coming to his baptisms, he spoke to them so that the multitude of people around him could hear:

You offspring of vipers, who told you to flee from the wrath to come. Produce a manner of life that shows you really want to change, and don't think that just because you are descendants of Abraham that God will save you.

*I tell you plainly that God is able to make children of **Abraham**† from the stones that are around you.*

Right now the ax lies at the root of the trees; every tree that doesn't produce good fruit is cut down and cast into the fire.

People in the crowd around John asked:

What must we do?

John told them:

Those of you that have two coats, give one to the person who has none. He that has an abundance of food, share it with those who have no food.

Publicans (**tax collectors for Rome**†) who had come to John to be baptized asked:

What must we do?

John said:

Don't steal money, but only collect the taxes that are due.

To the soldiers, John said:

Don't extort money by means of violence, and do not accuse anyone falsely or blackmail anyone. Be content with your wages.

John the Baptist's ministry created a great expectation. Many began to wonder if John might be the Christ.

John became aware of what they were thinking. He told them that he was baptizing with water to show repentance and demonstrate that a mightier man would succeed him - a man whose shoes he was not worthy to stoop down and unloose.

John said:

The one who is coming after me will baptize with the Holy Spirit and fire. The

† Further reading available at the end of this chapter.

winnowing shovel is in his hand and he will completely clean the threshing floor. He will gather his grain into his vault, but the chaff he will burn up with a fire that will not go out.

With many other exhortations, John preached good tidings to the people.

END OF CHAPTER TWO

CHAPTER TWO
COMPANION

ABRAHAM (page 34)

Father of the Jews and Arabs, and the 12 Tribes of Israel.

God made a covenant (contract) with Abraham that He would cause Abraham's descendants to become a great nation, and through them, everyone in the world would be blessed **(Genesis 12: 1-3).**

Abraham, by the Italian painter Guercino

The ultimate blessing that came through Abraham's descendants was Jesus, who came as God in the flesh to provide a way for everyone in the world for all time to have a relationship with God.

God also promised to give the land of Canaan to Abraham's descendants **(Genesis 17: 8),** but at the time, Abraham and his wife Sarah had no children and were both past childbearing age.

They got impatient, and Abraham had a child with Sarah's servant who was Hagar. The child was named Ishmael. Later, Sarah became pregnant and had Isaac. The Jews are descendants of Isaac, and the Arabs are descendants of Ishmael.

THE 12 TRIBES OF ISRAEL: God promised Abraham that He would make his descendants a great nation. That promise was passed to Abraham's son Isaac, then to Isaac's son Jacob.

Jacob's 12 sons are considered the beginning of the line of each of the twelve tribes of Israel and each tribe is named after the son from whom it descended.

However, there is one slight irregularity in this part of the family tree. Jacob had 12 sons, but two of the twelve tribes are named after his grandsons.

Levi did not get an inheritance of land because his descendants were responsible to assist the priests and maintain the temple, so their inheritance was the tithes and offerings of the people.

Jacob made Joseph equal with him as a patriarch because Joseph saved their family from famine when he was second in charge in Egypt and invited them to come and live near him in Egypt.

Jacob made Joseph's two sons Manasseh and Ephraim to each be the head of a tribe.

BAPTISM (page 33)

Baptism is a public ceremony indicating an inward decision of life changing importance. John the Baptist baptized people who repented (changed the way they lived). Jesus talks about baptism as being significant.

Pilgrims await baptism in the Jordan River

There are differences of opinion about whether a person should be sprinkled with water or immersed one or more times, and if it should happen when a person is an infant, or as a public statement indicating a conscious adult decision.

Baptism symbolizes your identification with Jesus and what has taken place spiritually in your life. When you are submerged under the water and then are brought up out of the water, it shows your identification with Jesus when he died, was buried and rose from the dead.

It is also symbolizes how you died to sin and your old way of life when you go under the water, and how your sins are washed away, and you are raised to a new life in Jesus as you come up out of the water.

The Bible teaches that it is not baptism which saves you, but instead putting your faith in Jesus and trusting in His death on the cross to pay the penalty for your sins so you can have a relationship with God.

Baptism is an opportunity for you to publicly acknowledge that you have put your faith in Jesus alone and that you want to live your life as his disciple.

ELIJAH (page 33)

Elijah was a prophet in Israel who lived about 800 years before Christ. He challenged and defeated more than 800 pagan priests in a dramatic contest in front of many people of Israel.

He was also taken to heaven in a fiery chariot, so he never died. Many people thought when they saw John the Baptist, that Elijah had returned to earth.

PHARISEES (page 34)

The Pharisees were religious leaders in the Jewish society at the time of Jesus. They were religious fundamentalists who focused on strict observance of the Jewish laws, ceremonies, and traditions. There were around 6,000 Pharisees during Jesus' time on earth. Pharisees were leaders in the local synagogue. Most every Jewish community had their own synagogue while there was only one temple, and it was in Jerusalem.

Pharisees by the Italian painter Duccio

Pharisees strongly encouraged the Jewish people to pursue righteousness by closely following the Jewish laws and not compromising with the beliefs and ways of the Romans. The Pharisees openly opposed Jesus for many reasons. They were particularly appalled at his acts of healing people on the Sabbath and his blatant claims to divinity.

Jesus denounced them as being hypocrites. They often lived moral lives, full of good deeds, but it was all outward actions with no thought given to the heart or motives of the actions.

REMISSION (page 33)

When you owe someone a debt, they expect you to pay it.

If someone else pays off your debt, your creditor is satisfied, and you don't owe anymore.

The penalty for our sin is death. We are sinners, and our penalty is death, but Jesus paid it for us. He is the only one who could because he is the only man who lived a perfect life.

REPENTANCE (page 33)

To repent is to change your mind and purpose.

Specifically in the Bible it means to turn away from sin and turn to God.

When we truly repent, we are conscious of our guilt and also of God's mercy. The result of true repentance is a change in behavior.

It is more than just feeling sorry about our sin or being sorry we got caught.

ROME (page 34)

A city in present-day Italy that grew to become an empire and ruled the western world for about 400 years, from about 150 years before Jesus was born.

The empire was still growing in the time of Jesus and would eventually consume far reaching outposts, including modern day England.

Romans were known for their military which was built on disciplined soldiers and effective tactics. Many countries didn't like being controlled by Rome because the Roman armies maintained order using brutal tactics like public crucifixions, which were not discontinued until the fourth century.

When Rome decreed that a census be taken, Mary and Joseph went to their ancestral home of Bethlehem, otherwise Jesus may have been born in Nazareth where they were living.

Pontius Pilate was a Roman governor in charge of Judea when Jesus was crucified. The Jews did not like being ruled by Rome and objected to their worship of idols and mythological gods.

Zealots were Jews who wanted to overthrow the Roman armies by armed rebellion.

SADDUCEES (page 34)

The Sadducees, Jewish religious leaders who were primarily from the upper-class, were much more sympathetic to the Romans and sought to maintain their aristocratic positions

The garb of a Sadducee

in society. They often disagreed with the Pharisees because the Sadducees rejected the oral traditions and much of the doctrine of the Pharisees.

The Sadducees were opposed to Jesus because there was the supposed threat that Jesus could potentially overthrow the Roman government, thus jeopardizing their positions of prestige. Sadducees lived primarily in Jerusalem and their lives were often focused around the happenings of the Jewish temple in Jerusalem.

The Sanhedrin (the judicial council of the Jewish people) was comprised primarily of Sadducees.

TAX (page 34)

Rome charged occupied countries to pay for the Roman legions stationed in the country and the cost of government as a whole. Rome was in control of Israel during the time Christ lived.

This tax had a complicated structure.

People in each country would work for Rome as independent contractors. Rome would designate a certain amount that had to come from each area. The tax collectors would often collect more than was required and keep the difference. Most Jews hated them because most were dishonest, plus they represented Roman oppression.

CHAPTER THREE

BEGINNING OF JESUS' MINISTRY

JESUS IS BAPTIZED BY JOHN

One day Jesus came from Nazareth to the **Jordan**†. He came to John to be baptized.

But John did not want to baptize Jesus and said to him:

I am the one that needs to be baptized by you, and you are coming to be baptized by me?

Jesus told John:

Permit it to fulfill all righteousness.

John did as he was asked.

After all the others had been baptized, it came time to baptize Jesus.

After Jesus had been baptized, and before he was out of the Jordan River, the heavens opened up and the Holy Spirit descended in bodily form as a dove.

A voice came out of the heavens, saying:

This is my beloved Son with whom I am well pleased.

Jesus was about 30 years old when he began to teach.

By then, Jesus was full of the **Holy Spirit**†.

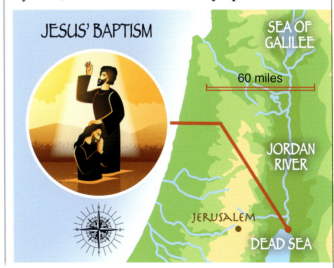

† Further reading available at the end of this chapter.

THE STORY OF JESUS

TEMPTED IN THE WILDERNESS

Immediately Jesus was led up by the Spirit into the wilderness to be tempted by the **devil**†. Jesus lived among wild beasts. He ate nothing for 40 days and 40 nights. Imagine his hunger.

The devil said to him:

If you are the Son of God, command these stones become bread.

Jesus said:

It is written that man shall not live by bread alone, but by every word that comes out of the mouth of God.

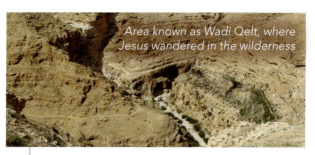

Area known as Wadi Qelt, where Jesus wandered in the wilderness

Then the devil led Jesus into Jerusalem and set him on the pinnacle of the temple and said to him:

If you are the Son of God, throw yourself down, for it is written, he will put his angels in charge of keeping him safe and guarding him from harm. The angels will not let you fall. They will hold you up with their hands so that you do not dash your foot against the stones.

Jesus answered:

It is written you shall not put the Lord your God to the test.

The devil took him to the top of a high mountain where he showed him all the kingdoms of the world in all their glory in a split second.

He said to Jesus:

I will give you authority over all these kingdoms, and you can have their glory for yourself. These are mine to give to

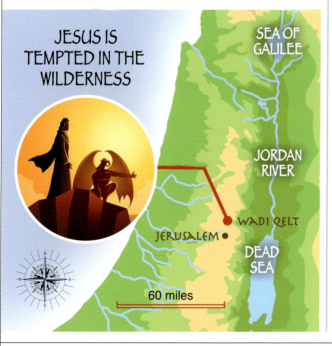

† Further reading available at the end of this chapter.

whomever I will. If you will fall down and worship me, this will all be yours.

Jesus answered:

Get away from me Satan, for it is written that you shall worship the Lord your God and him only shall you serve.

After Satan was done with his temptations, he left him for a season. The angels came to minister to Jesus.

JOHN CONFESSES THAT HE IS NOT THE CHRIST

The priests and the Levites came to the Jordan River in **Bethany**† to ask John the Baptist who he was. John told them in no uncertain terms that he was not the Christ.

They asked:

Are your Elijah?

John answered:

I am not.

They asked:

Are you the prophet?

John answered:

No.

They asked:

Then who are you?

John answered:

I am the voice of one crying in the wilderness. Make straight the way of the Lord.

Then they asked him:

Why do you baptize if you are not the Christ or Elijah?

John said:

I baptize with water. In the midst of you is standing someone who you do not know. He is the one for whom I am preparing the way. I am not even worthy to untie his shoes.

View of Jerusalem from Mt. Scopus

† Further reading available at the end of this chapter.

JOHN'S TESTIMONY

The next day John saw Jesus coming toward him and said:

*Behold the **Lamb of God**† who takes away the sin of the world! This is the one I spoke about when I said, 'He who comes after me has surpassed me because he was before me.'*

(John was six months older than Jesus and was explaining that Jesus was eternal and existed before anything else that was created.)

John then said:

I have seen the Spirit coming as a dove out of heaven and descending upon him.

I did not recognize who Jesus was, but the one who sent me to baptize with water said to me, When you see the dove descending and abiding on him then you will know that he is the one who will baptize with the Holy Spirit.

And I did see it with my own eyes and have given testimony to the fact that Jesus is the Son of God.

JESUS' FIRST DISCIPLES

The next day John was standing with two of his **disciples**†. He looked intently at Jesus as he walked by.

John said:

Behold the Lamb of God!

When the two disciples (Andrew and possibly John) heard this they followed Jesus.

Jesus turned and looked at them following and said to them:

What are you looking for?

They said to him:

***Teacher**† where are you staying?*

Jesus said:

Come and you will see.

So they did. It was about 4 p.m. Andrew went to find Peter to tell him that he had found the Messiah. He then brought Peter to Jesus.

Jesus looked at him and said:

You are Simon (the name means "hearing") the son of John. You shall be called

---

† Further reading available at the end of this chapter.

Cephas (Peter in Greek, and Stone in English).

JESUS FINDS PHILLIP

The next day Jesus decided to go into Galilee where he found Phillip.

Jesus said to Phillip:

Follow me.

Philip was from **Bethsaida**†, the same city where Andrew and Peter lived.

Phillip left Jesus to go and find his friend Nathanael in order to share the news that the Messiah had come, the one Moses and the prophets wrote about. He told Nathanael that the one who all Israel was waiting for was Jesus, the son of Joseph.

When Nathanael heard this, he asked:

Can anything good come out of Nazareth?

Phillip said:

Come and see.

Springtime in Galilee

Jesus saw Nathanael coming toward him and said to him:

Look, an Israelite in whom there is no deceit.

Nathanael said to Jesus:

How do you know me?

Jesus told him:

Before Phillip called you, when you were under the fig tree, I saw you.

† Further reading available at the end of this chapter.

Nathanael was stunned and said to Jesus:

Teacher, you are the Son of God. You are the king of Israel.

Jesus said:

Because I said to you, 'I saw you under the fig tree,' you believe in me? You will see greater things than these. I tell you the truth: You will see the heavens opened, and the angels of God ascending and descending on the Son of man.

FIRST MIRACLE

Three days after Jesus called Philip to follow him, there was a marriage in **Cana**† of Galilee that was being attended by Mary, the mother of Jesus. Jesus had also been invited, and his disciples were in attendance as well.

Church of the Miracle marks Cana as the site of Jesus' first miracle

Before the marriage festivities were over, they ran out of wine. Mary came to Jesus and told him that they had no more wine.

Jesus said to her:

Woman, what have I to do with you? My hour has not yet come.

Note: *Many people have misunderstood this part of the story of Jesus and have wondered why Jesus rebuked Mary.*

But notice that Jesus did not call Mary his mother. Instead, he called her 'Woman,' a term of courteous respect. Jesus was simply making the point that when it came to miracles, he was not acting under the authority of his mother and would not submit in the spirit of obedience.

This mild retort was meant to point us to the fact that Jesus operates under the authority of his Father in heaven and that his duties as a son of Mary and Joseph were subordinate to divine duties.

Jesus made the same point with Mary when

† Further reading available at the end of this chapter.

he was only 12 years old when he stayed in Jerusalem to be about his father's business in the temple, absent from the group returning to Nazareth.

It seems obvious that Mary had more in mind than just the gift of wine. She apparently wanted Jesus to reveal himself as the Messiah. His primary manifestation of himself as the Messiah was in his Passion. The time for this manifestation was yet to come.

His mother said to the servants:

Do whatever he tells you to do.

There were six stone water pots that the Jews used for ceremonial washing of hands before they ate. Each water pot held between 18 and 27 gallons of water.

Jesus told the servants to fill the water pots with water. They filled them to the brim. Jesus then told the servants to fill a cup from the water pot and take it to the ruler of the feast. They did as Jesus said.

When the ruler of the feast tasted the water that had become wine, not knowing where it came from, he called the bridegroom and said:

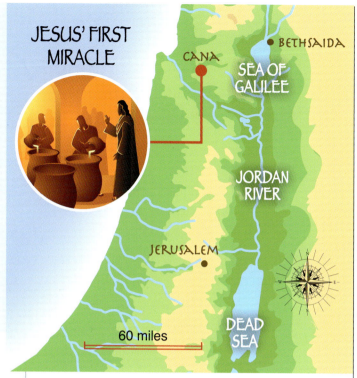

JESUS' FIRST MIRACLE

Usually, the good wine is brought out first, and then after everyone has had a chance to drink freely, the poorer quality wine is brought out. But you have kept the good wine for last.

This is the beginning of the signs that Jesus did in Cana of Galilee. The signs and wonders he did manifested his glory. And Jesus' disciples believed in him.

JESUS AT CAPERNAUM

After this, Jesus, his disciples and his mother went down to **Capernaum**†. They stayed there for many days.

END OF CHAPTER THREE

† Further reading available at the end of this chapter.

CHAPTER THREE COMPANION

APOSTLES & DISCIPLES
(page 46)

In a general sense, a disciple is a learner. In the gospel of John the word refers to people who believe that Jesus is who he claims to be (God in the flesh) and are trusting completely in him. A disciple is committed to learning about Jesus, trusting him, and following his teachings.

The word is also used interchangeably with "apostles" to describe the twelve men whom Jesus chose during his 3 1/2 years of earthly ministry.

The word itself means a "messenger," or "one who is sent out."

After the resurrection of Jesus, he spent 40 days on earth, and then ascended into heaven as the apostles watched. Jesus told them to wait until the Holy Spirit would fall upon them and give them God's power. This happened on the day of Pentecost.

After the Apostles were filled with the Holy Spirit, they went out and told people all over the world about Jesus.

The twelve:
- **Simon,** who is called Peter
- **Andrew,** brother of Simon
- **James,** son of Zebedee (nicknamed *sons of thunder*)
- **John,** brother of James (nicknamed *sons of thunder*)
- **Bartholomew,** also called Nathanael
- **Phillip**
- **Thomas,** also called *Didymus*
- **Matthew** the tax collector, also called *Levi*
- **James,** son of *Alphaeus*
- **Thaddaeus,** also called Judas (not Iscariot)
- **Simon the Cananaean** (the zealot)
- **Judas Iscariot** (the one who betrayed Jesus)

BETHANY (page 47)

Today this small village, east of Jerusalem, famous for the Tomb and Church of Lazarus, sits on the Jericho road.

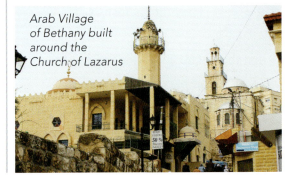

Arab Village of Bethany built around the Church of Lazarus

THE STORY OF JESUS

BETHSAIDA (page 47)

This ancient city lies under the fields of a local kibbutz, on the shores of the east side of the Sea of Galilee.

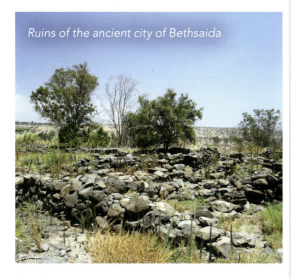
Ruins of the ancient city of Bethsaida

CANA (page 48)

Cana still exists, and is now called K'Far Kana. Northwest of Nazareth, a Franciscan Catholic Church commemorates Jesus' miracle of the turning water into wine.

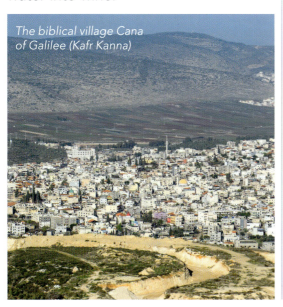
The biblical village Cana of Galilee (Kafr Kanna)

CAPERNAUM (page 49)

This ancient fishing village at the north end of Sea of Galilee has extensive archaeological excavations, examples of stone carving, and a reconstructed synagogue where tradition says Jesus taught.

Ruins of the ancient Great Synagogue at Capernaum

JORDAN RIVER (page 43)

The main river in Palestine.

It is in a deep valley and flows north to south, from north of the Sea of Galilee to the Dead Sea. In the course of about 100 miles, the riverbed drops more than 2,300 feet.

Jordan River, the main river in Palestine

THE STORY OF JESUS

God miraculously held back the Jordan River so the Israelites could walk across as if they were "on dry ground" (Joshua 3:17). John the Baptist baptized people in the Jordan River, including Jesus, when Jesus began his public ministry **(Mark 1:9).**

LAMB OF GOD & SACRIFICES
(page 46)

Sacrifices were used a symbol of removing sin from a person's life so they would be acceptable to God.

The purpose of sacrifices was to show that a deeper relationship with God is possible, but that it requires a need for continual cleansing of sin.

The sacrifices didn't have any value in themselves, but pointed worshippers forward to the coming of Jesus who would be offered once as the ultimate sacrifice to bear the sins of all the world for all time.

In the sacrificial system, when people wanted to dedicate themselves or re-establish their relationship to God, they would first admit that imperfections (sin) in their lives made them unacceptable to God.

They would confess (acknowledge) their sin to God, then lay their hands on the animal that was to be sacrificed as a symbol of identifying with the animal and recognizing that the penalty for sin is death.

The animal would then be killed, cut up and burned on the altar as an offering to God.

Sacrifices were established by God as early as Adam and Eve, when God clothed them with skins of animals and when their son Abel came to offer animals from his flock **(Genesis 4:4).**

Even then, God had planned for Jesus, and all these sacrifices were a symbol of Jesus who would come to offer himself as the perfect sacrifice. We can put our trust in Him because

The Lamb of God is depicted on a sacrificial altar in this detail from the famous Ghent Altarpice, by the VanEycks

by dying on the cross, His blood has paid the penalty for our sin. There is no need for any further sacrifice.

God set up specific rules for sacrificing animals, many of them recorded in the book of Leviticus that Moses wrote about 1,400 years before Jesus lived.

Even then, a lamb was required for most sin offerings. When Jesus began his public ministry, John the Baptist referred to his as, "the Lamb of God who takes away the sin of the world." *(John 1:29)*

Some people did not raise sheep and were too poor to buy a lamb, so God allowed them to use a dove to sacrifice instead. If they were too poor to buy a dove, they were allowed to offer a small amount of flour. God reached out to all of us, first in the sacrificial system, and then through Jesus, to make a way for our sin to be forgiven so we can enjoy a relationship with God. All he requires is that we confess (acknowledge) our sin and put our trust in Him.

In the Jewish sacrificial system, God also set up sacrifices to be offered on special occasions, and for repairing relationships with other people.

SATAN/ BEELZEBUB (page 44)

These are two names for the same thing. Satan was the highest angel in heaven when the universe was created.

He wanted to usurp God, and because of his sin of pride, he was thrown out of heaven along with a third of the angels who chose to follow him.

He is opposed to God and tried without success to get Jesus to go against God when Jesus was on Earth. Beelzebub comes from a word that means "lord of flies," or "lord or dung."

TEACHERS (page 46)

The word "teacher" usually comes from the Hebrew word, "Rabbi." Teacher is the term that Jews used to address their religious leaders. Because scribes were the most educated in the scriptures and fulfilled the role of instructing others, they were often addressed as "teacher."

Jesus was recognized as a Teacher who stood apart from other teachers. Most teachers would appeal to other teachers or famous scribes to support their statements while Jesus spoke as one who had authority in himself.

CHAPTER FOUR

FIRST TO THE SECOND PASSOVER

FIRST PASSOVER OF JESUS' MINISTRY

It was time for the Passover of the Jews, and Jesus went up to Jerusalem and into the temple.

Jerusalem's Old City at dusk

JESUS CLEANSES THE TEMPLE

In the temple were those selling oxen and sheep and **doves**†, and the **money changers**†.

Jesus made a whip of cords, and he drove those who were selling livestock and changers of money out of the temple. He turned over the table of the money changers.

He said to those who were selling doves:

Take these away from here and do not make my Father's house a house of merchandise.

His disciples remembered that it was written: *Zeal for God's house will consume me.*

The Jews came to Jesus and asked to show them a sign to convince them that he had the authority to interfere with the order of the temple.

Jesus told them:

Destroy this temple and in three days I will raise it up.

The Jews answered back:

† Further reading available at the end of this chapter.

THE STORY OF JESUS

It took 46 years to build this temple and you will raise it up in three days?

But Jesus was not talking about the temple in Jerusalem, he was talking about the temple of his body.

Jerusalem, archaeological excavations of the Israelite Period

Later, when Jesus was raised from the dead, his disciples remembered what he had said. They believed the **Scripture**†, and the words which Jesus had spoken.

While Jesus was in Jerusalem at the Passover, during the **feast**†, many believed in him because they witnessed the signs he performed.

But Jesus knew the hearts of men and did not trust them. He didn't need anyone to tell him what men were like.

NICODEMUS VISITS JESUS BY NIGHT

There was a Pharisee named Nicodemus, a ruler of the Jews, who came to visit Jesus by night.

Nicodemus said to Jesus:

Teacher, we know that you have come from God because no one can do the miracles that you are doing unless God is with him.

Jesus answered:

Pay attention to the truth I am going to reveal to you. Unless a person is **born again**†, he cannot see the kingdom of heaven.

Nicodemus asked:

How can a man be born when he is old? Can he enter into his mother's womb a second time and be born?

Walls of the old city of Jerusalem

† Further reading available at the end of this chapter.

Jesus said:

*Pay attention to the truth I am going to reveal to you. Unless you are born of water and the **Spirit**†, you cannot enter the kingdom of God.*

Everything that is born of the flesh is flesh; that which is born of the spirit is spirit. Do not be amazed that I say, 'You must be born again.' The wind blows wherever it will blow and you hear its sound, but you do not know where it came from or where it is going. So it is with everyone that is born of the Spirit.

Man in the modern dress of the Orthodox Jew enters the Zion Gate in Jerusalem

Nicodemus asked:

How can this be?

Jesus said:

Aren't you a teacher of Israel, and yet you do not understand these things? I am speaking about things that I know and telling you things I have seen, but you will not believe my testimony. If I told you about earthly things and you don't believe them, how will you believe if I tell you about heavenly things?

Jesus continued:

No one has ascended into heaven, except the one who descended out of heaven, the Son of man, who is in heaven.

*And just like Moses lifted up the serpent in the wilderness, in the same way so must the Son of man be lifted up; that whoever believes in him may have **eternal**† life.*

For this is the way in which God loved the world, he gave his only begotten Son so that whoever believes in him will not perish but have eternal life.

God did not send his Son into the world to judge the world but he sent him so that the world should be saved through him.

He who believes in him is not judged: He who does not believe has been judged

† Further reading available at the end of this chapter.

already, because he has not believed in the name of the only begotten Son of God.

This is the judgment. Light has come into the world, but men loved the darkness and avoided the light because what they were doing was evil and wrong.

But the person who approves and lives out the truth will come to the light so that his works may be made known and so that everyone can see that their works are done through God.

FIRST MINISTRY IN JUDEA

After this, Jesus and his disciples went to Judea where they began to baptize. John also continued to baptize in Aenon near Salim because there was a lot of water in that area.

Questions began to arise among John's disciples regarding purification.

They came to John and said:

The man (referring to Jesus) you testified about is also baptizing and everyone is going to him to be baptized.

Jesus' disciples were the ones doing the baptizing; Jesus did not baptize anyone.

John told his disciples:

A man cannot receive anything unless it is given to him from heaven. You heard what I testified; I am not the Christ, but the one sent ahead of him. The man who has the bride is the bridegroom.

The friend of the bridegroom, who stands by and hears him, is very glad to hear the bridegroom's voice. Therefore my joy is made full. He must increase, but I must decrease.

He who comes from above is above all, he who is on the earth is from the earth, and can only speak as a person on earth; he who comes from heaven is above all. What the man from heaven has seen and heard, he testifies about, and no one receives his testimony.

The ones who receive his testimony are putting trust in God and expressing that God is true.

The Father loves the Son and has given all things into his hand. He who believes in the Son has **eternal**† *life. But those who do not obey the Son shall not see life, but the wrath of God.*

JESUS GOES TO GALILEE

It was about this time that Herod, governor of Galilee, who had been reproved by John the Baptist for taking his brother's wife and for all the other evil things that he did, sent soldiers to arrest John.

View of ancient biblical excavation in Tel Hatzor, Galilee

After John was put into prison, Jesus left Judea and headed for Galilee. He knew that the Pharisees erroneously thought he was baptizing more disciples than John.

WOMAN AT THE WELL

In order to get to Galilee he needed to pass through **Samaria**†. Jesus and his disciples came to a city called **Sychar**†, which was near a field that the Jacob had given to his son Joseph.

Jacob's well was there. Jesus was tired from the journey, and he rested by the well.

He sent his disciples into town to buy food. While Jesus was sitting alone, a Samaritan woman came to draw some water.

† Further reading available at the end of this chapter.

THE STORY OF JESUS

Jesus said to her:

Give me a drink.

The Samaritan women was surprised and asked him:

How is that you who are a Jew would ask me, a Samaritan woman, for a drink? (The Jews did not associate with the Samaritans)

Jesus said to her:

If you only knew the gift of God and who it is that is asking you for a drink, you would have asked him and he would have given you living water.

The woman said to Jesus:

Sir, you have nothing to use to draw water out of the well, and the well is deep. Where are we going to get living water? Are you greater than our father Jacob, who gave us this well and drank from it himself, along with his sons and his cattle?

View of Olive groves in Samaria

Terraced hills with Olive trees in Samaria

Jesus said:

Everyone who drinks this water will thirst again: but whoever drinks the water that I will give him will never be thirsty again. The water that I give him will become a well of water in him springing up to eternal life.

The woman said:

Sir, give me this water so that I will never be thirsty again or need to come all this way to draw water from the well.

Jesus said to her:

Go call your husband and both of you come back here.

The woman answered:

I do not have a husband.

Jesus said to her:

You have answered correctly that you do not have a husband, for you have had five husbands and the man you're now living with is not your husband. You have told the truth.

The woman said:

I perceive that you are a prophet. Our fathers worshipped on this mountain; and you Jews say that Jerusalem is the proper place to worship.

Jesus said to her:

Woman, believe me, the hour is coming, when neither this mountain nor in Jerusalem shall be the place to worship the Father. You worship ignorantly: We worship intelligently, for salvation is from the Jews.

But the hour is coming, and now is here, when the true worshippers will worship the Father in spirit and truth. These are the kind of worshippers that the Father is seeking to worship him. God is Spirit and those who worship him must worship him in spirit and truth.

The woman answered him:

I know the Messiah, the one called Christ, is coming; when he comes, he will declare all things to us.

Jesus said:

I, the one who is speaking to you, am he.

The disciples were coming back from town, and they were amazed to see Jesus speaking to the woman. But no one said anything about it.

The woman left her water pot and went away to the city, and said to the townspeople:

Come see a man who told me all the things I ever did. Can this be the Christ?

People began leaving the city to find Jesus.

In the meantime, the disciples asked Jesus to eat. But he said to them:

I have food to eat that you do not know about.

The disciples began to ask one another:

Did someone bring him something to eat?

Jesus said to them:

My food is to do the will of him that sent me, and to accomplish his work. Do not say, 'Aren't there still four months before the harvest?'

I tell you, lift up your eyes and look on the fields, they are white and ready for harvest. He that reaps the harvest receives a wage, and gathers the fruit; the one that sows the seed and he that reaps the harvest will rejoice together. For here is a true saying: One sows and another reaps.

I send you to reap where others have sown the seed, and you have become a part of their labor.

Many of the Samaritans believed in him because of the Samaritan woman who testified that Jesus had told her everything she ever did.

When the Samaritans found Jesus, they asked him to stay with them. He did, for two days. Then many more believed because of his word.

They said to the woman:

Now we believe, not because of what you said. Now we believe because we have heard him for ourselves, and know that he is indeed the Savior of the world.

Samarian man harvesting olives

ARRIVAL IN GALILEE

After two days in Sychar, Jesus returned to Galilee in the power of the Spirit. He testified that a prophet does not have honor in his own country.

Jesus was received by Galileans who had seen all the things that he had done when he was last in Jerusalem at the feast.

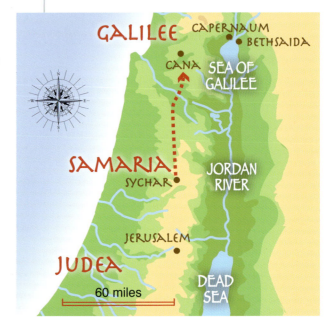

This was when Jesus began to preach the **Gospel**† of God. He also told the people that the kingdom of God was near, as prophesied.

Word of this spread throughout the entire region. He began to teach in their **synagogues**†, receiving glory and honor from all.

THE SECOND MIRACLE AT CANA

He returned to Cana where he had turned the water into wine. There was a nobleman in Capernaum whose son was sick.

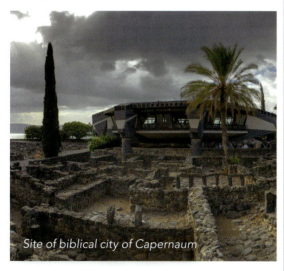
Site of biblical city of Capernaum

When he heard that Jesus was in the area, he found Jesus and begged him to heal his son, who was at the point of death. Jesus said to him:

Unless you see signs and wonders you will not believe.

The nobleman said:

Sir, come down or else my child will die.

Jesus said:

Go your way: your son is alive and well.

The man believed Jesus and went home.

As he was going to see his son, his servants met him with news that his son was fully recovered.

He asked his servants when his son had become well.

They told him that it was yesterday at the seventh hour that the fever left him.

† Further reading available at the end of this chapter.

The father knew that was at the same hour that Jesus had told him that his son was alive and well.

The nobleman believed in Jesus, as did his entire household.

This was the second sign that Jesus did after he came out of Judea into Galilee.

JESUS' TEMPORARY RESIDENCE

Jesus left Nazareth and made Capernaum his new headquarters. Capernaum is by the sea, within the borders of Zebulun and Naphtali. This fulfilled a prophecy of Isaiah. The people who lived there in darkness saw a great light.

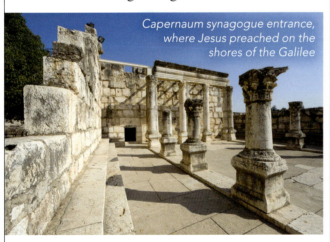

Capernaum synagogue entrance, where Jesus preached on the shores of the Galilee

JESUS CALLS FOUR FISHERMEN

As Jesus was walking along the **sea of Galilee†**, he saw two brothers, Simon, and his brother Andrew, fishing with nets in the sea.

Jesus said to them:

Come follow me, and I will make you fishers of men.

They followed Jesus.

As Jesus went a little farther, he saw two more brothers fishing, James, son of Zebedee, and his brother, John. They were both in the fishing boat with their father, mending their nets. Jesus called to them.

Fishermen on the Sea of Galilee

Great crowds had gathered around Jesus to hear him teach and preach the word of God as he was standing by the Sea of Galilee.

Jesus saw a couple of empty boats near the shore. He got into one of the boats, which belonged to Simon, and asked him to shove the boat a little ways from the shore. Jesus sat in the boat and began teaching to the crowd.

† Further reading available at the end of this chapter.

When Jesus was done teaching, he told Simon to get into the boat with his nets and head for deeper waters to put out his nets.

Simon said:

Master, we have worked hard all night and have been unable to catch any fish, but if you say so I will put the nets down as you wish.

As soon as Peter did as Jesus had requested, the nets were filled with many fish, so many that the nets started to tear. They called for their partners in a nearby boat to help. They came and filled up both boats with so many fish that the boats began to sink.

When Simon Peter saw this, he fell down at Jesus' knees and said:

Go away from me; for I am a sinful man, O Lord.

He was filled with amazement as was everyone else who saw all the fish that filled the boats. James and John were partners with Simon in the fishing business.

Jesus said to Simon:

Don't be afraid: From now on you will catch men.

And as soon as they got the boats to shore, they immediately left their nets and their boats and their father and followed Jesus.

HEALING A DEMONIAC

Jesus and the four fishermen whom he had called came into Capernaum.

That **Sabbath**†, Jesus entered into the synagogue and began teaching. The people there were astonished at this teaching, for he taught them with authority, not like the scribes taught.

While Jesus was teaching, a man with a wicked, **unclean spirit**† entered the synagogue and cried out with a loud voice:

Capernaum, the biblical site along the edge of the Sea of Galilee

† Further reading available at the end of this chapter.

THE STORY OF JESUS

Ah! What have we to do with you, Jesus you Nazarene, have you come to destroy us? I know who you are; you're the Holy One of God.

Jesus rebuked the demon within the man's body and told him not to say any more.

Jesus instructed the demon to come out of the man. The demon threw the man down and caused him to have convulsions and to cry with a loud voice.

But the demon departed as Jesus had commanded, leaving the man unhurt.

Everyone was amazed. They began to ask each other questions:

Who is this? What is this new teaching? With authority and power he commands even the unclean spirits to come out of a man and they obey him!

The news of this immediately spread. Rumors started concerning Jesus.

Everywhere in the region of Galilee and the outlying areas they were talking about Jesus.

HEALING PETER'S MOTHER-IN-LAW

After Jesus had healed the demoniac, he left the synagogue and went into the house of Simon and Andrew.

James and John were with him.

Jesus found Simon's mother-in-law sick with a high fever. All the members of the household asked Jesus to heal her.

Jesus stood over her, rebuked the fever and touched her hand. She immediately got up and the fever left her.

Stone arches over an alley in Safed, Galilee

Full of vigor, she began serving Jesus and his disciples.

News of where Jesus was staying spread quickly. As the sun set, people started bringing anyone sick or demon-possessed to Jesus. He healed them all.

This was a fulfillment of the prophecy in Isaiah that says, He himself took on our infirmities and he bore our diseases.

Soon, all the city's people gathered outside the house in which Jesus was staying.

Jesus healed those sick with many kinds of diseases and he cast out demons.

The demons came out of their victims, screaming and saying, *You are the Son of God*.

Jesus rebuked the demons and commanded them not to speak or declare that he was the Christ.

PREACHING TOUR THROUGH GALILEE

Early the next morning, Jesus got up and left the home of Simon Peter and headed for a deserted place where he prayed. Simon and those with him followed, and when they said:

Everyone is looking for you.

Jesus said to them:

Let's go into the next town where I can preach, for this is my mission.

The crowds looked for Jesus and when they found him they begged him not to leave their city.

But Jesus said to them:

I must preach the good news of the kingdom of God to the other cities also, this is why I was sent.

Jesus went all around Galilee teaching in their synagogues and preaching the gospel of the kingdom, casting out demons and healing all their sicknesses and diseases.

News of Jesus spread into all Syria, and people brought to Jesus all who were sick, those tormented by

Modern Kibbutz agriculture in Galilee

demons, the epileptic and palsied. He healed them all.

A great crowd followed Jesus from Galilee, **Decapolis**†, Jerusalem, Judea and from beyond the Jordan.

Streetscape in Galilee's Safed

JESUS HEALS A LEPER

While Jesus was in **leprosy**† one of the cities, a man full of came to him, and when he saw Jesus he cried out to him and knelt down in front of him and fell on his face and worshipped him, and begged Jesus:

Lord, if you are willing, you can make me clean.

Jesus was moved with compassion and stretched out his hand and touched him.

Jesus said:

I am willing. You are made clean.

Immediately, the leprosy was gone. Then Jesus sent him away, strictly instructing him not to say anything about what had happened, but to go to the priest and offer a sacrifice for cleansing, according to the law of Moses.

The man left Jesus and began to tell everyone what had happened to him and to spread the news of his deliverance from leprosy.

This caused much excitement and great crowds came to hear Jesus and to be healed of their infirmities.

The crowds became so large that Jesus could no longer enter openly into the city.

Jesus withdrew to a place in the desert where he prayed. But people pursued him from every part of the country.

† Further reading available at the end of this chapter.

JESUS HEALS A PARALYTIC

Days later, Jesus returned to Capernaum for more teaching. The crowds discovered the house where Jesus was staying.

The crowds trying to get into the house were so great that there was no room for anyone to squeeze even through a door. Jesus was teaching them the word of God. Pharisees and **doctors of the law**† had come from every village of Galilee, Judea and Jerusalem.

Jesus was displaying the Lord's power as he healed people of all sorts of sickness and disease.

Four men carried a man in a **bed**† who was paralyzed, but they could not reach Jesus because of the crowds.

So they carried the man up the stairs to the rooftop where they uncovered the roof tiles and let the man down through the hole in the roof. They let him down right in the middle of the crowd where Jesus was teaching and healing.

Jesus saw their faith and said to the paralyzed man:

Man, be of good cheer, your sins are forgiven.

Ancient holy city of Safed in Galilee

When some of the scribes and Pharisees who were sitting near Jesus heard what he had said to the paralytic, they spoke among themselves and wondered:

How can he say something like this? He is a blasphemer. Who is this person speaking blasphemies†? Who can forgive sins? Only God can forgive a man's sins.

Jesus knew what they were thinking and asked them:

Why are you thinking evil thoughts in your hearts? What is easier, to say to the paralyzed man, "your sins be forgiven," or to say, "stand up and take up your bed and walk"?

The man immediately stood up and took his bed and walked in front of everyone. He left for his house, glorifying God. Everyone was amazed, and when the

† Further reading available at the end of this chapter.

crowd saw what had happened, they were afraid.

They were filled with excitement and began glorifying God who had given such authority to a man.

THE CALL OF MATTHEW

After the healing of the paralytic, Jesus went to the seaside to walk along the shore. The crowds followed him and he taught them as he walked along the sea.

Jesus passed a man named Matthew, son of Alphaeus. Matthew was a tax collector and was sitting at his place of business.

Jesus said to him:

Follow me.

Matthew immediately left all his business, stood up, and followed Jesus.

END OF CHAPTER FOUR

CHAPTER FOUR
COMPANION

BED (page 69)

A bed in Jesus' time could be a mat, or a couple of quilts, or a cot with a light, portable frame, or a platform along the side of a house.

Most of the time it was much like a light blanket or two. When Jesus told a man who was healed to pick up his bed, he would have been rolling up a mat.

BLASPHEMY (page 69)

Speaking evil or insults about God or to God.

The Jewish religious leaders accused Jesus of blasphemy when he claimed he was equal with God. The fact that they accused him of blasphemy shows that they understood clearly that he was a man claiming to be God, not just a nice guy or a good teacher.

The fact that Jesus, who was obviously fully human, was claiming to be the God who created the universe, was considered by the Jewish religious leaders to be an insult to God.

DECAPOLIS (page 68)

It was a confederation often Hellenistic cities formed after Pompey took control of the area about 65 years before Christ was born. Most of the people in this region were Gentiles (anyone who wasn't a Jew was a Gentile), and many of them were Greek-speaking Roman soldiers.

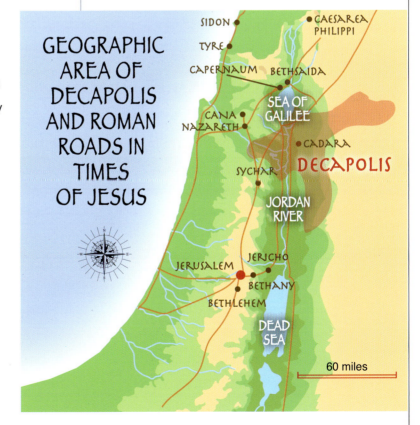

THE STORY OF JESUS

The cities had banded together to protect their citizens from Arabian tribes and militant Jews.

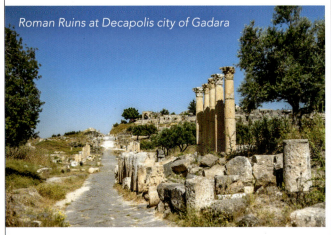
Roman Ruins at Decapolis city of Gadara

DEMON, OR UNCLEAN SPIRIT (page 65)

Demons are angels who chose to follow Satan and were banished from heaven with him.

They roam the earth and tempt people, and sometimes even control or possess them. They try to get us to choose against God and ultimately destroy ourselves and our relationships. Unclean spirits are the same thing as demons.

DOVES FOR SACRIFICE (page 55)

Some people did not raise sheep and were too poor to buy a lamb, so God allowed them to use a dove to sacrifice instead. If they were too poor to buy a dove, they were allowed to offer a small amount of flour.

God reached out to all of us, first in the sacrificial system, and then through Jesus, to make a way for our sin to be forgiven so we can enjoy a relationship with God. All he requires is that we confess (acknowledge) our sin and put our trust in Him.

In the Jewish sacrificial system, God also set up sacrifices to be offered on special occasions, and for repairing relationships with other people.

ETERNAL LIFE (pages 57 and 59)

The free gift given by Jesus to all who trust in Him.

It is endless life in the future with God and other believers in heaven, and also the joy and newness of life that faith in Jesus brings daily to those who trust Him.

FEAST OF THE TABERNACLES (page 56)

A yearly Jewish feast to commemorate the 40 years the Jews wandered in the desert after they came out of Egypt. It was also a thanksgiving for the harvest.

It is also called the "feast of booths" because the Jews stayed in booths (tents) for a few days to remember when they lived in tents for 40 years in the desert.

LAWYERS (page 69)

The lawyers in Jesus time were the scribes. Jewish scribes functioned not only to preserve the Scriptures by copying them and teaching them, but also by settling disputes and questions regarding the laws of Moses. See the definition of "scribe" for more information.

LEPROSY (page 68)

A disease that eats away at the skin, and eventually the nerves and bones.

Many lepers lose or damage limbs because when their nerves are damaged, they cut or burn themselves and don't feel it.

Lepers in Christ's time were required to live outside the city and yell "leper" anytime people came near, so they would not get close.

There was no known cure. It was even considered by some a judgment of God because, these people said, the leprosy that was visible was an indication of their rotten spiritual condition.

Lepers were left to fend on their own and to die a slow death. Jesus was compassionate to the lepers and showed that he cared about even the people that were considered the lowest on the social scale. He cared about them physically and spiritually.

MONEYCHANGERS (page 55)

Moneychangers were Jews who charged other Jews to change their currency into special temple currency. Many Jews traveled long distances to come to the temple in Jerusalem to sacrifice an animal as a symbol of the penalty for the sins they have committed. If it was too far to bring an animal, they had to buy an animal at the temple, but the people who sold the animals would only take temple currency.

Over the years, the moneychangers began to charge exorbitant fees for the exchange and the animal sellers were overcharging for the animals.

Many of the moneychangers were getting rich by overcharging poor people who were sincere about worshipping God. Jesus was upset with the moneychangers because they were not only profiting by being unfair to people who had no other options, but they were doing it on the temple property, which was supposed to be a place of worship.

REBIRTH (page 56)

Rebirth is when God gives us new spiritual life. It is called rebirth, or being "born again" because first we are born physically, and then by God's grace we are born spiritually.

We all begin this life "dead" spiritually because we are both sinners by birth and by practice. Sin separates us from God. Jesus paid the penalty for our sins when he lived a perfect life and died on the cross in order to pay the penalty for our sin and to become the mediator between us and God the Father.

When we by faith put our trust in Jesus, rather than our own efforts, we are brought into a right relationship with God. When this happens, we enter into eternal life, which means that we know and are known by God the Father, becoming one of his children.

The evidence that we are born again is that the Holy Spirit enters into our life and leads us into truth and enables us to produce "good fruit" including love, joy, peace, patience, and other "fruits of the spirit" in our lives *(Galatians 5:22-23)*.

We will not choose to pursue a lifestyle of sin as God gives us the power to resist temptation *(1 John 3:9; I Corinthians 10:13)*.

When we do sin we are promised that when we confess the sin that God will forgive us and cleanse us from it. Nowhere in the Bible does it teach that we are forgiven of sins by simply agreeing with God that we are sinners without repenting of the sin and being cleansed of its effect and delivered from its power over us by the power of God. *(1 John 1:9)*.

This does not mean that we do not repeat the same sins over and over, but only that true confession abhors the sin and begs God for both forgiveness and deliverance. Deliverance that God promises his people.

Being reborn into God family always produces the family traits of love, joy, patience, peace, long suffering, goodness, gentleness, faithfulness, meekness and self control.

As long as we are in this mortal body we will struggle with sin and its consequences. The Good News is that Jesus came to save sinners from past, present and future sins and that he indwells us for the purpose of changing us into his likeness.

One day, when we die in Christ, we will be delivered from the sin that struggles against the new nature that God has put in all his people. We will then live eternally free from both sin and its consequences, and in harmony with our God and Creator, to his everlasting praise and glory.

SABBATH (page 65)

The Sabbath is the last day of the week set aside by the Jews as a day of rest and worship. This is based on the fact that God rested on the seventh day when he was creating the universe.

The fourth of the Ten Commandments is to, "Remember the Sabbath day, to keep it holy. Six days you shall labor and do all your work, but the seventh day is a Sabbath of the Lord your God; in it you shall not do any work..." (*Exodus 20:8-10*).

Over the 1,200 years between the time the 10 commandments were given and the time Jesus lived, the Jews had developed elaborate rules and regulations to define "work." For instance on the Sabbath, a scribe was not allowed to carry a pen in his belt. A Jew was only allowed to travel 729 paces (about 2,000 cubits, or less than half a mile) without violating the law. They also made rules to get around the rules. For instance if you stashed some food in different places ahead of time to "establish residences," you could go from each of them another 2,000 cubits and still be legal.

The Jews were outraged at Jesus for healing on the Sabbath because he confronted them for making their rules more important than worshipping God. He was also claiming that he was God and the work that he was doing was just as important as what He did when He created the universe.

The religious leaders understood exactly what he was saying because they accused him of blasphemy and thought that he should receive the penalty of being killed by stoning.

It is still a commandment to rest every seventh day. Most Christians set aside Sundays because Jesus rose from the dead on the first day of the week.

SAMARIA (page 59)

People who lived in Samaria who were the result of intermarriage with Jews and Assyrians.

Assyrians invaded Israel about 700 years before Christ was born. They took many of the leaders as captives back to Assyria and transplanted Assyrians in order to change the Jewish culture in Samaria.

Landscape of the Mountains in Samaria

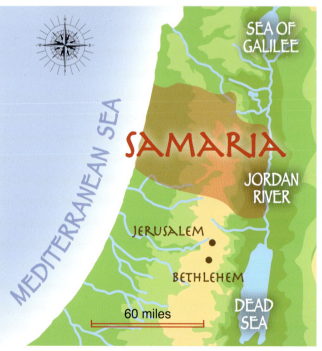

Jews came to view these people as inferior. They would even walk around a Samarian city instead of going directly through it just so they could avoid talking to or contacting a Samaritan.

SCRIPTURES (page 56)

A collection of sacred writings.

God communicated his message to specific people and they wrote it down **(2 Peter 1:21; 2 Timothy 3:16).**

When Jesus was living, the Scripture was considered what we call the Old Testament.

They are also referred to as the "Law and the Prophets." The New Testament was written by the apostles and people close to the apostles within a few years after Jesus died. Matthew, Mark, Luke and John are called the Gospels.

They are accounts of Jesus' life and ministry written from the perspective of each writer.

The Acts of the Apostles, or Acts for short, is the account of how the good news of Jesus was spread to different parts of the world.

Revelation is a record of a vision that the apostle John had about some of the churches in his day and about the end of the world when Jesus will return to earth, and create a new heaven and new earth.

The other books in the New Testament are letters written mostly by apostles to individuals or churches to give them instruction about the meaning of Jesus' life, death and resurrection, how the Holy Spirit works in our lives, and encouragement to act on what we believe.

SEA OF GALILEE (page 64)

Many of Jesus' disciples were fishermen on the Sea of Galilee. The lake was known for violent squalls that would come up with little warning.

One of the main industries was salting the fish to be exported across the Roman Empire. When Jesus was talking about the "salt of the earth" in **Matthew 5:13**, the people from that area knew about salt because it was their job, and they would see it every day.

SYCHAR (page 59)

Nothing remains of this biblical place, not even archaeological excavations.

Modern hill town in Samaria near ancient Sychar

SYNAGOGUE (page 63)

A place where Jews would gather to participate in services including prayer, the reading of the Scriptures (Old Testament), and exposition of the scripture that was read. They would sometimes be used as schools.

Sea of Galilee at Sunrise

CHAPTER FIVE

SECOND PASSOVER TO THE THIRD

◆◇◆

JESUS HEALS ON THE SABBATH DAY

The time of year had come for the feast of the Jews. Jesus went to Jerusalem on the Sabbath.

By the sheep gate in town was a **pool**†, which in Hebrew is called Bethesda. The pool had five covered porches, where many sick, blind, lame and withered people lived. One man had been there 38 years.

When Jesus saw him lying there, he said to the man:

Do you want to be healed?

The sick man said:

Sir, I don't have anyone to put me into the pool when the waters are stirred. Someone always goes in ahead of me.

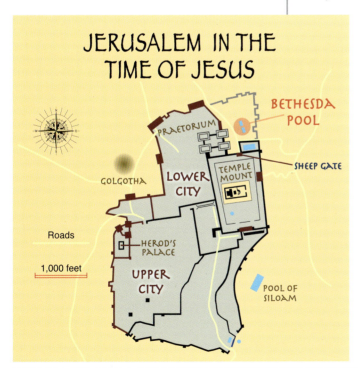

Jerusalem, ruins of the pool of Bethesda

† Further reading available at the end of this chapter.

THE STORY OF JESUS

Jesus said:

Stand up, take up your bed and walk.

Just like that, the man was healed.

When the Jews saw the man carrying his bed, they stopped him and told him that it was not lawful for him to carry his bed on the Sabbath.

But the man retorted:

The man who healed me told me to take up my bed and walk.

Who is this man who told you to take up your bed and walk?

The healed man did not know because Jesus had left the area.

Afterward, Jesus found the man in the temple and said to him:

Look, you are healed; do not sin anymore or else a worse thing will happen to you.

The man went away and found the Jews. He told them that it was Jesus who had healed him.

After learning this, the Jews began to persecute Jesus because he did this work on the Sabbath.

Jesus told them:

My Father is working even up until this moment, and I will work also.

The Jews took great insult at what Jesus said and became determined to kill him. They were angry because he made himself equal to God — not just that he had healed a man on the Sabbath.

Jesus responded, at great length:

Listen carefully to the truth I am going to declare to you: The Son can do nothing by himself, but only what he sees the Father doing.

Whatever the Father does, the Son will do the same. The Father loves the Son and shows him all the things that he does, and even greater works than what you have already seen will be done so that you will marvel.

Another view of the pool of Bethesda in Jerusalem

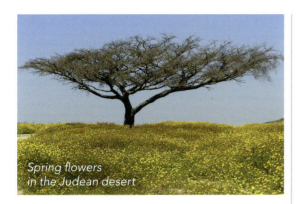
Spring flowers in the Judean desert

Just as the Father raises the dead and gives them life, in the same way, the Son will also give life to whoever he will.

The Father is not going to judge any man; he has given the authority to judge to the Son, so that all may honor the Son, just as they honor the Father.

The person that does not honor the Son, does not honor the Father who sent him.

Listen carefully to the truth I am going to declare to you. Whoever hears my word and believes in the Father who sent me has eternal life.

This person does not come into judgment but has passed from death to life.

The hour is coming, and now is here, when the dead will hear the voice of the Son of God.

Those who hear will live. Just as the Father has life in himself, in the same way, he gave to the Son life in himself and the Father has given the Son authority to execute judgment because he is the Son of man.

Don't be amazed at what I am saying to you: The hour is coming when all who are in the graves will hear his voice and they will come out, those that have done good, to the resurrection of life; and those that have done evil to the resurrection of judgment.

By myself I can do nothing: I judge only according to what I hear from the Father.

My judgment is right and perfect because it expresses the will of my Father, and my Father is the one that sent me to do his will, and it is his will I seek, not my own.

If I bear testimony of myself, then my testimony is not true. It is the Father that bears testimony, and I know that his testimony is true.

You have inquired of John the Baptist, and he has borne witness to the truth. But the testimony that I receive is not from a man. I am telling you these things so that you will be saved.

John the Baptist was like an oil lamp that burns and shines light, and you were willing to rejoice for a short time in his light.

THE STORY OF JESUS

But the testimony that I have is greater and more convincing than that of John the Baptist; for the works that the Father has given me to accomplish are the very works that I do, and they testify of me, and they prove that the Father has sent me.

The Father that sent me has testified of me. But you have not heard his voice at any time, nor have you seen his form.

You do not have his word living in you, and this is evidenced by the fact that you do not believe the one that the Father has sent.

You search the Scriptures because you think that in them you will find eternal life. These are the very Scriptures that testify and bear witness about me, but you will not come to me in order that you might have life.

I do not receive glory from people. I know you, and you do not have the love of God living in you.

I have come in my Father's name, and you will not receive me. If someone else comes in their own name, you will receive them. How can you believe, when you receive glory from one another, but refuse to seek the glory that comes from God?

Don't think that it is necessary for me to bring an accusation against you to my Father. There is already one that accuses you, and his name is Moses, the one on whom you have set your hopes.

JESUS DEFENDS HIS DISCIPLES

Jesus and his disciples were walking together on the Sabbath day through a grain field, probably on their way from Jerusalem to Galilee. His disciples, who were hungry, began to pluck grain, rub it in their hands and eat it.

Some Pharisees saw the disciples eating the grain and said to Jesus:

Look, your disciples are breaking the law of the Sabbath. Why are you doing what is unlawful to do on the Sabbath.

Jesus answered:

Haven't you read what King David did when he and his companions were hungry?

Remember how he came into the house of God, when Abiathar was the high priest, and took and ate the show bread and shared it with the entire company that was with him.

Was it lawful for David or his company to eat the show bread that was reserved for the priests alone?

Jerusalem, Tower of David

Have you not read in the law, that on the Sabbath day the priests in the temple engaged in chores and activities that were against the law for others.

Were they guiltless? I tell you this. Someone who is greater than the temple is here.

If you really knew what it meant when God declared through the prophet, I desire mercy, not sacrifice, you would not have condemned the guiltless.

The Son of man is Lord of the Sabbath.

The Sabbath was made for man, and not man for the Sabbath: The Son of man is Lord even of the Sabbath.

HEALING ON THE SABBATH

On another Sabbath day, Jesus entered into a synagogue and began to teach. There was a man in the synagogue with a withered right hand. The scribes and the Pharisees watched to see if Jesus would heal him on the Sabbath, so that they would have something to bring as an accusation against him.

They asked Jesus:

Is it lawful to heal on the Sabbath day?

Jesus knew exactly what they were thinking and said to the man with the withered hand:

Stand up and walk to the middle of the congregation.

The man did as Jesus said. Jesus spoke to them:

What man here who has one sheep that falls into a pit on the Sabbath day will not grab that sheep and pull it up out of the pit?

How much more valuable is a man than a sheep? It is lawful to do good on the Sabbath day. Is it lawful to do good on the Sabbath day, or to do harm?

To save a life or to destroy a life?

The scribes and the Pharisees said nothing.

Another view of the Tower of David

filled with anger and discussed with one another what they should do to Jesus. The Pharisees left the building and began conspiring with the secular powers under the authority of King Herod to figure out how they might destroy Jesus.

JESUS HEALS MULTITUDES

Jesus knew of these developments, and he withdrew with his disciples to the Sea of Galilee.

Many followed him who were from Galilee, Judea, Jerusalem and **Idumea**†, including crowds that were from beyond the Jordan and those around **Tyre**† and Sidon.

Jesus looked around at the congregation and became angry and grieved at the hardness of their hearts.

He said to the man in the midst of the assembly with the withered hand:

Stretch out your hand.

The man did as Jesus commanded. He stretched it out and it was restored, as whole as his other hand. The scribes and the Pharisees were

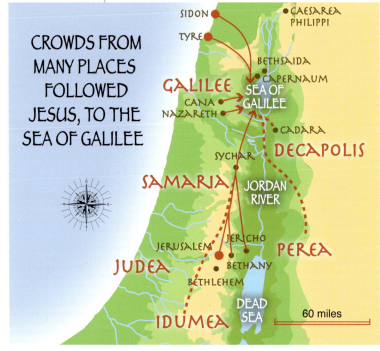

† Further reading available at the end of this chapter.

Jesus healed all those who were sick and diseased, but told them not to speak of it in order that the Scriptures would be fulfilled.

Again, it was Isaiah the prophet who said:

Look at my servant who I have chosen, my beloved in whom my soul is well pleased: I will put my Spirit on him, and he will declare judgment to the Gentiles.

He will not strive, nor cry aloud; neither will anyone hear his voice in the streets. A bruised reed he will not break, and smoking wick he will not extinguish, until the authoritative announcement of the divine purpose and will is sent out and has advanced to its final triumph.

The crowds were literally falling all over Jesus, so he asked his disciples to arrange for him to have a boat waiting on shore so he could escape the press of the crowd.

The demoniacally possessed fell down before Jesus and cried:

You are the Son of God.

Jesus continued to tell them not to speak. The sick, and even those with **plagues**† pressed from every side in order to get close enough to Jesus to touch him.

JESUS SELECTS TWELVE APOSTLES

Days later, Jesus went into the mountains to pray, and he continued to pray to God all night. When the morning came, he called his disciples and named the ones that he wanted to continue following him.

Here are the names of the apostles who Jesus chose:

- Simon, who is called Peter
- Andrew, brother of Simon

Flowering almond tree in desert

† Further reading available at the end of this chapter.

- James, son of Zebedee (nicknamed *sons of thunder*)
- John, brother of James (nicknamed *sons of thunder*)
- Bartholomew
- Phillip
- Thomas also called *Didymus*
- Matthew, the tax collector, also called *Levi*
- James, son of *Alphaeus*
- Thaddaeus
- Simon the Cananaean *(the zealot)*
- Judas Iscariot (the one who betrayed Jesus)

SERMON ON THE MOUNT

Jesus came down the mountain with his disciples and found a level place.

He was joined by a multitude of other disciples and a great number of people from all of Judea and Jerusalem, and crowds from the sea coast of Tyre and Sidon who had come to hear him and to be healed of their diseases. When Jesus saw the multitudes he healed those who were sick and diseased.

INTRODUCTORY STATEMENTS

After this, Jesus went up the mountain again and found a place to sit down. His disciples came to him. Jesus lifted his eyes and looked at them and began to teach them. This is what he taught.

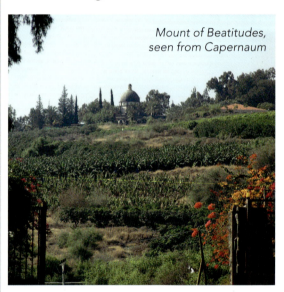

Mount of Beatitudes, seen from Capernaum

Beatitudes Chapel at the site of the Sermon on the Mount

BEATITUDES

Jesus said:

Blessed are the poor in spirit: for theirs is the kingdom of heaven.

Blessed are they who mourn: for they shall be comforted.

Blessed are the meek: for they shall inherit the earth.

Blessed are they who hunger and thirst for righteousness: for they shall be filled.

Blessed are the merciful: for they shall obtain mercy.

Blessed are the pure in heart: for they shall see God.

Blessed are the peacemakers: for they shall be called the sons of God.

Blessed are they that have been persecuted for righteousness' sake: for theirs is the kingdom of heaven.

Blessed are the poor: for theirs is the kingdom of God.

Blessed are you who hunger now: for they shall be filled.

View from Mount of Beatitudes

Blessed are you that weep now: for they shall laugh.

Blessed are you when men shall hate you, and when they exclude you from their company, and reproach you, and call out your name as evil, and persecute you, and say all kinds of evil against you falsely, for my sake.

Rejoice in that day, and be exceeding glad, and leap for joy; for your reward is great in heaven, for this is the same way their fathers treated the prophets and persecuted the prophets that came before you.

But woe to you who are rich! For you have received your consolation. Woe to you that are full now! For you shall be hungry. Woe to you that laugh now, for you shall mourn and weep.

Woe to you, when all men speak well of you! For this is the same way they treated the false prophets.

DUTIES OF MESSIAH'S SUBJECTS

Jesus said:

You are the salt of the earth; but if a salt loses its flavor, how can it be made salty again? It is good for nothing and is cast out and trampled under the feet of men.

You are the light of the world. A city set on a hill cannot be hidden. Nor do men light a lamp and put it under a pot. They put it on a lamp stand so that it can provide light for everyone in the house.

In the same way, you are to let your light shine before men; that they may see your good works and glorify your Father who is in heaven.

I tell you an important truth, until heaven and earth pass away, not one small stroke of the pen, or the smallest letter in the alphabet will be removed from the law until all things are accomplished.

*Whoever breaks even one of the least of the **commandments**†, and teaches men to break them, will be called the least in the kingdom of heaven:*

But, whoever teaches the law of God - and also does it - will be called great in the kingdom of heaven.

Unless your righteousness is greater than the righteousness of the scribes and Pharisees, you will not even enter the kingdom of heaven.

*You have heard it said for ages, You shall not kill; and whoever kills shall be in danger of the judgment. But I say to you that anyone who is angry with his brother shall be in danger of the judgment; and whoever says to his brother, 'Heretic' shall be in danger of the council; and whoever shall say 'You fool' shall be in danger of **hell**† commandments fire.*

If you are offering your gift at the altar, and while you are there you remember that your brother has something against

† Further reading available at the end of this chapter.

you, leave your gift at the altar and go find your brother and be reconciled, and then come off er your gift.

Agree with your adversary quickly, before he goes to the judge or your adversary will take you in front of the judge and the judge will tum you over to an **officer**† *of the court who will cast you into prison.*

Truly I tell you this, you will not escape your punishment until you have paid the last cent you owe.

You have heard that it has been said, You shall not commit adultery. But I say to you, anyone that even looks at a woman with lust for her, has already committed adultery with her in his heart.

If your right eye causes you to stumble, pluck it out and throw it away. It is better that a part of your body perish than your whole body be cast into hell.

If your right hand causes you to do evil, cut it off and throw it away: It is better that you cut off a part of your body and throw it away than your whole body be cast into hell.

It is said, Whoever divorces his wife, let him give her a writing of divorcement.

But I say to you, anyone who divorces his wife, except for fornication, makes her an adulteress: And whoever marries her after she is divorced commits adultery.

Again, you have heard the old saying:

'You shall keep the oaths made to God.'

And so you swear oaths in which God is not mentioned, thinking that you can avoid keeping your word. I say to you, do not swear an oath at all; not by heaven, for it is the throne of God; not by earth, for it is the footstool of God; not by Jerusalem, for it is the city of the great king. Do not swear an oath by your head, for you cannot make one hair white or black.

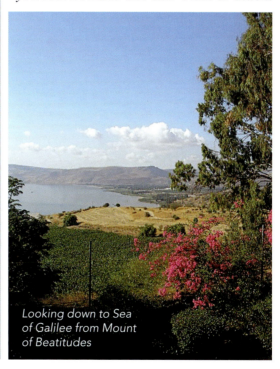

Looking down to Sea of Galilee from Mount of Beatitudes

† Further reading available at the end of this chapter.

Instead, let your speech be 'yes' and 'no.' Anything more than this is of the evil one.

You have heard that it is said, 'an eye for an eye and a tooth for a tooth.' But I tell you, do not resist the evil person. Whoever hits you on your right cheek, turn the other cheek to him. And if someone takes you to court to take away your coat, let him have your overcoat also.

If someone forces you to go a mile with him, go the second mile on your own.

Give to the person who asks you for something. If someone wants to borrow something from you, let him borrow it.

You have heard that it is said, 'you shall love your neighbor, and hate your enemy.' But I say to you who are listening, love your enemies, do good to them who hate you, bless them who curse you, and pray for them who persecute you and misuse you.

In this way, you may be sons of your Father who is in heaven. For he makes his sun to rise on the evil and the good, and sends rain on both the just and the unjust.

So, to the person who hits you on one cheek, offer the other; and to the person who takes away your coat, give him your overcoat also. Give to everyone who asks.

Do not try and recover your property from someone who borrows it and does not return it.

If you only love those who love you, what reward do you have? Even the tax collectors love their friends, and even the sinners love those that love them. If you only do good to those who do good to you, what reward do you have? Even the sinners do that.

If you lend to someone, expecting to receive it back, what reward to you have? Even sinners lend money expecting to get an equal amount or more back.

Love your enemies and do them good. Keep in mind that God is kind to the unthankful and the evil.

If you give a kind greeting to your friends and relatives only, what is noteworthy about that? Everyone does that.

You are to be merciful, even as your Father is merciful. You are to be perfect, as your heavenly Father is perfect.

ALMSGIVING, PRAYER, AND FASTING

Jesus said:

Be careful that you do not do your righteous acts only to be seen by men: If you do, you will have no reward from your Father who is in heaven.

When you give your gifts and **tithes**† do not sound a trumpet to announce your giving like the hypocrites do in the synagogues and in the streets, in order to be seen and receive glory from men. The truth you need to understand is that by giving in this way you have already received their reward.

Instead, when you give your gifts and tithes, do not let your left hand know what your right hand is doing. Do your giving in secret and your heavenly Father who sees in secret will reward you.

When you pray, go into a private place and shut the door in order that you might pray to your father who is in secret. Your heavenly Father, who sees all the secret and hidden things, will reward you.

Pathway to the Beatitudes Chapel

When you pray do not use vain repetitions, like the Gentiles do: They have the mistaken idea that they will be heard because they repeat their prayers over and over and speak a lot of words. Don't be like them. Your Father knows what you need before you even ask him.

This is way you should pray:

Our Father who is in heaven, hallowed be your name. May your kingdom come. May your will be done on earth as it is in heaven. Give us the bread we need for today. And forgive us our debts in the same way that we forgive those who owe us anything. And bring us not into temptation, but deliver us from the evil one.

For if you forgive men their trespasses, your heavenly Fat her will also forgive you. But if you do not forgive others their trespasses; your Father will not forgive your trespasses.

And when you fast, don't act like the hypocrites who put on a sad face and change their appearance in order to look glum and unkempt in order to be seen by men. The truth you need to understand is that they already have their reward.

† Further reading available at the end of this chapter.

*When you fast, **anoint**† your head and wash your face so that men will not notice that you are fasting. Your Father in heaven will know and he will reward you.*

HEAVENLY TREASURES

Jesus Said:

Don't put away treasures for yourself here on earth, where moth and rust consume and where thieves break in and steal.

Put away treasure for yourself in heaven, where there are no moths to consume and no rust to destroy, and no thieves to break in and steal. Where your treasure is, that is where your heart will be also.

The lamp of the body is the eye. If your eye is focused on eternal things then your whole body will be full of light. But if your eye is focused on evil things, then your whole body will be full of darkness. And great is that darkness.

No one can serve two masters, for either he will hate one master and love the other; or he will be loyal to one master and despise the other.

You cannot serve God and earthly riches.

The conclusion is this: do not be anxious about your life, what you eat or drink or the clothes you wear. Isn't life more than food, body and clothing?

Look at the birds in the sky. They do not plant or grow crops, nor do they gather provisions into barns. And your heavenly Father feeds them. Aren't you much more valuable than the birds?

Which of you, by being anxious, can add one minute to the length of his life? And why are you anxious about what you wear?

Consider the lilies of the field and how they grow.

Pathway to t Lilies of the field, poppies in bloom on the Mount of Olives, Israel

They don't labor or sew clothing and yet even Solomon, in all his glory, was not dressed like one of these.

If God takes care of the clothing for the grass of the fields, which is here today and tomorrow is thrown in the oven, won't he be even more concerned to clothe you?

Do not be anxious, saying, What shall we eat? or, What shall we drink? How will we be clothed? These are things that the Gentiles are seeking after.

Your heavenly Father knows that you have need of all these things.

But you should seek first his kingdom, and his righteousness; and all these things will be added to you. Do not be anxious about tomorrow; tomorrow will take care of itself.

There is enough trouble in one day without adding to it by borrowing trouble from tomorrow.

LAW CONCERNING JUDGING

Jesus Said:

Judge not so that you will not be judged. The judgments that you make will be the same judgments by which you are judged.

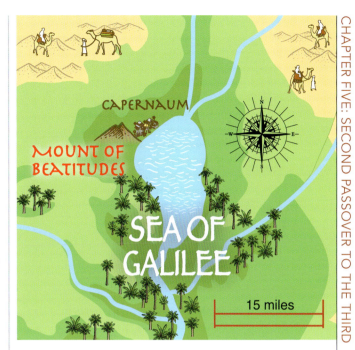

Whatever judgment you measure out will be the same judgment you receive. Do not condemn others and you will not be condemned. Be merciful and you will receive mercy.

Give and it will be given to you; all that you need, pressed down, shaken together, running over. For whatever measuring cup you use to give to others, the same measuring cup will be used to give to you.

Jesus then told his disciples a **parable**†: He asked them, *Can the blind lead the blind? Won't they both fall into a pit? The disciple is not greater than his teacher.*

And why are you looking at the small speck of sawdust in your brother's eye

† Further reading available at the end of this chapter.

and not considering the huge timber beam that is in your own eye?

How can you be of any help removing the speck from your brother's eye when you have a beam in your own eye? You hypocrite, remove the beam from your own eye so that you can see clearly to pick the speck out of your brothers eye.

Do not give things that are holy to vicious dogs, and do not cast your pearls before wild boars, for they will just trample them under feet and then turn on you to do you harm.

CONCERNING PRAYER

Ask and it will be given to you; seek, and you will find; knock and it will be opened up to you. For everyone who asks will receive. The person who seeks will find. The one who knocks will have the door opened.

Who among you, if his son should ask him for a loaf of bread, will give him a stone? Or if he asks for a fish, will give him a snake?

If you then, being evil, know how to give good gifts to your children, how much more will your Father who is in heaven give good gifts to those who ask him?

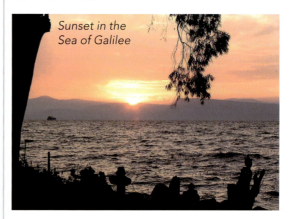

Sunset in the Sea of Galilee

THE GOLDEN RULE

Jesus Said:

Treat others in all the ways you would like others to treat you. This is the teaching of the law and the prophets.

THE TWO WAYS

Jesus Said:

Enter in by the narrow gate. Wide is the gate and broad is the way that leads to destruction, and there are many who enter that gate.

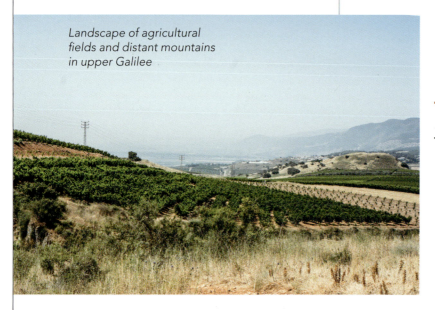

Landscape of agricultural fields and distant mountains in upper Galilee

Narrow is the gate and straight is the way that leads to life, and there are few who find it.

Beware of false prophets, who come to you in sheep's clothing, but inwardly are ravening wolves.

By their fruits, you will know them. Do men gather grapes from a thorn-bush or figs from thistles? In the same way, every good tree produces good fruit.

The corrupt tree produces evil fruit. The tree that produces corrupt fruit will be cut down and burned by fire.

Therefore, by their fruits you shall know them. The good man, out of the treasure of his heart, will produce what is good. The evil man will produce what is evil. Out of the abundance of the heart the mouth speaks.

Not everyone who calls me Lord will enter into the kingdom of heaven - only those who do the will of my father who is in heaven.

Many will say to me in that day of final judgment, Lord, didn't we prophecy in your name, didn't we cast out demons in your name and do many mighty works?

Fish pond on Kibbutz in Galilee

I will confess to them, I never knew you: Go away from me, you workers of lawlessness.

TWO BUILDERS

Jesus Said:

Why do you call me Lord and do not do the things which I told you to do?

Everyone who comes to me and hears my words and does them is like the builder who dug the foundation deep into the ground and laid its foundation on the solid rock.

The rains came and the floods poured down and the winds blew and beat against the house, but the house remained solid because its foundation was built on the rock.

Everyone who comes to me and hears my words and does not do them is like the builder who dug the foundation into the sand.

The rains came, and the floods poured down and the winds blew and beat against the house, and the house collapsed because its foundation was built on sand.

After Jesus finished these teachings, the multitudes were astonished because he taught them as someone with authority, not as their scribes.

HEALING THE CENTURION'S SERVANT

After Jesus had finished preaching in parables to the multitude, he went down the mountain and entered Capernaum. The multitudes followed him.

He was greeted by a delegation of Jews who asked him to heal a **centurion's**† gravely ill servant because he was a man who loved the nation of Israel and had built a synagogue with his own money.

Jesus agreed. But as he approached the centurion's home, the centurion sent out friends to ask Jesus not to trouble himself by coming into his home.

He then approached Jesus and said he did not feel he was worthy for Jesus to enter his home, nor even worthy to meet Jesus himself.

He asked Jesus just to say the word and his servant would be healed. The centurion said he had authority over soldiers who would obey him.

When Jesus heard this, he turned to the crowd that followed him and said:

Truly I say to you, I have not found faith this great, not even in Israel. And I tell you that many will come from the east and the west and will sit down

† Further reading available at the end of this chapter.

Roman ruins in Samaria

with Abraham, Isaac and Jacob, in the kingdom of heaven. But the sons of the kingdom, the Israelites, shall be cast into outer darkness, where there will be weeping and gnashing of teeth.

Jesus said to the centurion:

Go your way, it has been done just as you believed. And when the centurion returned to his house he found the servant healed and whole.

JESUS RAISES THE WIDOW'S SON

Soon after healing the centurion's servant, Jesus, his disciples and a great multitude went to a city called **Nain**†.

As he came near to the city gate, there was a funeral procession carrying a dead boy out of the city. The boy was the only son of a widow, and many of the people from the city were with her.

When Jesus saw her, he told her:

Don't weep.

He approached the coffin and those who were carrying the coffin stood still.

Jesus said to the young man:

I say to you, get up.

And the boy who had been dead sat up and began to speak. Jesus gave him to his mother.

Everyone became filled with fear, and they glorified God, saying:

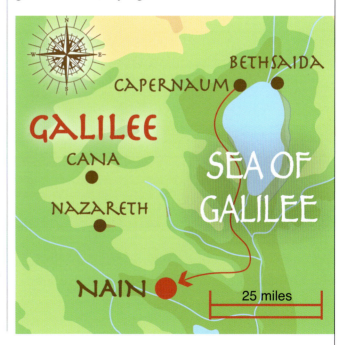

† Further reading available at the end of this chapter.

THE STORY OF JESUS

A great prophet has appeared among us, and God has visited his people.

The news of the dead boy being raised to life spread out to all of Judea and beyond.

QUESTION FROM PRISON

John the Baptist had been thrown into prison.

John's disciples kept him updated on what Jesus was teaching and the miracles that he was working.

John sent two of his disciples to ask Jesus:

Are you the Messiah we have been expecting or should we be looking for someone else?

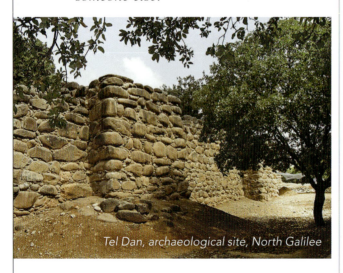
Tel Dan, archaeological site, North Galilee

John's disciples found Jesus, and as they waited for an answer to take back to John the Baptist, Jesus cured many diseases, healed those with the plague, cast out demons, and restored sight to the blind.

Jesus then answered the disciples of John by saying:

Go and tell John the things you have seen and heard, the blind receive sight, the lame walk, the lepers are cleansed, the deaf hear, the dead are raised to life, and the poor have good news preached to them. Tell John that blessed is the person who finds no reason to disbelieve in me.

When John's messengers left, Jesus began to teach the crowds regarding John the Baptist:

What did you go out in the wilderness to look at? A reed shaken by the wind? A man dressed in expensive clothes? Those who are finely dressed are in kings' houses. What did you expect to see? A prophet?

Yes, I tell you that John the Baptist was much more than a prophet.

He was the one the prophets wrote about when they said:

Behold, I send my messenger before your face, and he will prepare the way ahead of you.

The truth that you need to understand is that of all born of women there has never been a prophet greater than John the Baptist, and yet the most humble and least important person in the coming kingdom is greater than he.

All the common people who heard this agreed with God's wisdom in sending John to baptize in order that men might repent and get ready for the kingdom.

But the Pharisees and lawyers rejected the whole idea that John's baptism was necessary or important.

Then Jesus taught them and said:

This generation is like two groups of children sitting in the marketplace. One group called to the other to play with them, but the other group was sullen and stubborn and would not play.

The one group said to the other, we played music but you would not dance: We wailed, but you would not weep.

Jesus continued teaching:

John the Baptist came neither eating or drinking and they say his has a demon. The Son of man has come eating and drinking, and you say, Look, a gluttonous man and a drinker, a friend of tax collectors and sinners!

Jesus then spoke about the cities in which he did most of his miracles:

*Woe to you, **Chorazin**† ! Woe to you Bethsaida! If the mighty works that were done in your city had been done in Tyre and Sidon they would have repented in sack **cloth and ashes**† long ago. When the day of judgment comes, Tyre and Sidon will be judged more lightly than you.*

*And will Capernaum be exalted to heaven? No, it will be cast down to hell. If the mighty works that had been done in Capernaum, had been done in **Sodom**†, they would have repented, and the city would be standing today. It will be more tolerable for the land of Sodom at the day of judgment than for you.*

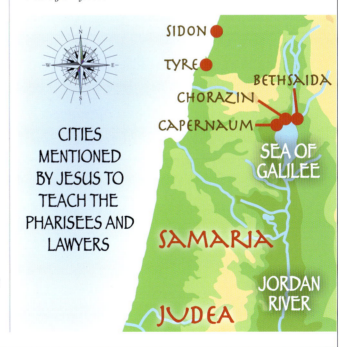

CITIES MENTIONED BY JESUS TO TEACH THE PHARISEES AND LAWYERS

† Further reading available at the end of this chapter.

THE STORY OF JESUS

Springtime in Galilee

Jesus then stopped and prayed out loud to his heavenly Father and said:

I thank you, O Father, Lord of heaven and earth, that you have hidden these things from the wise and the educated and that you revealed them to the pure and childlike. Yes, Father, for this is what pleases you.

Jesus continued:

All things have been given to me by my Father. No one knows the Son except the Father; and no one knows the Father but the Son, and those to whom the Son decides to reveal him.

Come to me, all of you whose souls labor and are burdened down, and I will give you rest.

Take my yoke upon you, and learn about me: for I am gentle and lowly in heart; and you will find rest for your souls.

My yoke is easy, and my burden is light.

JESUS' FEET ANOINTED

One of the Pharisees invited Jesus to his home. Jesus accepted and went to the Pharisee's home to eat a meal with him.

A woman who was known as a sinner found out that Jesus was in the house.

She entered the house carrying an alabaster bottle of ointment perfume. She went to the end of the couch that Jesus was reclining on and stood weeping so that her tears wet Jesus feet.

She then began to wipe Jesus' feet with her hair, kissed his feet and anointed them with the **perfumed oil**†.

The Pharisee said to himself:

If this man were a prophet he would have known that this is a sinful woman and would not allow her to touch him.

Jesus knew what his host was thinking, and said:

† Further reading available at the end of this chapter.

Simon (that was the Pharisee's name), I have something to say to you.

Simon said:

Teacher, tell me what is on your mind.

Jesus said:

A lender had two debtors: One owed him 500 shillings and the other owed him 50. Neither of the debtors was able to pay the lender back, so he forgave both debts. Now let me ask you a question: Which of the debtors will love the lender the most?

Simon answered:

I suppose the one who was forgiven the most.

Jesus said:

You have given the right answer.

Turning to the woman, he said to Simon:

Do you see this woman? I came into your house and you gave me no water to wash my feet, but she has wetted my feet with her tears and wiped them with her hair.

You did not give me a greeting kiss; but she, since the time I came into your house has not stopped kissing my feet. You did not anoint my head with oil, but she has anointed my feet with ointment.

I say to you, her sins, which are many, are forgiven because she loved much. But to whom little is forgiven, little love is shown.

Jesus said to the woman:

Your sins are forgiven.

Those who were at the table with Jesus began to say to each other:

Who does he think he is, that he can forgive sins?

Jesus said to the woman:

Your faith has saved you. Go in peace.

Harvesting olives in Samaria

JOURNEYING ABOUT GALILEE

After this, Jesus began preaching and bringing the good news of the kingdom of God to all the cities and villages in Galilee. His disciples were with him.

Jesus and his disciples were supported by Mary Magdalene, the woman Jesus had healed of evil spirits, Joanna, the wife of King Herod's steward, Susanna, and many others. They provided the disciples' meals and helped support their ministry.

As Jesus entered a home for a meal, the crowds flocked to him with such enthusiasm and so pressed in around Jesus that he could not even eat.

Jesus' brothers and mother went to try and rescue Jesus. They lacked faith and believed that Jesus was being swept away by a religious zealousness that was putting his safety in danger.

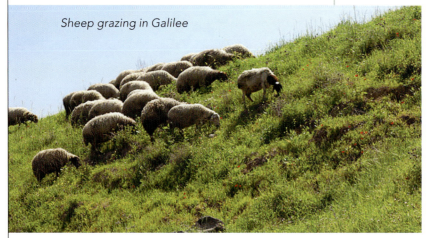

Sheep grazing in Galilee

But Jesus continued to heal and cast out demons. They brought a demon-possessed man to Jesus who was both deaf and blind. Jesus healed him, and the man was restored to his right mind and began to speak and to see.

The crowds were amazed, and some began to say:

Could this be the son of David?

ACCUSATIONS OF THE JEWS

When the scribes and the Pharisees heard this, they said:

This man casts out demons by the power of Beelzebub, the prince of demons.

Others tried to get Jesus to perform a heavenly sign to show that the Pharisees were mistaken.

Jesus, understanding everything they were thinking, called them together and told this parable:

How can Satan cast out Satan? A city or a house divided against itself cannot stand. A kingdom that is divided against itself cannot stand.

If Satan is divided against himself, then how will his kingdom stand? And if Satan has risen up against himself, he cannot stand but will come to an end.

If I am casting out demons by the power of Beelzebub, then by whose power are your disciples casting demons out? They will be your judge.

But if, by the power of the Holy Spirit of God, I cast out demons, then the kingdom of God has come upon you.

Galilee's landscape

When a strong man who is fully armed guards his home and belongings, his home is safe. But if a stronger man comes and defeats him, he takes away the armor that he was trusting in steals his goods and wrecks his home.

This can only happen if the strong man is bound and defeated.

He who is not with me is against me, and the person who is not gathering with me is scattering.

The truth you need to understand is this: Every sin and blasphemy will be forgiven. But the blasphemy against the Holy Spirit will not be forgiven. Anyone that speaks a word against the Son of man can be forgiven.

But anyone that blasphemes against the Holy Spirit can never be forgiven and has committed an eternal sin. This is a sin that will not be forgiven in this world or in the world to come.

This was Jesus' response to those who said he had an unclean spirit.

Jesus continued:

Be honest, say that the tree is good and produces good fruit or say that the tree is corrupt and produces corrupt fruit.

You children of snakes: how can you, being evil, speak good things? For out of the abundance of your heart your mouth speaks.

The good man, out of the good stored in him, produces good things. The evil man, out of the evil stored in him, produces evil things.

I tell you this, every careless word that a man speaks, he will give an account for it on the day of judgment. Your words will either justify you or they will condemn you.

SIGN SEEKERS

Again, the multitudes gathered together and came to Jesus. Some of the scribes and Pharisees questioned Jesus and asked for a miraculous sign.

But Jesus told them:

*This generation is evil, it looks for a sign. Only an evil and adulterous generation looks for signs. No sign will be given to you, except the sign of **Jonah**† the prophet.*

Jonah was in the belly of the great fish for three days and three nights.

In the same way, the Son of man will be three days and three nights in the heart of the Earth. Just like Jonah was a sign to the Ninevites, so will the Son of man be a sign to this generation.

*The men of **Nineveh**† will stand in judgment and condemn this generation, for they repented when Jonah preached to them: O look, someone greater than Jonah is here with you.*

The queen of the south will rise up in judgment with this generation and condemn it. She came from the ends of the earth to hear the wisdom of Solomon. And look, someone greater than Solomon is here with you.

When an unclean spirit goes out of a man he goes through desolate places and finds no rest. Then he says to himself; I will return to my old house that I left. And when he returns he finds the house empty and swept clean and decorated.

He then goes and finds seven other evil spirits more evil than himself and they enter the house and become residents. The last state of the man is worse that the first. It is the same way with this generation.

While Jesus was speaking, a woman in the crowd lifted up her voice and said:

Blessed is the womb from which you were born, and the breasts that nourished you.

Olive trees in Galilee

† Further reading available at the end of this chapter.

Jesus answered her and said:

Blessed are those that hear the word of God and obey it.

No one lights a lamp and puts it in his cellar, or under a pan, but on a lamp stand so that everyone that comes into his house can see the light.

The lamp of your body is your eye: When your eyes are focused on the right thing your whole body is full of light. But when your eyes are focused on what is evil, your entire body is full of darkness.

Look at yourselves and examine whether you are full of light or darkness.

THE TRUE FAMILY

While Jesus was still teaching the multitudes, his mother, and his brothers stood outside the house where Jesus was, wanting to talk to him.

Because the crowd was too thick to come into the house, they sent word through the crowd that they were calling him.

There was a great number of people sitting around Jesus, and as the word was passed along, someone said to Jesus:

Look, your mother and your brothers are looking for you, they are outside the building waiting to see you and they want to speak to you.

Jesus answered and said to the one who spoke:

Who is my mother? And who are my brothers? My mother and my brothers are those who hear the words of God and do them. For whoever does the will of my Father in heaven is my brother, and sister and mother.

Blooming chrysanthemums in the Galileean wilderness

JESUS DENOUNCES THE PHARISEES

While Jesus was teaching, one of the Pharisees in the crowd asked him to come have dinner with him.

Jesus accepted the invitation and entered his home.

When the Pharisee saw that Jesus did not wash his hands before sitting down to eat he was amazed.

Jesus said to him:

You Pharisees clean the outside of the cup and plate, but the inward parts are full of greed and wickedness.

You fools! Didn't the one who made the outside also make the inside? Give your inner life as an offering and everything is clean.

But woe to you Pharisees! You tithe with an exactness that is so precise that you give the tenth part of a seed or a herb.

But you ignore doing justice to others and loving God. Those are the things you should be giving, and not the other.

Woe to you Pharisees! You love the important seats in the synagogues and fancy greetings in the marketplace.

Woe to you! You are like tombs that have been whitewashed on the outside but are full of corruption and dead bones on the inside.

Purple flowers for export growing of a kibbutz

One of the lawyers who was listening, said to Jesus, Aren't you being hasty in your condemnation?

Jesus said to him:

Woe to you lawyers also! You load up men with burdens too heavy to carry, while you will not lift a finger to carry your own burdens.

Woe to you! You decorate the tombs of the prophets that your fathers killed. So you are witnesses and agree with the works of your fathers. Your fathers killed the prophets and you decorate their tombs.

Jesus then summarized the words spoken by the prophets of old and said:

I will send to them prophets and apostles, and some of them they will kill and per-

secute. The blood of the prophets, which was shed from the beginning of the world will be required of this generation.

*From the blood of **Abel**† to the blood of Zacharia, who was killed between the altar and the sanctuary, yes, I say to you, it will be required of this generation.*

Woe to you lawyers! You took away the key to understanding Scripture. You didn't even use the key to enter into the kingdom yourself, and you make it difficult for others to enter.

When Jesus was finished speaking, he left the building. The scribes and the Pharisees pressed hard against him to try and provoke him to say something that they could use against him.

A palm in the Judean desert

HIS APPROACHING PASSION

In the meantime, the crowds continued to grow to many thousands. There were so many people that they could hardly move without stepping on someone.

With the crowds nearby, Jesus began teaching his disciples. Jesus told them:

*Beware of the **yeast**† of the Pharisees, which is hypocrisy. There is nothing that is now concealed that will not be revealed, and nothing is hidden that will not be made known.*

Remember that whatever you have said in darkness will be heard in the light, and things which you have spoken in the most secret place will be broadcast on the housetops.

I say to you my friends, Do not be afraid of those who kill the body, because that is all they can do. But I warn you to be afraid of he who has the power not only to kill the body but to cast the soul into hell. Fear him.

Aren't five sparrows worth about two cents?

And not one of them is forgotten in the sight of God. Every hair of your head is numbered, Fear not: You are more valuable than many sparrows.

† Further reading available at the end of this chapter.

And I tell you this, everyone who acknowledges me before men, I will acknowledge him before the angels of God. But the person who denies me in the presence of men, he will be denied before the angels of God.

Everyone who speaks a word against the Son of man will be forgiven. But if a person blasphemes the Holy Spirit, will not be forgiven.

When they bring you before the synagogue and the rulers and the authorities, do not be anxious about how you will answer their charges, or what you should say, for the Holy Spirit will teach you what to say at the time when you are required to speak.

One of the people in the multitude shouted out:

Teacher, tell my brother to divide the inheritance with me.

Jesus told him:

Who made me a judge or a divider over you?

He turned to the crowd and said:

Pay attention and keep yourself from covetousness.

A man's life is not measured by the number of things that he owns.

Jesus then told them a parable:

There was a rich man who had a tremendous harvest. He said to himself:

What should I do since I have no place to store all the harvest.

And he said to himself:

This is what I will do: I will pull down my barns and build bigger barns; I will put all my grains and my goods in the new barns. I will say to my soul,

Soul you have much wealth laid up for many years to come, take your ease, eat drink and be merry.

Camels crossing the Judean desert

But God said to him:

You foolish man, this very night your soul is required of you; the things that you have stored up for yourself, whose will they be?

This is just like the person who stores up treasure for himself but is not rich toward God.

And he said to his disciples:

Listen to what I say. Do not be anxious about your life, as to what you are going to eat; or about your body, as to what you will wear. Life is more than food and clothing.

Think about the ravens, they do not plant or reap, they have no barns to store up grain, and yet God feeds them.

How much more valuable are you than the birds? Who among you, by being anxious, can add one minute to the length of his life?

You cannot affect even the smallest thing by being anxious. Why be anxious about everything else?

Think about the lilies of the field. They do not labor or make their own clothing, and yet Solomon and all his glory was not dressed like any of them.

If God clothes the grass of the field, which is here today and gone into the furnace tomorrow, how much more will he clothe you? Oh, you of little faith.

Don't worry about what you are going to eat or drink, and don't be anxious in your minds about the future. For this is how the world responds to life. Seek the kingdom and all these other things will be taken care of.

Do not be afraid, little flock, for it is your Father's good will to give you the kingdom. Sell what you have, and give gifts to God and his service.

Make for yourselves purses that do not wear out, and a treasure in heaven that will never run out, where there is no thief who will steal it or moths that will consume it. Wherever your treasure is, that's where your heart will be.

And be prepared to move quickly and keep your lamps burning.

Keep alert like men who are waiting for the groom to return to the marriage feast, so that when he comes and knocks on the door you are ready to answer it and let him in quickly.

Blessed are the servants who the Lord finds waiting for his return. When he comes, he will gather his faithful servants together and sit down to a meal with them and serve them.

Blessed are the servants who are ready for their Lord to come, even when he is least expected. So be ready, for he will come at a time when you don't think he is coming.

Peter then asked the Lord if these parables were for the disciples only or for everyone.

Jesus answered:

Blessed is the wise steward who is found doing his master's will when he comes. That faithful servant will be put in charge of much more after the master returns.

But woe to the servant who thinks, My Lord is going to be late coming, so I may mistreat the servants under me, and eat and drink and becomes drunk without any regard for the Lord's coming.

The Lord will come on a day that the servant does not expect and he will be punished severely.

The servant who acts disobediently, out of ignorance, will receive a lesser punishment.

To everyone who has been given much, much shall be required.

I came to rouse men to spiritual conflict. Do not think that I have come to give peace on the earth. No, but rather division.

In the future, five in one house will be divided; three will be of one mind and two of another.

A desert flower in Judea

A father will be divided against his son, and a son against his father; mother against daughter and daughter against her mother; mother in law against her daughter in law, and the daughter in law against her mother in law.

Then Jesus spoke to the crowds and said:

When you see a cloud rising in the west, you know that it is going to rain. And so it does. And when you see the south wind blowing, you say, There will be a scorching heat; And so it happens.

You hypocrites, you know how to interpret the weather and the sky; but you don't know how to interpret these present times.

Fig tree bearing fruit

BARREN FIG TREE

As Jesus was preaching about the signs of the times, there were some present who told Jesus about the Galilaeans, whose blood **Pilate**† had mingled with their sacrifices.

Jesus heard this and said:

Do you think that these Galilaeans were greater sinners than others? Unless you repent, you will also perish.

Regarding those 18 whom the tower of Siloam fell on and killed, do you think they were greater sinners than all the rest of the men who live in Jerusalem? Unless you repent you will also perish.

Then Jesus told this parable:

A man had a fig tree planted in his vineyard. The season for it to bear fruit came, but when the man examined the tree, he found no fruit.

He said to the gardener in charge, I have come and examined this tree for three years and for three years it has not produced any figs.

I want you to cut it down so that it stops blocking the light and taking up the space that the other fruit-bearing trees need.

The gardener said, Lord, please leave it growing for another year. I will dig around it and fertilize it, and if still does not produce fruit, then I will cut it down.

FIRST PARABLES

Jesus left the house he was staying in and went down to the seaside where he began to teach.

A great multitude came to be with Jesus and hear him teach. The crowd was so

† Further reading available at the end of this chapter.

great that Jesus got into a boat and pushed it a little ways offshore.

Then Jesus sat in the boat while the crowd stood on the beach. And Jesus began to teach them using parables.

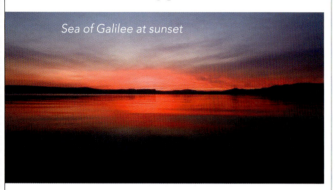
Sea of Galilee at sunset

PARABLE OF THE SOWER

Jesus taught:

Look, The sower went out to sow his seed, and as he sowed, some seeds fell along the path and were trodden under foot, and the birds of the sky came and ate the seeds.

Some of the seeds fell among the thorns and grew up among the thorns. But the thorns choked out the plants so that they did not produce any fruit.

Some of the seeds fell on the good soil and grew and some produced 100-fold and some produced 60-fold and some produced 30-fold.

And Jesus cried out:

Anyone that has ears to hear let him hear.

When Jesus was alone, the 12 disciples came to him and asked him what the parables meant and why he was speaking in parables?

Jesus told them that they would be told the mystery of the kingdom, but that the others who heard the parables would not understand them. Jesus told them that this was in fulfillment of the prophecy of Isaiah who said:

By hearing you will hear, but you will not understand. For this people's heart is hardened and their ears are dull, and their eyes have been closed.

Because if they did hear, and see and understand with their hearts, they would repent and I would heal them.

Pomegranates, a biblical fruit

Apple tree in a Kibbutz of Galilee

But, blessed are your eyes, for they see; and your ears, for they hear.

This is a truth you need to understand. Many prophets and righteous men desired to see the things that you are seeing and to hear the things that you are hearing.

Now this is how you are to understand this parable and all the parables I teach.

Therefore hear the parable of the sower.

The seed is the word of God. The sower sows the word. The seeds that land on the way side and are eaten by the birds, are the words that are heard.

After the words are heard then Satan immediately comes and snatches it away from them, so that it does not take root in their heart. Once the word is snatched away then they cannot believe and be saved.

The seed that is sown in the rocky place are like those who hear the word and believe it for a while; then difficulties and trials come because of the word, and they stumble and fall away.

The seed that is sown among the thorns is like the word that is heard and begins to take root, but the cares, deceitfulness of riches and the lusts of this world choke out its life.

The seed that is sown on the good ground are those with honest hearts, who hear the word and hold it fast and accept it.

They produce fruit, some 100-fold, some 60 and some 30.

Biblical garden plants: almond tree flowers

PARABLE OF THE SEED

And Jesus said:

The kingdom of God is like a man who cast seed upon the earth.

THE STORY OF JESUS

The man goes to sleep and rises again the next day, and the seed springs up and grows, but the man does not know how it grew.

The earth bears fruit with out any help from the man, it does it by itself.

First the blade, then the ear, the full grain. But when the fruit is ripened, he takes a sickle and harvests the grain.

PARABLE OF THE WEEDS

Jesus told them another parable:

The kingdom of heaven is like a man who sows good seed in his field.

But as he slept the enemy came in and sowed weeds among the wheat, and then slipped away.

As soon as the blades of grain started showing, so did the weeds. The servants came and asked the owner of the field:

Didn't you plant good seed? Why are weeds growing up among the wheat? The man said:

The enemy has done this.

The servants asked if they should go and gather up the weeds. The man said:

No, you might destroy some of the good wheat.

Let them grow together until the harvest, and at harvest time I will tell the reapers:

Gather up the weeds and tie them in bundles and burn them. Then gather the wheat and put it into my barn.

Mustard seeds

PARABLE OF THE MUSTARD SEED

Jesus told them another parable. He said:

To what can we compare the kingdom of God? What parable can explain its excellence?

The kingdom of heaven is like a grain of mustard-seed, which a man took and planted in his field. A mustard seed is the smallest of seeds grown in the garden.

But once it starts growing, it gets bigger and bigger, bigger than any of the other plants in the garden. Finally, it grows to the size of a tree and puts out large branches.

The birds come and take refuge and find shade and make their homes in its branches.

In another parable, Jesus said that the kingdom of heaven is like the yeast that a woman hid in three measures of flour, and it was mixed into and permeated all of the dough.

Jesus told all these parables to the multitudes, and he only taught them in parables with no explanation. This was a fulfillment of the prophecies found in the Psalms that said:

I will open my mouth in parable; I will say things hidden since the foundation of the world.

But to his own disciples he explained everything.

PARABLE OF THE WEEDS EXPLAINED

Jesus left the multitudes and came in the house where he was staying with his disciples.

And the disciples came to Jesus and asked him to explain the parable of the weeds in the field.

Jesus told them that the one planting the good seed is the Son of man - the field is the world:

A wheat field in Galilee

The good seed is the sons of the kingdom.

And the one who sows the weeds is the evil one, and the enemy who sowed them is the devil.

The harvest is the end of the world, and the reapers are angels.

The weeds that are gathered and burnt with fire is a picture of what it will be like at the end of the world. The Son of man will send out his angels, and they will gather all the things that are evil and cause people to stumble.

Beautiful landcape in Israel

PARABLES OF TREASURE

Jesus then went on to teach that the kingdom of heaven was like a treasure hidden in a field that a man finds. Once he finds the treasure he sells everything that he has and buys the field:

The kingdom of heaven is also like a merchant who is looking for precious pearls.

When he finds one pearl of great value, he sells everything that he has and buys it.

The kingdom of heaven is also like a net that is cast into the sea: it gathers every kind of fish.

When the net is pulled in, the fishermen sit down and sort out the good fish they want to keep from the worthless ones.

This is how it will be at the end of the world. The angels will come and separate the righteous from the wicked. The wicked will be cast into a furnace of fire where there is weeping and gnashing of teeth.

Then Jesus asked his disciples:

Have you understood all these things?

They answered:

Yes

Plate of figs, nuts, apricots and raisins

JESUS STILLS THE STORM

Later on, when it was about sunset, there was a great crowd gathered around Jesus.

Jesus got into a boat with his 12 disciples and told them to take the boat to the other side of the sea.

As they were preparing to shove off, a scribe came up to Jesus and said:

Teacher I will follow you wherever you go.

Jesus said to him:

The foxes have dens and the birds of the sky have nests; but the Son of man has no place to lay his head,

After this, one of Jesus' disciples said to him:

Allow me to go and bury my father.

But Jesus said to him:

Follow me; and let the spiritually dead bury their own dead.

Jesus then entered the boat that his disciples had prepared and began to travel to the other side of the lake. They left the crowd on the shore.

As the boat sailed off toward the other shore, Jesus fell asleep in the boat.

While Jesus slept a great windstorm came up on the lake. The waves began to beat against the boat and fill it up with water.

The disciples became afraid, to the point of thinking they would be lost in the storm. But Jesus lay asleep at the back of the boat.

The disciples came to Jesus and woke him, saying:

Lord, we are perishing! And Jesus stood up and rebuked the wind and the sea and the raging water.

He said to the sea:

Peace, be still.

The storm ceased and there was a great calm. Jesus said to his disciples:

Why are you so fearful? Don't you have faith yet?

Oh, you of little faith.

The disciples, still afraid, began to marvel, saying to one another:

Who is this man that even the wind and the seas obey him?

Jesus stills the storm

THE STORY OF JESUS

JESUS HEALS TWO DEMONIACS

After the storm, they came to the other side of the lake to a region called the **Gadarenes**†.

As Jesus and his disciples came out of the boat, they were met by men who came out from the caves and the tombs.

These men had unclean, evil spirits that had great power over them, so great that even when they had been bound with chains, they were able to break the iron.

No man was strong enough to tame these men possessed by demons.

They spent their time crying out and doing harm to themselves by cutting themselves with stones. They wore no clothes.

When they saw Jesus, they ran to him and fell down before him and worshipped him. They cried out with a loud voice and said:

What do you want with me, Jesus, Son of the most high God?

As Jesus was commanding the unclean spirits to come out, they begged Jesus not to torment them.

Jesus asked them:

What is your name?

The demon replied:

My name is Legion, for we are many.

The demons begged Jesus not to send them out of the country and they begged Jesus not to send them to the abyss.

Off in the distance was a great herd of pigs feeding on the hillside. The demons begged to enter the swine,

† Further reading available at the end of this chapter.

saying, If you do cast us out send us into the herd of swine.

Jesus told them:

Go.

Dote palms in modern Israel

They came out of the men and entered into the herd of about 2,000 pigs. Once this happened, the entire herd rushed down the steep cliffs and hurled themselves into the sea and drowned.

When the herdsmen saw what had happened they fled to the city and told everyone what they had witnessed.

Those who lived in the city came to see what had happened. They came to Jesus and found the men who had been possessed by the unclean spirits sitting on the ground, clothed and in their right minds.

The herdsmen told how the demons possessed the pigs and how the herd of pigs threw themselves into the sea and drowned.

And they told the men from the city how those who had been filled with the unclean, evil spirits had been healed. And they were afraid.

All the people of the city of Gadarenes began to ask Jesus to leave their country. They were full of fear.

Jesus and his disciples headed toward the boat in order to leave the region. One of the men who had been possessed by the unclean spirits begged Jesus to let him come along with him.

But Jesus told him that he could not, that he must return to his home and his friends and tell them the great things that God had done for him and how God had shown him great mercy.

The man went his way, declaring throughout the entire city what Jesus had done for him.

As Jesus crossed to the other side of the lake, a great multitude was waiting for him by the shore. They welcomed Jesus as he returned. They had been there all that time, waiting for Jesus to come back.

THE STORY OF JESUS

MATTHEW'S FEAST

Matthew who is also called Levi, was the last of the 12 disciples Jesus had called while he was collecting taxes near the Sea of Galilee. Matthew made a great feast for Jesus at his house.

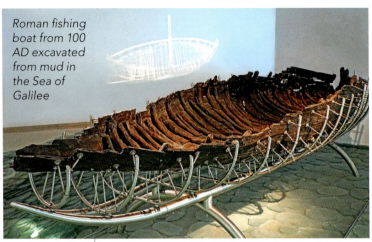
Roman fishing boat from 100 AD excavated from mud in the Sea of Galilee

The other disciples joined Jesus, along with Matthew's old friends and acquaintances, which included tax collectors and other people of low reputation.

When the religious leaders (Pharisees and teachers) saw Jesus eating and drinking with tax collectors and other outcasts of society, they began to criticize Jesus and his disciples by asking:

Why do you eat and drink with tax collectors and sinners?

When Jesus heard what they were saying, he replied:

It isn't people who are well that need a doctor, but those that are sick. I haven't come to call the righteous; I have come to call sinners to repentance. Go and learn what this means. I desire mercy and not sacrifice.

John's disciples and some of the Pharisees were fasting. Some of John's disciples came to Jesus to ask him why his disciples did not fast.

Jesus replied:

Do the friends of the bridegroom mourn (fast) as long as the bridegroom is with them? No. As long as the bridegroom is with them, they cannot fast.

But the day will come when the bridegroom will be taken away from them, and then they will fast.

He told this same story to the disciples of John. Jesus said:

No one takes a piece of cloth from a new garment and sews it on an old garment.

No man puts new wine into old wineskins, or else the new wine would burst the skins, and the wine would be spilled and lost. But they put new wine into new wine skins.

JAIRUS' DAUGHTER

While Jesus was speaking to John's disciples, a man named Jairus came up to Jesus and fell at his feet in worship.

Jairus was one of the rulers of the synagogue. Jairus begged Jesus to come and heal his 12-year old daughter:

Come and lay hands on her and she will live, for she is at the point of death.

Jesus got up and started toward the home of Jairus. His 12 disciples followed him. The multitudes also followed him and pressed him from every side.

There was a woman in the crowd who for 12 years had been afflicted by a disease that discharged blood. She had spent everything she earned paying physicians to cure her but to no avail.

Stone carving of a Menora from a synagogue in Capernaum

She had heard about Jesus and said to herself:

If only I can touch the border of his garment, I would be made whole.

She forced her way through the crowd and got behind Jesus and reached down and touched his garment, and she was immediately healed.

Jesus turned around and said:

Who touched my garment?

Everyone denied it.

Peter and the other disciples came to Jesus and said:

The crowd is pressing you from all sides. What do you mean when you ask who touched me?

Jesus answered and said:

I know that someone touched me because I felt the power go out from me.

He looked all around to find the person who had touched him. When the woman realized that she could no longer hide, she came to Jesus, trembling with fear. She fell at his feet and confessed that she was the one who had touched him.

She told Jesus and the crowd why she had touched him and that she was healed immediately.

Jesus said to her:

Daughter, be of good cheer; your faith has healed you. Go in peace and be healed.

The woman left, completely healed.

While Jesus was speaking to the woman, someone came from the house of Jairus and said to him:

Your daughter is dead; you do not need to trouble the teacher any further.

When Jesus heard this, he said:

Don't be afraid, simply believe and the girl will be healed.

When Jesus entered Jairus' house, he told everyone to stay out except for the father and mother of the dead girl, along with Peter, James and John. When he entered the house, the funeral party was already there, weeping and wailing, playing the flutes.

Jesus told them to stop all the commotion. He told them that girl was not dead, just asleep. When the funeral party heard this, they started laughing and mocking Jesus.

He insisted they all leave, and finally they did. Jesus then took the father and mother and went into the room where the child was lying. He took the child's hand and spoke to her.

He said:

Little girl, I say to you, get up.

Immediately her spirit returned, and she got up and walked around. Jesus told them to bring her food.

Her parents were stunned. But he told them not to tell anyone what they had witnessed. Nevertheless, Jesus' fame spread through all the country.

Blue colors on the sea of Galilee

HEALING BLIND MEN

Jesus left the house of Jairus, and as he was leaving, two blind men followed him, crying out:

Have mercy on us, son of David.

The blind men followed him to his destination. He said to them:

Do you believe that I can give you sight?

And they said:

Yes, Lord.

He touched their eyes and said to them:

Let it be done to you according to your faith.

Their eyes were opened, and they saw. Jesus sternly told them not to tell anyone what he had healed them.

But instead of doing as Jesus had asked, they went and told everyone they met that Jesus had restored their sight.

Jesus continued walking and ran into a man who was dumb and possessed by a demon.

When Jesus cast out the demon, the man began to speak. The crowds that witnessed this marveled. Some of the people said that had never happened before in Israel.

But the Pharisees rebutted them, saying:

He casts out demons by the prince of demons.

Stars in the sky of Israel

JESUS IS REJECTED

Jesus left the area of Galilee and returned to his hometown of Nazareth. His 12 disciples followed him.

When the Sabbath came, Jesus entered the synagogue, as was his custom, and stood to read the Scriptures. He was handed the book of the prophet Isaiah.

He opened the book and found the place where it is written:

The Spirit of the Lord is upon me because he anointed me to preach good news to the poor, he has sent me to pro-

claim release to the captives, and recovery of sight to the blind, to set at liberty those that are oppressed, to proclaim the year of the Lord's favor.

Jesus closed the book and handed it back to the attendant and sat down. All eyes were fixed on Jesus as he said to them:

Today this Scripture has been fulfilled in your ears.

Those who heard him asked each other:

Where did he get this power, and how does he do these mighty works? Isn't this the son of the carpenter, Joseph, the son of Mary? Where did he get all these things?

They were offended.

Jesus said to them:

I tell you this truth: a prophet is not without honor except in his own country and among his relatives. No prophet is acceptable in his own country.

Try and understand the truth I am about to share with you. In the days of Elijah when the heavens were shut up and it did not rain for three and a half years and a great famine was upon all the land, Elijah was not sent to anyone from his home country.

He was sent to a widow from Zaraphath, in the land of Sidon, and she was saved from the famine by the miracle from God.

And although there were many lepers in Israel at the time of this tribulation, only one leper was healed by Elijah. He was Naaman, a man from Syria.

When they heard this, they became furious. They rose up against Jesus and led him to the edge of the hill upon which their city was built with the intention of throwing him down the cliff to his death.

But Jesus simply passed through the middle of them and went on his way.

Jesus performed few mighty works in Nazareth because of the residents' lack of faith and unbelief. He left Nazareth and returned to Capernaum.

A beautiful olive tree in Galilee

THE TWELVE SENT OUT

Jesus continued his travels to many cities and villages, teaching in their synagogues and preaching the Gospel of the kingdom, and healing all kinds of diseases and all kinds of sickness.

But when he saw the crowds, he was moved with compassion for them. They were distressed and scattered, like sheep without a shepherd.

Jesus said to his 12 disciples:

The harvest is huge, but the harvesters are few. Pray to the Lord of the harvest and ask him to send laborers into his harvest.

Jesus called his 12 together and began to send them out two by two. He told them to heal the sick and to preach the good news of the kingdom.

He told them that they should take nothing for the journey, except a staff. They were not to take bread or money. Instead they were to go out in sandaled feet without so much as an extra coat.

He told them not to go to the Gentiles, and not to go to the cities of Samaria, but instead to concentrate on the lost sheep of the house of Israel.

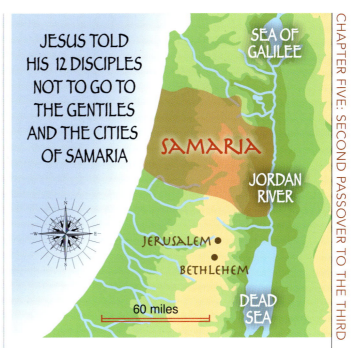

As they went out, Jesus reminded them that they had received freely and they were to give freely.

Jesus told them to find someone worthy in a city and stay with that family. If the house was worthy, they were to salute it with a proclamation of peace. If it was not worthy, then no peace would be upon the house.

Jesus said:

Wherever you go, stay in one house until you leave the city. If they do not receive you and your preaching, then shake off the dust that is under your feet as a testimony against them.

The truth you need to understand is that it will be better for the land of Sodom and Gomorrah in the day of judgment than for the city that rejects your testimony that the kingdom of God is near.

I am sending you out as sheep among wolves; be wise as serpents and as harmless as doves. But beware of men, for they will deliver you over to the courts, and they will whip you in their synagogues.

A model of Jerusalem in Jesus' time

You will be brought before governors and kings for my sake, as a testimony to the Gentiles.

But when they deliver you up, do not be anxious, and do not worry about what you are going to say. You will be given the words to say by the Spirit of God — when the time comes.

Brother will deliver brother up to death, and a father will deliver up his own child, and children will rise up against their parents and cause them to be put to death for my name's sake.

He that endures to the end will be saved.

When they persecute you in one city, flee to the next. I tell you this truth: you will not have gone through all the cities of Israel, before the Son of man comes.

If they have called me the master of the house of Beelzebub, you cannot expect better treatment.

Do not be afraid of them. There is nothing covered that will not be revealed.

Everything that is hidden will be known. What I tell you in the darkness, speak it in the light.

Do not be afraid of those who can kill the body but not the soul. Fear God who can cast body and soul into hell.

He who does not take his cross and follow after me is not worthy of me. He who finds his life will lose it; and he who loses his life for my sake will find it.

He who receives you receives me. He who receives me receives the one who sent me.

If a person receives a prophet in the name of the prophet, he will receive a prophet's reward. If you receive a righteous man in the name of a righteous man, you will receive the reward of a righteous man.

The disciples departed and went out throughout the villages and preached that men should repent. They preached the good news. They cast out demons, anointed the sick with oil and healed them.

After Jesus gave his disciples these instructions, he left to preach and teach in the cities.

Herodian desert palace and fortress

HEROD ANTIPAS

About this time, King Herod Antipas, the tetrarch, heard about all the things that Jesus was doing. He was perplexed because some thought Jesus was John the Baptist risen from the dead. Others thought that Jesus was Elijah or some other prophet. Herod began to ask if John the Baptist, whom he beheaded, had risen from the dead.

Herod had arrested John and put him in prison for the sake of Herodias. Herodias had been the wife of his brother Phillip.

John the Baptist had spoken up and said that it was not lawful or right for Herod to take his brother's wife.

Herodias hated John the Baptist and was looking for a way to kill him. Herod feared John, but nevertheless spent time talking with him.

Herodias got her chance to kill John on Herod's birthday. All the highest-ranking people in the land were invited. When it came time for entertainment, Herodias had her daughter dance for Herod, and he was very pleased.

Herod promised her with an oath in front of everyone that he would give her anything she wanted, up to half his kingdom. She conspired with her mother and asked Herod for the head of John the Baptist on a platter.

Herod was very grieved at this, but because he was afraid of losing face and for the sake of his oath, he commanded that John's head be cut off and brought to the party on a platter.

One of Herod's soldiers went to the prison where John was, beheaded him, put his head on a platter and gave it to the girl who then gave it to her mother, Herodias.

The disciples of John collected his body and buried it. They told Jesus what had happened.

WITHDRAWAL FROM HEROD'S TERRITORY

All the apostles (12 disciples) came together after having been sent out by Jesus to preach the coming of the kingdom.

They told Jesus all the things that they had seen and done. They told him how the sick were healed and the demons cast out. They shared what they taught and preached regarding the kingdom.

When John the Baptist's disciples told Jesus about the death of John, Jesus gathered his disciples and withdrew to the other side of the Sea of Galilee to Bethsaida.

FEEDING THE FIVE THOUSAND

But when the multitude heard that Jesus was crossing the lake, they followed him. Many others ran from all the surrounding cities to find Jesus.

When Jesus saw the crowds, he had pity on them and he welcomed them. Jesus taught them and healed all their diseases.

Later on, he and his disciples went into the mountain, and Jesus sat with them. The time for the feast of the Passover was near.

As the day wore on, the 12 disciples came to Jesus and said:

Send the multitudes away, it is getting late and they need to leave so that they can go into the villages and towns nearby to buy food and find lodging.

But Jesus said to them:

There is no reason for them to go away.

Jesus lifted his eyes and looked over the crowd coming to him. He said to Phillip:

Where can we buy bread enough for all these people to eat?

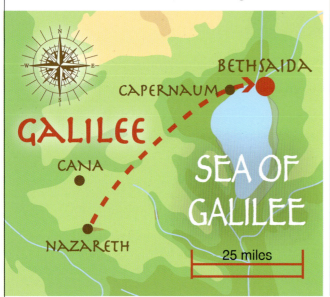

Jesus already knew what he was going to do, but said this to test Philip. Philip answered and said:

Everyone ate until they were filled

Even if everyone only had a small piece of bread, it would cost thousands of dollars to feed them.

Jesus said to his disciples:

Give them food to eat. They asked him, Do you want us to go and spend thousands of dollars on bread?

Jesus asked them:

How many loaves of bread do you have?

Simon Peter's brother said to Jesus:

There is a young lad who has five barley loaves and two fish.

But there are about 5,000 men to feed What good would a couple loaves of bread and two fish do?

Jesus told them to bring him the five loaves and two fish. When they had done this, Jesus commanded all the people to sit down on the grass in groups of 50.

He took the bread and fish and looked up to heaven. He blessed the food and broke the loaves. He gave the loaves and fish to the disciples to distribute to the crowd.

Everyone ate until they were filled.

Once they were full, he told his disciples to gather up everything that was left over. They gathered up all the remaining loaves and fish, and it filled 12 baskets.

When the people saw this miracle they said:

This is truly the Messiah who has come into the world.

JESUS WALKS ON WATER

Jesus knew that these crowds of people wanted to take him by force to make him King.

He told his 12 disciples to get into the boat and go ahead of him to the shore on the other side of Bethsaida, the town next to Capernaum. He then sent the multitude away.

Jesus then went up into the mountain to pray. The evening came, and Jesus was alone.

As the disciples rowed to Capernaum, a great wind blew up. They were about three and a half miles across the lake, about half way to where Jesus had told them to go.

Jesus looked across the lake and saw that his disciples were in trouble, trying to row the boat against the wind.

Jesus walked on the water toward the disciples.

When the disciples saw Jesus walking on the water in their direction, they were afraid. They thought it was a ghost, and they cried out with fear.

But Jesus spoke to them and said:

Take heart, it is I, do not be afraid.

They started preparing for Jesus to enter the boat. But Simon Peter said to Jesus:

If it is you, then ask me to come meet you on the water.

Jesus said:

Come.

Peter went over the side of the boat and walked on the water toward Jesus. But when he saw the force of the wind, he was afraid and began to sink.

He cried out:

Lord save me!

Immediately Jesus stretched out his hand and took hold of Peter. He said to Peter:

Oh you of little faith, why did you doubt?

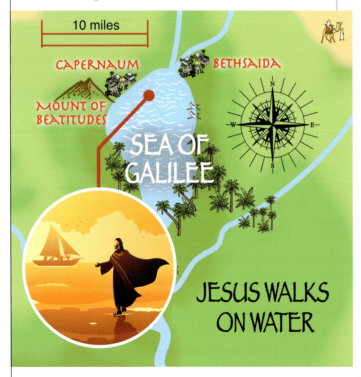

JESUS WALKS ON WATER

Sea of Galilee at sunset

As soon as Jesus and Peter went into the boat, the wind stopped blowing. The disciples were amazed and began worshipping him, saying:

It is the truth; you are the Son of God.

When they had crossed the lake, they came to the land of **Gennesaret**†, where they moored their boat.

As soon as Jesus and his disciples left the boat, the people recognized who he was and began sending word around the region that Jesus was there.

Jesus went about healing the sick, and many asked Jesus if they could touch the border of his garment. All who did were made whole.

PETER'S CONFESSION

The day after Jesus had feed the 5,000, the crowds that had been on the other side of the shore realized that Jesus had left. They began looking for him, and once they figured out where he had gone, they got into their boats and rowed across the lake to Capernaum to find him.

When they found Jesus on the other side of the shore, they asked him:

Teacher, why did you come here?

Jesus answered them and said:

I am going to tell you an important truth that you need to understand.

You are looking for me not because you saw a miracle, but because you ate loaves of bread and your hunger was satisfied.

Don't work for the food that spoils but for the food that gives life for eternity, which only the Son of man can give you.

A Judean field cultivated with wheat

† Further reading available at the end of this chapter.

For I am the only one the Father has commissioned to give eternal life.

They asked:

What must we do in order to earn this food that gives life for eternity?

Jesus said to them:

The work you can do to please God is to believe on the one whom God has sent.

They said to him:

What sign are you going to do so that we will believe in you? What wonders will you work? Our fathers ate manna in the wilderness, just as it is written. He gave them bread out of heaven to eat.

Jesus said to them:

It was not Moses that gave you the bread out of heaven, but my Father gives you the true bread out of heaven. The bread of God is the one that comes down out of heaven and gives life to the world.

They said to Jesus:

Lord, give us this bread always.

Jesus said to them:

I am the bread of life. He who comes to me will not hunger, and he who believes on me will never thirst.

But I say to you, You have seen me, and you still do not believe in me. All those who the Father gives to me will come to me. He who comes to me I will never turn away.

For I have come down from heaven, not to do my own will, but to do the will of him who sent me. This is the will of him who sent me, that I lose none of all he has given to me, but that I will raise them up at the last day.

For this is the will of my Father, that everyone who looks to the Son, and believes on him, will have eternal life. I will raise him up in the last day.

The Jews began to start grumbling about Jesus because he said he was the bread of life that came down from heaven.

They said:

Isn't this Jesus, the son of Joseph? Don't we know his father and mother? How can he say he came down from heaven?

Jesus answered them:

Stop grumbling among yourselves. No one can come to me unless the Father, who sent me draws him. I will raise him up in the last day. It is written in the prophets: they will all be taught by God.

Every one who has heard from the Father, and has learned, comes to me. Not that anyone has seen the Father, except he who is from God; he has seen the Father.

I am going to tell you a very important truth: He who believes in me has eternal life. I am the bread of life.

Your fathers ate manna in the wilderness, but they all eventually died.

I am the living bread that comes down from heaven and once a man eats it he will never die, but live forever. The bread that I give is my flesh, given for the life of the world.

Judean desert in spring, flowering after rains

The Jews began to discuss what these mysterious words meant:

How can a man give us his flesh to eat?

Jesus said to them:

Again, I tell you a very important truth, unless you eat the flesh of the Son of man and drink my blood, you will not have life. He who eats my flesh and drinks my blood has eternal life, and I will raise him up at the last day.

For my body is true food and my blood is true drink. The person who eats my flesh and drinks my blood remains in me, and I in him.

I live because the living Father sent me. The same is true for the person who partakes of me; he will live because of me.

This is the true bread that comes down from heaven. Unlike the bread your fathers ate in the wilderness and died, the person who eats this bread will live forever.

These are the things that Jesus taught in the synagogue while he was in Capernaum.

Many of the followers of Jesus, other than his disciples were offended when they heard this teaching.

Jesus knew what they were grumbling about and said to them:

Does this cause you to stumble? What would happen if you saw the Son of man ascend to where he came from?

It is the Spirit who gives life; the flesh is of no profit. The words that I have spoken to you are spirit and life. But there are some of you who do not believe. (Jesus knew from the very beginning who didn't believe and who would reject him.)

Jesus said to them:

This is the reason that I told you that no one can come to me unless the Father reveals the truth to him and draws him to me.

After this, many people went back to their homes and stopped following him.

Jesus called his 12 disciples together and asked them:

Do you want to go away, too?

Simon Peter answered:

Lord, to whom would we go? You are the one with the words of eternal life. We believe in you and know that you are the holy one of God.

Jesus answered them:

Did not I choose all 12 of you, and one of you is a devil?

He was speaking of Judas, the son of Simon Iscariot, for he was the one of the 12 who would betray Jesus.

END OF CHAPTER FIVE

CHAPTER FIVE
COMPANION

ABEL (page 107)

Adam and Eve's second son. His older brother Cain killed him in anger. Abel followed God's instructions for sacrificing a lamb.

Cain was a farmer and offered God produce but God didn't accept it because that wasn't what God told him to do. Cain became jealous of Abel and killed him.

Abel's sacrifice of the lamb showed that God required a blood sacrifice in order to take care of sin, and was a foreshadowing of Jesus Christ, who was the perfect Lamb of God, sacrificed as a blood offering for our sin.

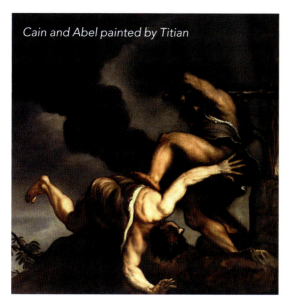
Cain and Abel painted by Titian

CENTURION (page 96)

A Roman officer in charge of a hundred men. It's the same root word as "century," which is 100 years. Centurions were often chosen because of their character and leadership qualities as well as their ability in battle.

Tombstone of a Centurion from Ludgate Hill in the Museum of London

CHORAZIN (page 99)

Overlooking the north end of Sea of Galilee, this ancient city made of black volcanic stone is an extensive archaeological excavation with city streets and a reconstructed synagogue from the time of Jesus.

Black volcanic rocks were used to build this Biblical City

THE STORY OF JESUS

COMMANDMENTS (page 88)

Usually refers to the 10 commandments that God gave to Moses as basic moral guidelines for the Israelites to follow. **(Exodus, chapter 20)**

1. Thou shalt have no other gods before me.
2. Thou shalt not make unto thee any graven image.
3. Thou shalt not take the name of the LORD thy God in vain.
4. Remember the sabbath day, to keep it holy.
5. Honour thy father and thy mother.
6. Thou shalt not kill.
7. Thou shalt not commit adultery.
8. Thou shalt not steal.
9. Thou shalt not bear false witness against thy neighbor.
10. Thou shalt not covet any thing that is thy neighbor's.

GADARA (page 118)

Located at the northern end of modern day Jordan and just south of the Golan Heights, Gadara was in the time of Jesus a town in the region of The Gadarenes in Decapolis. The Gadarenes, on the southeast end of the Sea of Galilee, was the scene of one of Jesus' miracles. It was there that Jesus cast out the demons from a group of men who lived in caves.

Gadara (Umm Qais) ruins

GENNESARET (page 131)

This ancient city lies under the fields of a local kibbutz, on the shores of the west side of the Sea of Galilee.

The ancient city was on the shores of the Sea of Galilee at this site.

HEALING POOLS (page 79)

Bethesda and Siloam were two pools in Jerusalem during the time of Jesus' public ministry.

It is difficult to know exactly what they were like because the Romans were thorough in destroying Jerusalem about 70 years after Jesus was born.

They were both fed by streams outside the city. Siloam was the only permanent water source for Jerusalem.

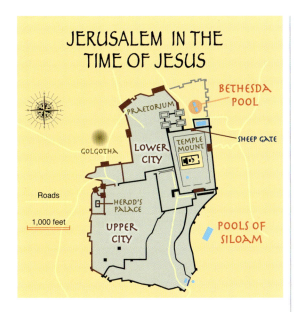

The water came into the city through Hezekiah's tunnel, which was dug 800 years before Jesus was born.

The pool of Bethesda was probably more of a bath, which would have been typical in Roman times.

It had five porches and was located on the east side of Jerusalem near the Fortress of Antonia.

The Bible records that at this pool, an angel would move the waters at certain times and the first person to enter the water when that happened would be healed of their sickness. Jesus healed a lame man here *(John 5: 1-9).*

HELL (page 88)
Hell is a place of permanent separation from God.

Three different words in the New Testament refer to different aspects of hell:

Sheol has the idea of insatiable unfulfilled desires.

Hades is similar to sheol, with the added burden of prison with bars and locks.

Gehenna refers to the place of the lost with terrible conditions.

Dante, C.S. Lewis and other authors also created frightening descriptions of hell. Permanent separation from total love, goodness, and peace is impossible for us to fathom, but possible to avoid by putting your trust in Jesus.

IDUMEA (page 84)
A province to the south of Judea. Also known as Edom. The people were descendants of Jacob's brother Esau.

Jacob and Esau's father was Isaac, Abraham's son, so they were Abraham's grandsons. Jacob and Esau were twins and were trying to get the best of each other their whole lives.

The competition began, seemingly, even when their mother was giving birth to them (See Genesis chapter 25 beginning at verse 22). Jacob, the younger son stole Esau's birthright (See **Genesis chapter 27**).

Years later, when Jacob's descendants the Israelites had left Egypt, they were on their way north and the Edomites refused to let them pass through their land. They fought battles back and forth for many years after that.

Herod the Great was Idumean and when he and his descendants were rulers in Israel, the Jews hated them because of their heritage and because they cooperated with the Romans.

JONAH (page 104)

A prophet of God who was reluctant to go where God sent him. He lived about 800 years before Jesus was born. You can read the story of Jonah in the Old Testament book named after him. He is best known for being swallowed by a large fish that God sent.

NAIN (page 97)

Nothing remains of this biblical place, not even archaeological excavations.

This is the place where the people of Galilee tell their visitors that there was Nain

NINEVEH (page 104)

The capital city of Assyria when it was a powerful empire about 800 years before Jesus was born.

God told Jonah to go there and preach to the Ninevites. At first Jonah refused and tried to run away from God, but ended up being thrown in the ocean and swallowed by a big fish.

Jonah changed his mind, and when the fish spit him up on the shore three days later, he went to Nineveh. Many people in Nineveh listened to his message and followed God **(see the book of Jonah).**

OFFICERS OF THE PHARISEES (page 89)

Temple guards who were probably Levites who served as temple security guards.

Especially around the time of the Passover when there was a lot of activity with crowds from out of town and animals being bought and sacrificed, it would be important to have a group in charge of keeping order.

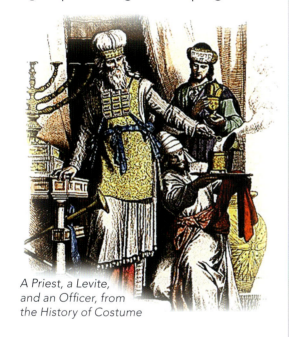

A Priest, a Levite, and an Officer, from the History of Costume

PARABLE (page 93)

A story about earthly things with a spiritual meaning.

Jesus used parables by describing things that were familiar to people. This helped them understand spiritual truths.

Parables are different from allegories in that parables have one point and the details are important but secondary, while in an allegory, every detail has significance. Pilgrim's Progress is an allegory.

One of the most well known parables is the Good Samaritan. Jesus is making the point that your neighbor is anyone who is in need who you can help, regardless of their nationality or how they have treated you.

The fact that the hero in the story is a Samaritan is an important part of Jesus' main point because the Jews despised the Samaritans, and yet he was the only one to stop and help a Jew in need, and he did it generously **(Luke 10:25-37).**

PERFUMED OIL (page 100)

Throughout the Bible, oil symbolizes the Holy Spirit. Before Christ, God mandated that oil was to be used in ceremonies to anoint or set someone apart for a special job, such as a prophet, priest or king. Anointment symbolized that they would receive special abilities and wisdom from God.

It was also used in common situations like perfume or personal hygiene.

Some perfumed oils were used along with cloths in the embalming process. Jesus' anointment symbolized that he came to the world as prophet, priest, and king.

PHOENICIA

Phoenicia is the Greek name for the region that now includes the coastal regions of present-day Syria, Lebanon, and Israel. This is roughly the same area sometimes referred to as Canaan. These people were known for purple dyed goods and for being great sailors and traders.

Modern Mediterranean port of Acre (Akko) lies at southern tip of old Phoenicia

PILATE (page 111)

Pontius Pilate was the governor of Judea for 10 years. He had entered public life not for pure of lofty reasons but to advance his own career and serve his own selfish purposes. He was ruthless and murderous, with a reputation among the Jews he ruled as being tyrannical and tempestuous. He had a very low and corrupt character.

PLAGUES (page 85)

An affliction or disease.

When Moses came to Pharaoh to ask him to let the Jews leave Egypt, Pharaoh refused at first because the Jews were a source of slave labor to him.

God sent "plagues" on Egypt to convince Pharaoh of his power and to persuade him to let the Jews leave **(Read beginning with Exodus 7:14).**

Many of the plagues showed God's power over gods the Egyptians worshipped, like the first plague turning the Nile into blood and the ninth plague, darkness, showed power over the Sun god.

The tenth plague also showed God's power over Pharaoh's own family when his firstborn son was killed, as was the firstborn in all of Egypt, except for the Jews.

SACKCLOTH AND ASHES (page 99)

Cloth made of goat or camel hair that was uncomfortable because it caused skin irritation.

It was worn during times of repentance and mourning and covered the body from neck to ankles as if for burial. It was a sign of deep humility.

People would often put ashes on their heads as a further sign of humiliation and self abhorrence.

SODOM (page 99)

A city in the plains near the Dead Sea where Lot lived.

God destroyed it because of the rampant immorality and violence of its residents. That's the origin of the word sodomy. **(See Genesis chapters 18 and 19.)**

TITHE (page 91)

An offering of one tenth of a crop or income set aside to give to God as a demonstration of thanks and to recognize that everything we have is a gift from God. Jesus sometimes criticized the religious leaders because they would tithe to make themselves look good and not to worship God.

TYRE (page 84)

The Phoenician city of Tyre, located on the eastern shore of the Mediterranean Sea, stood as one of the most ancient and prosperous cities in history. Herodotus, known as the father of modem history, lived and wrote between about 490 B.C. and 425 B.C. During a visit to the temple of Heracles in Tyre, Herodotus inquired about the age of the temple, to which the inhabits replied that the temple was as old as "Tyre itself, and that Tyre had already stood for two thousand three hundred years." From Herodotus, then, it can be supposed that the city goes back to 2,700 B.C.

Rosh Hanikrah, Israel. The Mediterranean coastline south of Lebanon near site of Tyre.

WASHING FEET, AND ANOINTING WITH OIL (page 92)

Washing feet was commonly done by servants for guests entering a wealthy person's house. Most people wore sandals, and the roads were dusty so when travelers arrived, someone would wash their feet.

Anointing usually involved pouring oil on someone's head or body as a sign of being set apart to be a prophet, priest or king.

People would also put oil on their bodies to refresh themselves or for medicinal purposes. It was also use to embalm dead bodies. When the woman anointed Jesus' feet, she used costly perfume along with her tears and hair. This was done in light of Jesus impending death on the cross. It can also be seen as a symbol of his being set apart as prophet, priest and king.

YEAST (page 107)

A symbol of sin throughout the Bible.

In the Passover meal, the bread is unleavened **(leaven is another word for yeast; see Exodus 12:15-20).**

At the last supper with his disciples, Jesus held up a piece of unleavened bread and said, "This is my body which is given for you ... " showing that the bread represented him, and that he was without sin. **(Luke 22: 19)**

When Jesus says in **Luke 12: 1**, "Beware of the leaven (yeast) of the Pharisees, which is hypocrisy," he is saying that just like yeast pervades dough and puffs up the whole loaf, sin (in this case hypocrisy) gets in our life, pervades and contaminates us, and causes us to get "puffed up" (prideful and selfish).

When we are full of ourselves, we don't love God or others, which goes against the greatest commandments that are to love God and love others.

CHAPTER SIX

THIRD PASSOVER UNTIL JESUS' ARRIVAL AT BETHANY

SCRIBES CRITICIZE JESUS

Jesus returned to Galilee where he continued his ministry. But he did not return to Judea because the Jews were determined to kill him.

A group of Pharisees came from Jerusalem and joined some scribes. They began to question Jesus. They had seen some of Jesus' disciples eat their food with unwashed hands. They considered this a defilement and rebellion against **the tradition of the elders**†.

The Pharisees and the scribes asked Jesus:

Why don't your disciples follow the traditions of the elders?

Jesus told them:

Why do you disobey the commandment of God? Because of your traditions? You

† Further reading available at the end of this chapter.

THE STORY OF JESUS

hypocrites. The prophet Isaiah was right about you when he said:

This people honors me with their lips, but their heart is far from me.

They worship me in vain, teaching instead the precepts and principles of men.

You push away the commandments of God and hold fast the traditions of men. You would rather obey man than obey God.

For God, through Moses, said:

Honor your father and your mother, let anyone who speaks evil of his father or mother be put to death.

But you have undone the clear intention of God's law with your own traditions.

You refuse to support your parents in their old age by calling the money that should be used for your parents a special gift to God.

That allows you to keep the gift for yourself instead of using it to support your parents.

In this way you insult God and create a tradition that undoes God's purpose that you should support your parents in their old age.

This is just one example of the ways you subvert the true intentions of God's commands with your own traditions.

Jesus called the crowds of people to him.

Jesus said to them:

It is not what goes into a man's mouth that corrupts or defiles him, it is what comes out of his mouth that corrupts and defiles.

Jesus then entered into the home where he was staying. His disciples came to him and said:

Did you know that you greatly offended the Pharisees by what you said?

Jesus said:

Every plant that my heavenly Father has not planted will be rooted up. Leave the Pharisees alone; they are blind guides. The blind guides and the blind who they lead will both fall into a pit.

Peter said to Jesus:

Tell us the meaning of what you said to the Pharisees.

Jesus said:

You don't understand that it is not the outside things that defile a man but the things that are in his heart.

If a man eats meat, it goes into his stomach and through his digestive system and is then flushed out of his system. It does not go through the heart of a man.

It is what comes out of a man that makes him unclean, and they are:

Evil thoughts
Fornications
Theft
Murders
Adulteries
Covetousness Wickedness
Deceit
Sensuality and envious eye
Lying
Temper tantrums
Pride

All these evil things are produced from inside a man. Eating with unwashed hands does not defile a man.

WITHDRAW FROM HEROD'S TERRITORY

Then Jesus left Galilee and withdrew into the borders of Tyre and Sidon.

PHOENICIAN WOMAN'S DAUGHTER

Jesus found a house to stay in so that he could escape the public eye. But his fame was too great and it soon became known to the people in the region where Jesus was staying.

Almost immediately, a **Canaanite**† woman, whose daughter had an unclean spirit, heard that Jesus was nearby, and found him.

She said to Jesus:

Have mercy on me, Oh Lord, son of David. My daughter is grievously tormented by a demon.

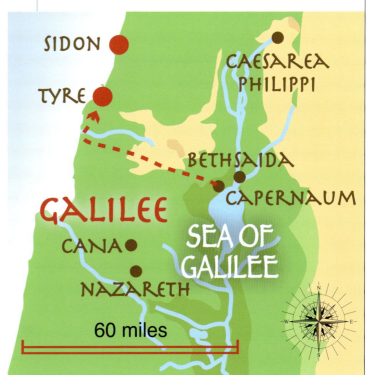

† Further reading available at the end of this chapter.

But Jesus didn't say a word to her.

The woman was a **Greek**†, a Syrophenician by race.

The woman kept begging Jesus to cast the demon out of her daughter. Finally, the disciples came to Jesus and complained that she was making a nuisance of herself and creating a disturbance every where they went.

Jesus said to the 12 disciples:

I was sent to the house of Israel.

But the woman came and fell down at Jesus' feet and worshipped him, saying:

Lord help me.

Jesus said to her:

Let the children first be filled, for it is not becoming to take the children's food and cast it to the dogs.

She responded:

Yes Lord; but the dogs under the table eat the children's crumbs even while the children eat.

Jesus said:

Woman, your faith is great; let it be done as you wish. The demon has gone out of your daughter.

The woman returned home and found her daughter lying on her bed, completely healed.

AVOIDING OF HEROD'S TERRITORY

Jesus left the border region of Tyre and came through Sidon to the Sea of Galilee.

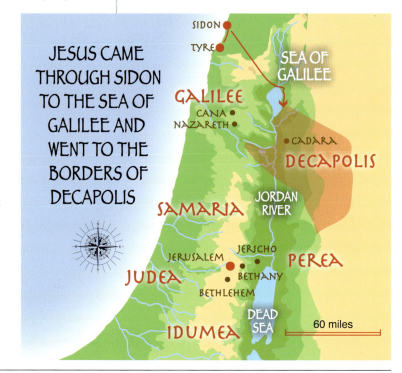

† Further reading available at the end of this chapter.

He went through the middle of the borders of Decapolis and up into the mountain where he sat down.

Stacked loaves in an Old City Market

FOUR THOUSAND FED

Jesus was directed to a man who was deaf and spoke with an impediment.

They asked Jesus to lay hands on him. Jesus took him away from the crowd that had gathered around him.

Jesus put his fingers into the man's ears and spat and touched his tongue. Looking up to heaven, Jesus sighed and said in Aramaic:

Be opened.

The man's ears were immediately opened. The speech impediment was healed and the man spoke plainly.

He told the man not to tell anyone what had happened. But the man went away and told everyone he met.

Everyone was astonished and began to say:

He can even make the deaf to hear and the dumb to speak.

When the crowds saw the lame walking and the blind seeing, and the deaf hearing, they glorified the God of Israel.

The crowd that came to Jesus had grown to about 4,000 men. They stayed with Jesus for three days.

On the third day, Jesus spoke to his 12 disciples and told them that he had compassion for the crowds.

Jesus knew that they had not eaten in three days and he did not want to send them back to their homes until they had eaten and regained some of their strength.

Jesus did not want them to faint from hunger on their journey back home, for some had traveled a great distance.

The disciples asked Jesus where they were going get enough bread to feed such a large crowd, since they were in a desert area with no provisions nearby.

Jesus asked his disciples how many loaves of bread they had. The disciples answered that they had seven loaves and a few small fish.

Jesus took the loaves, gave thanks and broke the bread into pieces and gave it to his disciples to distribute to the multitude. Jesus took the few small fish and blessed them, and gave them to the disciples to give to the multitude.

Everyone ate until they were full. The disciples then gathered up all the bread and fish that remained, and there were seven baskets full. After this miracle of feeding the 4,000, he sent them their homes.

Judean countryside

A BLIND MAN HEALED

Jesus went immediately into the boat with his disciples and went to the borders of Magadan, which is in Dalmanutha.

The Pharisees and Sadducees found Jesus and began to question him. They wanted Jesus to show them a sign from heaven.

Jesus was deeply grieved in his spirit at their unbelief.

Jesus said:

Why is this generation looking for a sign? When it is evening you look at the sky and see that it is red, and you predict good weather.

In the morning you look at the sky and see that it red and lowering and you predict foul weather.

You know how to discern the face of the sky and yet you cannot see the signs of the times.

An evil and adulterous generation looks for a sign. The truth is that no sign will be given to this generation except the sign of Jonah.

So Jesus left that area and went to the boat and sailed to the other side of the Sea of Galilee with his 12 disciples.

The disciples forgot to bring any bread along for the trip. When they mentioned it to Jesus he said:

Beware of the yeast of the Pharisees and the Sadducees. Beware of the yeast of Herod.

The disciples, not quite understanding what Jesus was talking about, wondered if he was saying these things to them because they forgot to bring bread.

Jesus knew what they were thinking and said to them:

You have so little faith, why are you worrying about not having any bread? Don't you understand yet?

Don't you remember the five loaves and the five thousand it fed, with an abundance left over?

Don't you recall the seven loaves and the four thousand it fed with an abundance left over?

Why is it that you do not understand that what I am telling you is not about bread.

Have your hearts been hardened? Do you have eyes and yet do not see? Do you have ears that do not hear? Don't you remember anything?

Then the disciples understood that Jesus was not talking about bread, but that he was warning them to beware of the teaching of the Pharisees and Sadducees.

Once they landed on shore, Jesus and his disciples went to Bethsaida - not the suburb of Capernaum but Bethsaida Julias, which is a town on the east side of the Jordan River near where it flows into the sea of Galilee.

A blind man was brought to Jesus for healing. Jesus took the man's hand and led him outside the village. Jesus then spit into his eyes and laid his hands on his eyes, and asked:

Do you see yet?

The man looked up and said:

I see men, but they look like walking trees.

Then Jesus laid his hands on his eyes again and when the man opened his eyes everything became perfectly clear.

Jesus sent the man to his home and gave him instructions not to enter the village.

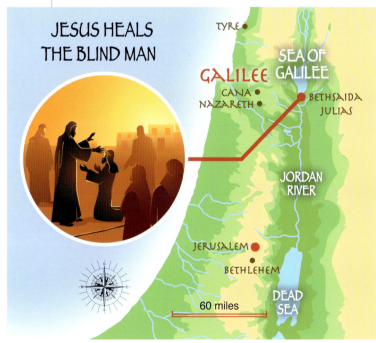

THE GREAT CONFESSION

Jesus went out with his disciples into the villages of **Caesarea and Philippi**†. Having spent time in prayer with his disciples, he asked:

Who do men say that I am?

His disciples answered:

Some say that you are John the Baptist, others say you are Elijah, others say that you are Jeremiah or one of the other old time prophets come back to life.

Jesus asked them:

But who do you think I am?

Simon Peter said:

You are the Christ, the Son of the living God.

Jesus said to him:

Blessed are you, Simon, son of Jonah: For flesh and blood did not reveal this to you, but my Father who is in heaven.

I tell you that your name is Peter (petros - a small loose stone), and upon this Rock (petra - bedrock or foundation stone) I will build my church and the gates of hell shall not prevail against it.

I will give to you the keys of the kingdom of heaven and whatever you bind on earth will be bound in heaven; and whatever you loose on earth will be loosed in heaven.

He then told his disciples not to tell anyone that he was the Christ.

PASSION FORETOLD

From that time on Jesus began to plainly tell his 12 disciples that he was going to suffer greatly.

He told them that he must go to Jerusalem and be rejected and be tormented by the elders, chief priests and scribes. He told them that he was going to be killed, and that he would rise again on the third day.

† Further reading available at the end of this chapter.

Flowers that bloom in Galilee

Peter took Jesus aside and began to rebuke him, telling him that the things Jesus was predicting would never happen.

Jesus turned around so that all his disciples could hear him and he said to Peter:

Get behind me, Satan! You are a stumbling block to me. You are not thinking about this the way God does. You are talking about things that concern men.

After this, Jesus called the multitude along with his disciples together and began to speak to them.

He said:

If anyone would follow after me, he must deny himself and take up his cross daily and follow me.

For whoever would save his life will lose it, and whoever would lose his life for my sake and the sake of the Gospel, will save it.

What does it profit a man if he gains the entire world but forfeits his own life? What can a person exchange for his life?

Whoever in this adulterous and sinful generation is ashamed of me and my words, the Son of man will also be ashamed of him when he comes with the holy angels, in his own glory and the glory of the Father.

The truth is that some of you who stand here will be alive to see the kingdom of God coming with power.

THE TRANSFIGURATION

Six days later, Jesus took Peter, James and John to a mountain where they could be by themselves and pray.

While they were praying, the clothes that Jesus was wearing dazzled, and he was transfigured before them.

His face shone like the sun, and his clothes became white as light.

Before long, two more men appeared with Jesus. Moses and Elijah-and they began talking with Jesus.

The two men also had a glorious appearance and they spoke about the death of Jesus and what he was going to accomplish in Jerusalem.

The three disciples saw this and were amazed and afraid. Peter, not knowing what he was really saying, said:

Let's built three tabernacles; one for you, one for Moses and the other for Elijah.

While Peter was still speaking, a bright cloud came over them and they were very afraid. A voice came out of the cloud and said:

This is my beloved Son, and I am very pleased with him; listen to him.

The disciples fell on the faces with fear. Jesus touched each one of them and told them to stand up and not be afraid.

Suddenly the disciples looked around and everyone was gone except for Jesus and themselves.

As they traveled down the mountain, he told the three that they should not tell anyone about this until after he had risen from the dead.

So they kept this to themselves, but wondered what Jesus meant when he said he would rise from the dead.

Later his disciples asked him why the scribes kept saying that Elijah must come before the Messiah.

Jesus told them:

Yes, it is true that Elijah must come first to restore all things. But I tell you that Elijah has already come, and they did not recognize him.

The disciples understood that he was talking about John the Baptist.

HEALING THE DEMONIAC BOY

The next day, after coming down off the mountain, Jesus saw a multitude of people. He saw that the scribes were questioning his 12 disciples.

When the crowd saw Jesus, they were amazed because Jesus' face was shining.

Jesus asked the multitude and his disciples what questions were asked by the scribes.

One of the men in the crowd knelt before Jesus and said:

Teacher, I have brought my son, who has an evil spirit that keeps him from talking; he also has epilepsy and is suffering greatly. The evil spirit throws him down, and he gnashes his teeth and he foams at the mouth.

He is badly bruised from all the abuse and is full of sores. I brought the boy to your disciples, but they could not cast out the evil spirit.

Jesus told the man:

Oh faithless and perverse generation, how long will I be with you? How long must I put up with you? Bring your son to me.

They brought the boy to Jesus and when the boy saw Jesus, the demon threw him to the ground and he began thrashing about and foaming at the mouth.

Jesus asked the father:

How long has your son been like this?

The father replied:

Since he was a young child. Sometimes the unclean spirit throws him into the fire and sometimes he throws him into water.

If you can do anything for him, please have compassion on us and help us.

Jesus answered:

If I can! All things are possible to the one who believes.

Immediately the father of the child cried out to Jesus:

I believe, please help my unbelief!

When Jesus saw that people where running from everywhere to join the crowd, he rebuked the unclean spirit, and said to him:

You deaf and dumb spirit, I command you to come out of him and do not enter him again.

The unclean spirit caused a great deal of torment as he obstinately came out of the boy, and the boy lay still on the ground as if he were dead.

Jesus took the boy by the hand, pulled him up, and he was healed. Jesus gave the boy to his father.

All were astonished at the majesty of God. Afterwards, Jesus went to the house where he was staying. His disciples came to him and asked him:

How come we could not cast out the unclean spirit?

Jesus said to them:

Because of your little faith. Listen to this truth and pay attention, for if you had faith as a grain of mustard seed you will say to this mountain, move to another place, and it will move.

If you have faith, nothing will be impossible for you.

Then he said to them:

This kind of demon can only come out with prayer.

Sun over Galilean valleys

RETURN TO GALILEE

On his way to Capernaum, Jesus passed through Galilee. He tried to keep his trip anonymous, seeking rest from the crowds.

He began to teach his 12 disciples, saying to them:

The Son of man will be delivered up into the hands of men.

While the multitudes marveled all the things that Jesus did, he said to his disciples:

Let these words really sink into your mind, for the Son of man will be delivered up into the hands of men. They will kill him, and after he is dead for three days, he will rise again.

The disciples were grieved by what Jesus was telling them.

They did not really understand what Jesus was telling them because it was hidden from them by God. They were afraid to ask Jesus for the details.

Rendering of the Tribute Money, by Masaccio

TRIBUTE MONEY

When Jesus and his disciples arrived in Capernaum the people collecting the temple tax came to Peter and asked:

Doesn't the teacher pay the temple tax?

Peter answered:

Yes.

When they came into the house where they were staying, Jesus asked Peter:

What do you think, Simon? Who do the kings of the Earth receive their tax, toll or tribute from? From their sons or from strangers?

Peter answered:

From strangers?

Jesus said:

So the sons are free. But in order not to cause them to stumble, go to the sea and cast a line with a hook on it, and then open the mouth of the first fish you catch.

In it you will find enough to pay the temple tax. Take it and give it to those who are collecting the tax.

CHILDLIKENESS

The disciples began to argue with each other about who was going to be the greatest in the kingdom. Jesus asked them:

On the way here, were you talking among yourselves about who would be the greatest?

But they kept silent.

Jesus sat down and called the 12 to come and sit around him. He told them:

THE STORY OF JESUS

If a man would be first, he will be last of all and the servant of all.

Later on that day, the disciples came to Jesus and asked:

Who, then, is the greatest in the kingdom of heaven?

Jesus called over a small child and set him by his side while he sat in the middle of the disciples. He took the child into his arms and said:

Unless you change and become as a little child you will not enter the kingdom of heaven.

Whoever humbles himself as this little child, that person is the greatest in the kingdom of heaven.

Jesus continued:

Whoever receives a little child in my name, receives me. Anyone who receives me, does not only receive me but also receives the one who sent me.

The one who is the least among you, is the one who is great.

John said:

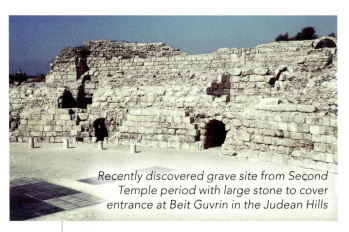

Recently discovered grave site from Second Temple period with large stone to cover entrance at Beit Guvrin in the Judean Hills

Master, we saw someone casting out demons in your name and we told him to stop, because he was not one of us.

Jesus said to them:

Don't stop him. No one who is doing mighty works in my name will be quick to speak evil of me. The person who is not against us is for us.

Whoever gives you a cup of water to drink because you belong to me; truly, he will not lose his reward.

Whoever causes one of these little ones that believes in me to stumble, it would be better for him if a great millstone were hung around his neck and he was thrown into the sea to sink to the bottom.

The wickedness of man makes sin inevitable, but that does not remove the responsibility from the person that causes others to sin.

If your hand causes you to stumble, cut it off. It is better for you to enter into life maimed than to have two hands and go into hell.

If your foot causes you to sin, cut it off. It is better for you to enter into life limping on one leg than to have both your feet and to be cast into hell.

If your eye causes you to sin, pluck it out. Better to enter into life with only sight in one eye than to have two eyes and enter into hell.

In hell the worm never dies, and the fire never goes out.

For everyone is salted with salt, but if the salt has lost its saltiness then how will it be seasoned? Have salt in yourselves and be at peace with one another.

See that you do not despise these little ones.

What do you think? If a man has 100 sheep and one of them goes astray, won't he leave the 99 and go find the missing sheep?

When he finds the lost sheep, won't he be happier about finding it than the 99 that had not gone astray? It is the will of your Father in heaven that not one of these little ones should perish.

FORGIVENESS BETWEEN BRETHREN

Jesus said:

If your brother sins against you, go to him and show him his fault, between you and him alone.

If he listens, you have gained a brother.

But if he will not listen then take one or two more witnesses with you, so that the matter is made clear.

A roman city under excavation in Israel

If he still refuses to hear then take the matter to the church.

If he refuses to hear the church, then leave him alone and stop having any dealing with him and treat him like an outsider.

The important truth that you need to understand is that whatever you bind on earth will be bound in heaven, and whatever you loose on Earth will be loosed in heaven.

Again I tell you if any two of you will agree on anything that you ask, it will be done for you by my Father who is in heaven.

Where two or three have gathered together in my name, I am among them.

Then Peter came and asked:

Lord, how often should I forgive my brother when he sins against me? Should I forgive him seven times?

Jesus said to Peter:

Not seven times, but 70 times seven times.

The kingdom of heaven is like a king who called upon all of his servants to account for the debts they owed him.

One of the servants who was brought to the king owed the equivalent of $1.5 million.

Because the servant could not pay the debt, the king commanded that the servant's land and property all be sold and that he and his family be sold as slaves in order to settle the debt.

The servant fell down and worshipped the king, and begged him to have patience with him, promising to pay it all.

The king was moved with compassion and released him from bondage and forgave him the entire debt.

That day, the servant went out and found another fellow servant who owed him $500. He grabbed the servant by the throat and told him that he must pay what he owed.

The fellow servant fell down and begged the man to have patience with him, and he would pay what he owed. But instead of showing him mercy, he had the fellow servant thrown into prison.

When the other servants saw how their fellow servant had been treated they were very upset, and they went to the king and told him everything that the unforgiving servant had done.

Galilean red poppies

The king then summoned the unforgiving servant and said to him:

You wicked servant, I forgave you the all the debt you owed because you pleaded with me to do so. Shouldn't you have had mercy on your fellow servant, just as I had mercy on you?

The king became very angry with the wicked servant and had him taken to the tormentors† until he could pay all that was due.

Then Jesus said:

Your heavenly Father will treat you the same way if you do not forgive you brother from your hearts.

JESUS' BROTHERS ADVISE HIM

The feast of the tabernacles was at hand. Jesus' brothers came to him and said to him:

Leave this place and go to Judea so that your disciples can see the works that you do.

For no man does anything in secret while he seeks to be known openly. If you are going to do these things, make yourself known to the world.

Even his own brothers did not believe in him.

Jesus said to them:

My time has not yet come, but your time is always ready. The world cannot hate you, but it hates me because I testify that its works are evil.

You go up to the feast: I will not go up to the feast because until the right time.

After saying these things, he stayed in Galilee.

THE PRIVATE JOURNEY TO JERUSALEM

After his brothers had left for Jerusalem to go to the feast, Jesus also went, not publicly, but in secret.

The time had come when Jesus was about to embrace his final mission on Earth.

Jesus set his face toward Jerusalem and sent messengers ahead to the village of the Samaritans to make things ready for

† Further reading available at the end of this chapter.

THE STORY OF JESUS

him. But when Jesus arrived in Samaria, he was not welcomed or received.

When James and John saw how their Lord was treated, they asked if they could call down fire from heaven on them. Jesus rebuked them for this, and went on to the next village.

JESUS SENT MESSENGERS AHEAD TO THE VILLAGE OF THE SAMARITANS

SACRIFICE FOR CHRIST'S SERVICE

As they went on their way through Samaria to Jerusalem, a man came up to them and said that he would follow Jesus wherever he went. Jesus turned to the man and said:

The foxes have holes and the birds of the sky have nests but the Son of man has no where to lay his head.

Jesus said to another:

Follow me.

The man replied:

I will follow you, but first let me say goodbye to my relatives.

But Jesus said to him:

If a man puts his hand to the plow and looks back he is not fit for the kingdom of God.

THE FEAST OF TABERNACLES

The Jews from Jerusalem who were at the Feast of the Tabernacles kept looking for Jesus. They asked:

Where is he?

There was a lot of murmuring and rumors among the multitudes about Jesus. Some said:

He is a good man.

Others said:

No, he leads the people astray.

But no one spoke openly about Jesus for fear of the Jews of Jerusalem.

During the middle of the feast, Jesus went up into the temple and taught. The Jews from Jerusalem were amazed:

How is this man so learned and wise since he has had no formal education?

Jesus told them:

The teaching is not mine; it comes from the one who sent me.

The person who speaks for himself is looking for his own glory, but he who seeks the glory of the one who sent him, is a man of truth and no unrighteousness is in him.

Didn't Moses give you the law, and yet none of you keep the law? Why do you want to kill me?

The multitude answered:

You have a demon. Who is trying to kill you?

Jesus answered:

I did one work, and you all marvel because of it. Moses gave you circumcision, and you circumcise a man on the Sabbath.

If a man is circumcised on the Sabbath, so the law of Moses is not broken, then why are you infuriated with me for making a man completely whole on the Sabbath?

Stop judging things by their appearance, but judge by what is right.

Some of the people in Jerusalem said:

Isn't this the man they are trying to kill? Look, he speaks openly and they don't say anything to him. Could it be that the rulers know that he is the Christ?

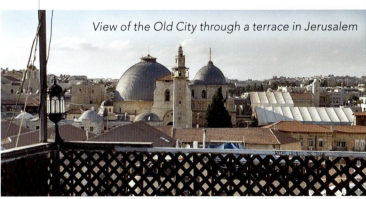

View of the Old City through a terrace in Jerusalem

THE STORY OF JESUS

How is it that we know where this man comes from? But when the Christ comes, no one will know where he came from.

Jesus, in the temple, said:

You know me, and you know where I came from. I have not come of myself but the one who sent me is true, and you do not know him; because I am from him, and he sent me.

They tried to capture Jesus, but no one could lay a hand on him, because his time had not yet come.

Many in the multitude believed in Jesus, and they said:

When the Christ comes, will he do more signs than this man has done?

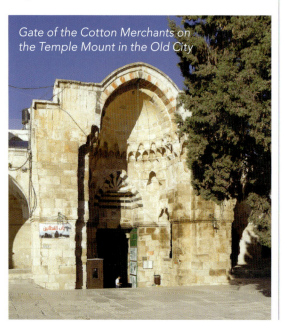
Gate of the Cotton Merchants on the Temple Mount in the Old City

The Pharisees heard what the crowds were saying about Jesus, and they sent the officers to capture him.

Jesus knew that his time was short and said:

I am only going to be with you a little while longer, and then I will go to the one who sent me. You will look for me, but you will not find me. Where I am going you cannot come.

The Jews from Jerusalem said to themselves:

Where will this man go that we cannot find him? Will he go to the be with the Jews who live among the Greeks, and teach the Greeks?

What does he mean when he says, You will look for me but you will not find me; and where I am going you cannot come?

Now on the last day of the great feast, Jesus stood and cried, saying:

If anyone thirsts, let him come to me and drink. The person who believes in me, as the Scriptures say, from within him will flow rivers of living water.

Jesus spoke these things of the Holy Spirit, which those who believe in him were going to receive. For the Holy Spirit was not yet given, because Jesus was not yet glorified.

Some of the multitude, when they heard Jesus, said:

This is truly a prophet.

Others said:

This is the Christ.

But some said:

What, does the Christ come from Galilee? Doesn't the Scripture say that the Christ is going to come from the seed of David and from Bethlehem, the village where David lived?

So there was a division among the people because of Jesus.

Some wanted to arrest him; but no man laid a finger on him.

When the officers sent to arrest Jesus returned empty handed, the chief priests and the Pharisees asked them why.

The officers said:

We have never heard a man speak like this man.

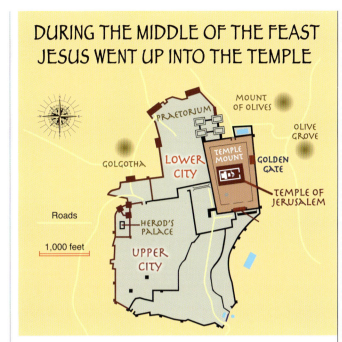

The Pharisees answered them and said:

Have you also been led astray? Have any of the rulers believed in him?

Have any of the Pharisees believed in him? The crowd is ignorant of the law and under a curse.

Nicodemus (the ruler who came to Jesus by night) said to them:

Does our law judge a man before it hears the case and learns the facts?

They answered Nicodemus:

Are you also from Galilee? Search the Scriptures and you will find that no prophet arises out of Galilee.

THE STORY OF THE ADULTERESS

The assembly of chief priests and Pharisees broke up and went home. But Jesus went to the **Mount of Olives**†.

Damascus Gate into the Old City of Jerusalem

Early the next morning he returned to the temple.

People came to him, and he sat down and began to teach them.

The scribes and the Pharisees brought a woman who had just been caught in the act of adultery and put her in the middle of the group that Jesus was teaching.

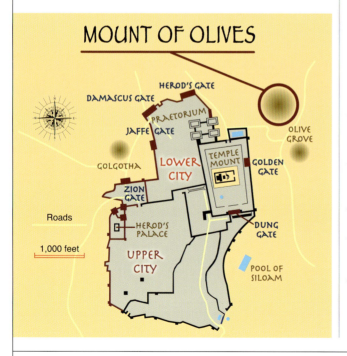

They asked Jesus:

*The law of Moses commands us to **stone**† adulterers. What do you say about it?*

Jesus stooped down, and with his finger, he wrote on the ground. They continued to taunt Jesus with the question.

Jesus stood up and said to them:

He who is without sin among you, let him be the first one to throw a stone at her.

Again Jesus stooped down and continued writing on the ground. The scribes and Pharisees, after hearing Jesus' answer, were silent.

They left Jesus, starting with the oldest and ending with the youngest.

Then Jesus stood up and asked the woman:

Where are the ones who accuse you?

† Further reading available at the end of this chapter.

Does no man condemn you?

She said:

No man, sir.

Then Jesus said:

Neither do I condemn you. Go your way. From now on sin no more.

Zion Gate in Jerusalem

ATTEMPT TO STONE JESUS

Jesus continued to teach in the temple in Jerusalem.

Jesus said:

I am the light of the world. Whoever follows me will not walk in darkness, but will have the light of life.

The Pharisees said to him:

You are testifying about yourself; your testimony is not true.

Jesus answered:

Even if I do bear witness of myself, my testimony is true, for I know where I came from and I know where I am going.

But you do not know where I came from or where I am going.

You judge superficially and according to appearances. I judge no man, but if I do judge, my Judgment is true; for I am not alone, the Father has sent me.

In your law, it is written that the witness of two men is true. I am the one who bears witness of myself and the Father that sent me also bears witness of me.

They said to him:

Where is your Father?

Jesus answered:

You do not know me or my Father. If you knew me, you would know the Father also.

Jesus spoke these words in the treasury where the chests for offerings were placed, in the most public part of the temple. No one came to arrest him because his hour had not yet come.

Jesus continued:

I will go away and you will look for me but you will die in your sin. Where I am going, you cannot come.

The Jews began asking among themselves:

Will he kill himself? Is that what he means when he says:

Where I am going, you cannot come?

Jesus said to them:

You are from below; I am from above. You are of this world; I am not of this world.

This is what I have to say to you. Unless you believe that I am who I say that I am, you will die in your sins.

Then they asked Jesus:

Who are you?

Jesus said to them:

I have told you who I am from the beginning. I have many things to say and to judge concerning you.

A traditional Israeli tomato and cucumber salad in a bowl

He who sent me is true and the things that I heard from him are the things I am telling the world.

Finally! They understood that Jesus was speaking of God the Father.

Jesus said to them:

When you have lifted up the Son of man, then you will know that I am he, and that I do nothing of myself, but I only do what the Father has taught me.

The one who has sent me has not left me alone, and I always do the things that please him.

As Jesus spoke these words, many believed him.

Jesus said to the Jews from Jerusalem who had believed him:

If you remain in my word, then you are truly my disciples and you will know the truth and the truth will make you free.

They answered Jesus:

We are Abraham's seed and have never been in bondage to any man. What do you mean when you say:

You will be made free?

Jesus answered:

Every one who commits sin is in slave to sin. The slave does not live in the house forever, but the Son lives forever.

So if the Son shall make you free, you will be free indeed.

I know you are Abraham's seed, yet you are trying to kill me because my words have not changed your hearts.

I speak about things that I have seen with my father, and you do the things that you have heard from your father.

They answered Jesus:

Our father is Abraham.

Jesus said to them:

If you really were Abraham's children, you would do the works of Abraham.

But now you are looking for a way to kill me, a man who has told you the truth that I have heard from God. Abraham would not act this way. You do the works of your Father.

They said to him:

We were not born -out of an act of fornication, we have one Father, even God.

Jesus said to them:

If God really were your Father, then you would love me, for I came from God. I have not come on my own. God sent me.

Why don't you understand the words that I am saying? It is because you cannot hear my word.

You are from your father, the devil, and the lusts of your father are what it is your will to do.

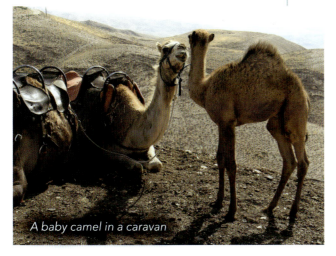
A baby camel in a caravan

THE STORY OF JESUS

He was a murderer from the beginning, and never did what was true because there is no truth in him. When he speaks a lie it is his nature, for he is a liar and the father of lies.

Because I tell you the truth, you do not believe me. Which one of you can convict me of sin?

I tell you the truth. Why is it that you do not believe me? The person who is of God hears the words of God.

The reason you cannot hear these words is because you are not of God.

The Jews of Jerusalem answered by saying:

Aren't we right about you when we say that you are a Samaritan and have a demon?

Jesus answered:

I do not have a demon. I honor my Father, and you dishonor me. I am not seeking my own glory.

I am going to tell you an important truth, so you need to pay attention. If a man cherishes and obeys my words, he will never see death.

The Jews said to Jesus:

Now we know you have a demon. Abraham is dead, and so are all the prophets. You say that if a man keeps your word he will never taste death.

Are you greater than our father Abraham, who died, and the prophets who died? Who are you making yourself out to be?

Jesus answered:

If I glorify myself, my glory is nothing. It is my Father who glorifies me, the same one who you say is your God. You do not know him, but I do.

If I said I did not know him I would be a liar like you are liars. But I know him and I keep his word. Your father Abraham rejoiced to see my day, and he saw it by faith and was glad.

The Jews said to him:

You are not even 50 years old, and you have seen Abraham?

Jesus said to them:

I am going to tell you a truth that is very important. Pay attention! Before Abraham was born, I am.

The Jews took up stones and threw them at Jesus, but Jesus hid himself from them and went out of the temple.

A MAN BORN BLIND

As Jesus passed by, he saw a man who was blind from birth.

His 12 disciples who were with him asked:

Teacher, whose sin caused this man to be born blind — his own or his parents?

Jesus answered:

Neither. He was born blind so that the works of God could be displayed in him. We must do the work of him who sent me while it is daytime.

The night is coming when no man can work. When I am in the world, I am the light of the world.

After Jesus had said these things he spat on the ground, and made clay and anointed the man's eyes with it. He told the man to go to the pool of Siloam.

The man did as Jesus said and came away seeing.

The neighbors of the blind man who had known him for a long time and had seen him often begging for a living said:

Isn't this the blind man who sat and begged?

Others said:

It is.

Others disagreed.

But the man himself declared:

I am the man.

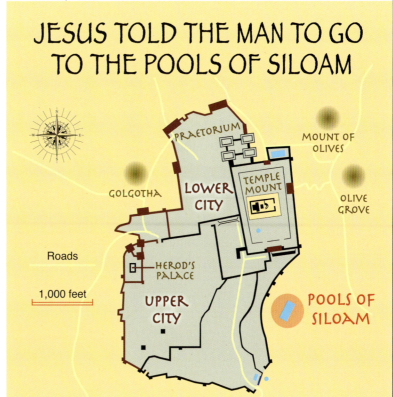

JESUS TOLD THE MAN TO GO TO THE POOLS OF SILOAM

They asked him:

How is it that you can now see?

He said:

The man called Jesus made clay and anointed my eyes and told me to go wash at the pool of Siloam. I did what Jesus said, and now I can see.

The people asked:

Where is Jesus?

The man answered: I do not know.

The people brought the blind man to the Pharisees to see how they would respond to the man who had been born blind.

Jesus did this miracle on the Sabbath day.

So the Pharisees asked the man how he had received his sight. He told them the same story he had told his neighbors.

When they heard this, some of the Pharisees said:

This man is not from God because he does not keep the Sabbath day.

Other Pharisees said:

How is it that a man who is a sinner can do such miracles?

So they questioned the blind man again.

The man who had been blind said:

He is a prophet.

The Jews did not believe that the man had actually received his sight. They called his parents and asked them how he had received his sight.

His parent answered:

Yes, this is our son, and he was born blind. But we don't know how he has received his sight. He is old enough, ask him yourself.

The parents feared the Jews because they knew that they had already agreed among themselves that anyone who confessed that Jesus was the Christ would be thrown out of the synagogue.

That is why they told the Pharisees to ask their son how he had received his sight.

So the Pharisees called a second time for the man who had been born blind. They said to him:

Give glory to God, not Jesus, because we know he is a sinner.

The man answered:

Whether he is a sinner or not, I do not know, but I do know one thing, I was blind, and now I can see.

They said to him:

What did he do to you?

The man answered:

I have told you over and over what he did. Do you want to hear it again? Would you like to become one of his disciples?

The Pharisees, after hearing this, reviled the man and said:

You are his disciple, but we are disciples of Moses. We know that God spoke to Moses, we don't know who this man is.

The man said:

Why, here is a real mystery. He opened my eyes and yet you do not know who he is.

We know that God does not listen to sinners, but if anyone is a true worshipper of God and does his will, he will listen to that man.

Since the world began, I have never heard of a man who was born blind

The Blind Man Washes in the Pool of Siloam, painted by James Tissot

who had his eyes opened and received his sight.

If Jesus were not from God, he could do nothing.

They told him:

You were born into sin, and you presume to teach us?

They threw him out.

Jesus heard that they dismissed from the assembly and he went and found him.

Jesus said to the man:

Do you believe in the Son of God?

He answered:

Who is the Lord, that I might believe in him?

Jesus said:

You have both seen him and he is the one who is speaking to you right now.

The man said:

Lord, I believe.

The man worshipped him.

Jesus summed it up by saying:

Judgment came into this world so that those who could not see can now see, and those who can see have become blind.

There were Pharisees nearby who heard what Jesus said. They asked Jesus:

Are you saying that we are blind?

Jesus answered:

If you were blind, you would have no sin. But because you say that you see, your sin remains.

THE GOOD SHEPHERD

Jesus continued to teach the Pharisees who were questioning him:

The person who does not enter the sheepfold by the door, but instead climbs in by some other way, is a thief and a robber.

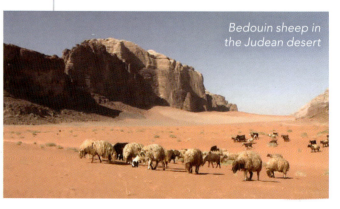
Bedouin sheep in the Judean desert

But the one who enters in by the door, he is the shepherd of the sheep.

The gatekeeper opens the door to the shepherd from the inside, and when the sheep hear the shepherd's voice as he calls his own sheep by name, they follow.

They recognize the shepherd's voice, and they follow him. They will not follow a stranger but will flee from him, because they do not recognize his voice.

Jesus spoke to them in parables, but they did not understand what he was saying. He tried again:

I am the door to the sheep. Everyone who came before is a thief or robber, and the sheep did not hear them.

I am the door. If anyone enters in through me, he will be saved, and will go in and out, and will find pasture.

The thief only comes to steal and to kill and to destroy. I have come that you might have life, and have it more abundantly.

I am the good shepherd. The good shepherd lays his life down for the sheep. The hired hand will not lay his life down for his sheep.

If the wolf comes, the hired hand runs away and lets the sheep be scattered and killed. He runs because he does not care about the sheep; he is just a hired hand.

I am the good shepherd, and I know my own, and they know me. Just like the Father knows me, and I know the Father. I lay down my life for the sheep.

I have other sheep that are not of this fold. I must be their shepherd also. They will hear my voice, and they will follow me. They will all become one flock with one shepherd.

The Father loves me because I lay down my life, so that I can take it up again. No one is going to take it away from me but I will lay it down myself.

I have the power to lay it down, and I have the power to take it up again. This commandment I received from my Father.

These words caused a division among the Jews of Jerusalem. Many said:

He has a demon, or he is insane, why are you listening to him?

Others said:

These are not the words of a demon. Can a demon open the eyes of the blind?

JESUS SENDS OUT 70

Now after this, Jesus appointed 70 messengers in addition to the 12 disciples.

He sent them two-by-two into every city and place that he was going to visit.

He told them:

The harvest is great, but the laborers are few. Pray that the Lord of the harvest would send out laborers into the harvest.

Go on your way. Look, I am sending you out like lambs in the midst of wolves. Do

Road through Armageddon, Megiddo, Israel

not carry any money or extra shoes, and don't talk to anyone on the way.

Whatever house you enter, first say:

Peace be to this house.

If you are received then your peace will rest upon that house. If you are not received, then there will be no blessing on that house.

Stay in the same house, and eat and drink what they give you, for a laborer is worthy of his hire. Do not go from house to house.

Whatever city you enter, receive whatever they put in front of you and eat what you are served.

Heal the sick and tell them, The kingdom of God is very near to you.

If you go into a city and are not received, then go into the streets

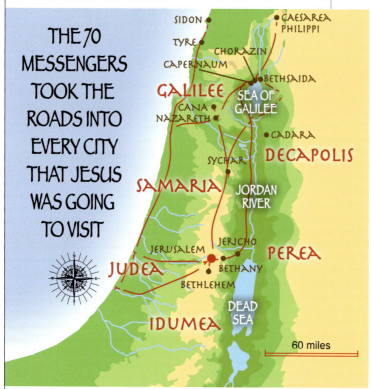

THE 70 MESSENGERS TOOK THE ROADS INTO EVERY CITY THAT JESUS WAS GOING TO VISIT

and shake the dust off your feet as a testimony against them. Tell them that the kingdom of God is very near.

I tell you that it would be more tolerable for Sodom in the day of judgment than for that city.

Woe to you, Chorazin!

Woe to you Bethsaida! If the mighty works that were done in you were done in Tyre and Sidon they would have repented, sitting in sackcloth and ashes.

What about Capernaum, will it be exalted to the heavens? Or will it be brought down to hell?

The person who hears you is hearing me, and the person who rejects you is rejecting me. The person who rejects me, rejects the one who sent me.

The 70 went out and did as Jesus had commanded them. When they returned to Jesus, they were full of joy:

Lord, even the demons are subject to us in your name.

Jesus said to them:

I saw Satan falling as lightning from heaven. Look, I have given you the authority to tread on serpents and scorpions, and to trample over all the power of the enemy. Nothing can hurt you.

But do not be happy that the spirits are subject to you, but rejoice that your names are written in heaven.

In the same hour, Jesus rejoiced in the Holy Spirit and said:

I thank you Father, Lord of heaven and Earth, that you have hidden these things from the wise and educated, and have revealed them to babes. Yes, Father, for this was well pleasing to you.

All things have been given to me by my Father, and no one knows who the Son is, except the Father and whoever the Son reveals himself to.

Turning to the disciples he said privately:

Blessed are the eyes that see the things that you see. I tell you this, many prophets and kings have desired to see and hear the things that you have seen, and they didn't see or hear them.

PARABLE OF THE GOOD SAMARITAN

There was a lawyer who stood up and tried to put on trial the skill of Jesus to answer a difficult question:

Teacher, what shall I do to inherit eternal life?

Excavation of biblical site on the road to Jericho

Jesus answered him:

What is written in the law? How do you read it?

The man said:

You shall love the Lord you God with all your heart, and with all your soul, and with all your strength, and with all your mind. You should love your neighbor as you love yourself.

Jesus said to him:

You have answered correctly. Do this and you will live.

But trying to justify himself, he said to Jesus:

Who is my neighbor?

Jesus told the man:

A man was going down from Jerusalem to Jericho†, and he was attacked by robbers who stripped him and beat him, leaving him half dead.

By chance, a priest was going down the same way and when he saw the man he walked on the other side of the road and passed him by.

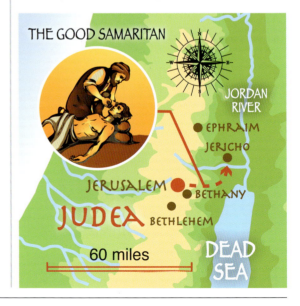

† Further reading available at the end of this chapter.

*A little later a **Levite**†, also traveling down the road, saw the man and moved to the other side of the road and ignored him.*

*But a Samaritan, who was traveling down the same road, saw the injured man and had compassion on him. He bound up his wounds and poured oil and **wine**† on them.*

He then put the man on his donkey and brought him to the closest inn, and took care of him.

The following day he took out a day's wage from his purse and gave it to the innkeeper with instructions to take care of the man.

He also told him that if he needed more money, he'd repay him on his next trip.

Jesus asked:

Which of the three proved to be the neighbor to the man who was attacked by the robbers?

The lawyer replied:

The one who showed him mercy.

Then Jesus said to him:

You go and do the same.

JESUS, THE GUEST OF MARTHA AND MARY

As Jesus and his disciples went on their way, he entered the village of Bethany. A woman named Martha received him into her house.

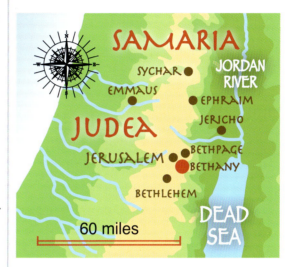

She had a sister named Mary, who sat at the feet of Jesus to hear him teach.

Martha was very busy serving. She came to Jesus and said:

Lord doesn't it bother you that Mary has left me alone to serve?

Jesus answered and said:

Martha, Martha, you are anxious and troubled about many things, but one thing is the most important: Mary has chosen what is important, and I will not take it away from her.

† Further reading available at the end of this chapter.

THE STORY OF JESUS

PRAYER TAUGHT

Jesus and his 12 disciples were praying, and after the prayer, one of the disciples said to the Jesus:

Lord teach us to pray, just like John the Baptist taught his disciples.

Jesus said to them:

When you pray, say, Father, Holy be your name. May your kingdom come. Give us today our daily bread, and forgive us our sins, for we also forgive everyone that is indebted to us. Bring us not into temptation.

Then Jesus said to them:

Which one of you who has a friend? Would you go to him at midnight and say to him:

> *Friend, lend me three loaves of bread. A friend of mine has just arrived from a journey, and I do not have anything to feed him.*

Would the friend answer:

> *Don't bother me now, all my children are in bed, and it is too late. I cannot get up and help you?*

I tell you this, even though he would not get up and help you because of your friendship, he would get up just to get rid of the nuisance and noise you caused at the midnight hour.

I say to you:

Ask, and it will be given to you.

Seek, and you will find.

Knock, and it will be opened to you.

If a son asks for a loaf of bread will the father give him a stone? Or if he asks for a fish, will he give him a serpent? Or if he asks for an egg will he give him a scorpion?

If you, who are evil, know how to give good gifts to your children, how much more will your heavenly Father give the Holy Spirit to them who ask him?

A beautiful sunset in Judea

WOMAN HEALED ON THE SABBATH

Jesus was teaching in the synagogue on the Sabbath day. There was a woman who had been suffering for 18 years from an infirmity that left her twisted so badly that she could not stand up straight.

Jesus saw the woman, called her over and said:

Woman, you are set free from your infirmity.

He laid hands on her, and she was immediately healed. She was able to stand tall, and she began glorifying God.

The ruler of the synagogue became indignant at Jesus because he had healed on the Sabbath day.

The ruler said to the crowd:

There are six days in which to do your work and you can be healed on any one of those days, but not on the Sabbath.

Jesus answered him:

You hypocrites, doesn't each one of you lead your ox or your donkey to water on the Sabbath?

Shouldn't this woman, a daughter of Abraham whom Satan had bound for 18 years, be freed from her bondage on the day of the Sabbath?

Colonnade along excavated Roman street

As Jesus said these things, his adversaries were put to shame, and the whole crowd rejoiced because of all the glorious things that Jesus did.

Jesus continued:

What is the kingdom of God like? What should I compare it to?

It is like the grain of the mustard seed, which a man took and threw into his garden and it grew, and it became like a tree.

Then the birds of the sky made homes in its branches.

What else can I compare the kingdom of heaven to? It is like yeast, which a woman hid in three measures of flour, until it permeated all of the dough.

THE JEWS ATTEMPT TO STONE JESUS

It was the time of the feast of dedication at Jerusalem. It was winter, and Jesus walked in the temple in Solomon's porch.

The Jews came around him and said to him:

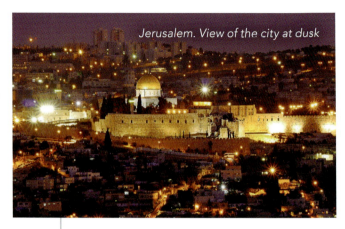
Jerusalem. View of the city at dusk

How much longer will you hold us in suspense? If you are the Christ, tell us plainly.

Jesus answered them:

I told you and you did not believe. The works that I do in my Fathers name, they testify to who I am. But you don't believe because you are not my sheep.

My sheep hear my voice, and I know them, and they follow me. I give them eternal life and they will never perish, and no one can snatch them out of my Father's hand. I and my Father are one.

Hearing this, the Jews took up stones and tried to kill him.

Jesus said to them:

Many good works I have you shown you from the Father. And for which of these good works are you going to stone me?

The Jews answered by saying:

We will not stone you for one of your good works, but for blasphemy, because you, being a man, make yourself out to be God.

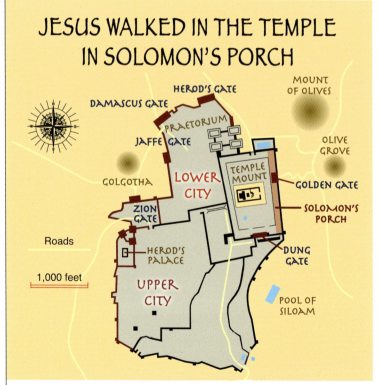

JESUS WALKED IN THE TEMPLE IN SOLOMON'S PORCH

Jesus answered them:

*If he called them gods, the ones to whom the word of God came. Are you going to say to the one the Father **sanctified**† and sent into the world, You are blaspheming, because I said:*

I am the Son of God.

If I do not do the works of my Father, don't believe me. But if I do the works of my Father, even if you do not believe my testimony, believe me because of my works.

Then you will know and understand the Father is in me and I am in the Father.

The Jews put down their stones and decided to arrest Jesus instead. But Jesus left without them being able to put a hand on him.

Jesus went to the area where John the Baptist had started baptizing, and he stayed there.

Many came to Jesus and said:

John the Baptist did no miracles, but everything he spoke about Jesus is true.

Many more came to believe on Jesus.

THE STRAIGHT GATE

Jesus went on his way through the cities and villages, teaching and making his way back to Jerusalem.

Someone said to him:

Are there only a few who are saved?

Jesus said to them:

Strive to enter in by the narrow door, for many will seek to enter and will not be able.

Gaze at the lovely Jerusalem archways

Once the master of the house has risen up and has shut the door, many will stand on the outside and knock, saying:

Lord, open up to us. - The Master will say:

I do not know who you are. Then they will say:

We ate and drank in your presence, and you taught in our streets.

† Further reading available at the end of this chapter.

THE STORY OF JESUS

The Master will say:

I tell you, I do not know you; go away from me all of you who do evil.

There will be weeping and gnashing of teeth when you see Abraham, Isaac and Jacob, and all the prophets in the kingdom of God, but you are kept out.

They will come from the east and the west and from the north and the south, and they will all sit down in the kingdom of God. The last will be first and the first will be last.

During the same hour that Jesus was teaching this, a group of Pharisees came to Jesus saying:

Get out of here, for Herod wants to kill you.

Jesus said to them:

- Go and say to that fox:

- Look I cast out demons and perform many healings today and tomorrow, and the third day I am perfected.

I must go on doing what I am doing until the time comes for me to suffer martyrdom in Jerusalem.

Oh Jerusalem, Jerusalem, you kill the prophets and stone them that are sent to you! How often I would have gathered your inhabitants together, even as a hen gathers her brood under her wing, but you would not!

Look, your temple is left desolate, I tell you, You will not see me until you say:

Blessed is he that comes in the name of the Lord.

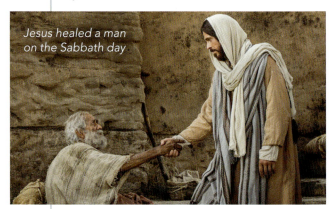

Jesus healed a man on the Sabbath day

SABBATH HEALING

The time came when Jesus went into one the rulers of the Pharisees home to eat bread on the Sabbath day. They were watching him to see what he would do.

And a man with the **dropsy**† came and stood before Jesus.

† Further reading available at the end of this chapter.

Jesus knew what the Pharisees were thinking, and said:

Is it lawful to heal on the Sabbath, or not?

The Pharisees didn't say a word.

Jesus then healed the man.

Then he said to the Pharisees:

Which one of you whose ox or donkey fell into a well on the Sabbath day would not immediately pull him out?

They couldn't answer him.

When Jesus saw how the Pharisees honored themselves by taking the chief seats. He told them a parable.

Jesus said:

When you are invited to a marriage feast, don't sit in the place of honor, or someone who is more important than you will come in and you will be asked to move to one of the lesser seats.

But instead, find the lowest seat you can and take it so that when the host comes he will invite you to take a better seat next to the host, and you will receive honor from everyone there.

Everyone who exalts himself will be humbled, and he who humbles himself will be exalted.

And then he said to the Pharisee who had invited him to eat:

When you make a dinner or a supper, don't call your friends, or your brothers, or your relatives or your rich neighbors. They can all pay you back with the same hospitality.

When you make a feast, invite the poor, the injured, the lame and the blind. You will be blessed because they do not have any way to repay you. You will receive a reward in the resurrection of the just.

One of the guests at the meal with Jesus, after hearing what Jesus said, exclaimed:

Blessed is the person that eats bread in the kingdom of God.

But Jesus answered him:

A man made a great supper, and he invited many to come. He sent his servants out to ask his friends to come because the feast was just about ready.

But the friends began to make excuses as to why they could not come.

One invited guest said:

I have just purchased a field, and I need to go see it, please excuse me from coming.

Another invited guest said:

I have just purchased five yoke of oxen, I need to go and try them out, please excuse me.

And another said:

I have just gotten married, and I cannot come.

When the servant came to his master and told him how his invited guests had replied, the man became very angry. He said to his servant:

Go quickly into the streets and lanes of the city and bring in the poor, the maimed and the blind.

After that had been done, there was still room at the feast. So the servant was sent to find guests in the highways and hedges until the man's house was full.

The Master of the feast said:

None of those men who were first invited will ever taste my feast.

COST OF DISCIPLESHIP

A great multitude followed Jesus. So Jesus turned around and said to them:

If any man comes to me and does not hate his own father and mother and wife and children and brothers and sister, and even his own life cannot be my disciple.

Dead Sea's shore

Whoever does not bear his own cross, and come after me, cannot be my disciple.

Which of you wanting to build a tower, does not first sit down and count the cost to make sure he has enough money to complete it?

Otherwise, after he has laid the foundation, and runs out of money to finish the project, everyone will mock him. They will say:

The man began to build, and he was not able to finish.

What king goes to war against another king without first sitting down and considering the odds of winning the battle?

If he only has ten thousand soldiers and his enemy has twenty thousand, perhaps he should send an ambassador to make peace.

If you do not renounce everything that you have, you cannot be my disciple.

Salt is only good as long as it has flavor. If salt loses its flavor, how will it be seasoned? It is not good for anything and will be thrown into the trash heap.

He that has ears to hear, let him hear.

SECOND GROUP OF PARABLES

Now all the tax-collectors and sinners were coming to see and hear Jesus.

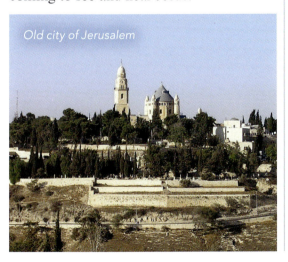
Old city of Jerusalem

But the scribes and Pharisees were offended by the company that Jesus kept, and said:

This man hangs around with sinners and eats with them.

Judean Sheep

THE LOST SHEEP

Jesus spoke to them in a parable and said:

Who among you who has one hundred sheep, and if one of them gets lost, does not leave the ninety-nine and go looking for the lost sheep until he finds it?

And when he finds that sheep he carries it on his shoulders, rejoicing.

When he comes home, he calls his friends and neighbors together and rejoices with them. He says:

   I have found the sheep that was lost.

I tell you that in heaven there is great joy over one sinner who repents, more than the ninety-nine righteous persons who do not need repentance.

THE LOST COIN

Jesus said:

There was a woman with ten pieces of silver. If she loses one of the silver coins, won't she look for it diligently until she finds it?

And when she has found it she will call her friends and neighbors together and ask them to rejoice with her because she found the valuable coin that was lost.

I tell you there is joy in the presence of the angels of God over one sinner that repents.

THE LOST SON

Jesus said:

A man had two sons. The younger son said to his father:

> *Give me my inheritance.*

And the father did as the son requested and divided his inheritance and gave his portion to the youngest son.

A couple days later, the young son gathered all his things together and took a journey into a faraway country.

When he arrived in the far country, he spent his entire inheritance on wild living. And after he had spent everything he had, there came a mighty famine in the land, and the son began to go hungry.

So he joined himself to one of the citizens of the country who sent him into his pasture to feed the pigs.

And the son was so hungry that he started thinking about eating the husks that were being feed to the pigs. No one would help him.

After a while, he came to his senses and said:

> *My father's hired hands have bread to spare and lack of nothing, and I am here dying of hunger. I will get up and go to my father's house and tell him that I have sinned against heaven and in his sight.*
>
> *I will tell him that I am not worthy to be his son, and beg him to hire me on as a servant.*

So he got up and went to his father.

And while he was off in the distance, a ways from his father house, his father saw him and was moved with compassion for him. He ran and met him, and hugged and kissed him.

The son said to the father,

> *I have sinned against heaven and in your sight, I am not worthy to be called your son.*

But the father interrupted the son and said to his servants:

> *Bring out the finest clothes and dress my son, put a ring on his hand and new shoes on his feet. And pick out the finest calf and kill it and make a feast.*

> *Let's celebrate, for this was my son who was dead, and he is now alive. He was lost, and now he is found.*

And they had a celebration.

But the oldest son was in the field, and when he came near the house and heard the music and saw the dancing, he called one of the servants aside to find out what was happening. And the servant told him.

The older brother became angry and would not go into join the celebration.

His father came out to talk with him and asked him to join the celebration, but he would not.

He said to his father:

> *I have served you faithfully for all these years and never disobeyed any of your rules. You never gave me a baby goat, much less a calf, that I might have a celebration with my friends.*

> *But your son, who has wasted his inheritance and spent his money on prostitutes, has been given a party. You have killed a calf for him and made a feast.*

The father said:

> You are always with me and everything I have belongs to you. But it was good to have a celebration for you younger brother. Your brother was dead and is now alive.

> *He was lost, but now he is found.*

THE UNRIGHTEOUS SERVANT

Jesus said to his disciples:

There was a rich man who had a steward. This steward was accused of wasting his goods. The rich man called in the steward, and asked about the rumors he was hearing.

He required an accounting, and told the steward that he could no longer manage his affairs.

The steward said to himself:

> *What should I do, since my job of managing this rich man's estate is going to be taken away? I am not strong enough to get a job digging up fields and I am too ashamed to beg.*

> *I know what I will do while I still have authority over my masters financial matters.*

Then he called on each person that owed his rich employer money and asked them how much they owed.

He went to one debtor and asked:

> *What do you owe?*

The man replied:
> *I owe 450 gallons of olive oil.*

The steward said:

> *Here, I will reduce the debt to 225 gallons of olive oil.*

He came to another person that owed his master and asked:

> *What do you owe?*

The man replied:

> *I owe a barn full of wheat.*

Stone Olive press with rolling stone for crushing olives to express oil.

Wheat field in Israel

The steward said:

I will reduce the debt to a half barn full of wheat.

The steward did this with all his master's debtors, putting all of them in debt to him. When the rich man discovered what his dishonest steward had done he commended the unrighteous steward for his shrewdness:

For the sons of this world are wiser than the sons of light.

Then Jesus said to them:

Use the resources you have been given in such a way that you will have a reward in the future, for this world will fail you.

He who is faithful in a very little is faithful also in much: and he who is unrighteous in a very little is unrighteous in much.

If you have not been faithful in the temporal and the transitory, who is going to trust you with true lasting riches? If you have been unfaithful using someone else's possessions, who is going to trust you with your own?

No servant can serve two masters for either he will hate the one and love the other, or else he will hold to one and despise the other.

You cannot serve God and material possessions.

The Pharisees, who loved money, scoffed at the teaching of Jesus.

And Jesus continued teaching them.

Jesus said:

You justify yourselves in the sight of men, but God knows your hearts.

Don't you understand that those things that are exalted by men are an abomination in the sight of God?

For everyone who divorces his wife and marries another commits adultery.

And the person who marries the one who has been divorced from the husband commits adultery.

THE RICH MAN AND LAZARUS

Jesus said:

There was a rich man, and he was clothed in the purple robes and wore the finest linen, eating sumptuous meals every day.

And a beggar named Lazarus was laying at the gate of the rich man's resort, full of sores.

The beggar was hoping to eat some of the crumbs that fell from the rich man's table. While he lay at the gate in his misery, the dogs would come and lick his sores.

One day the beggar died and the angels carried him into Abraham's bosom.

Walls of Old City

The rich man also died and was buried, and found himself in Hell. As he was being tormented, he lifted his eyes and saw Abraham off in the distance, and Lazarus in his bosom.

And the tormented man cried and said:

Father Abraham, have mercy on me, and send Lazarus that he may dip the tip of his finger into the water and cool my tongue. I am in anguish in this flame.

But Abraham said:

Son, remember that you in your lifetime received good things, and Lazarus received evil things. But here, he is comforted, and you are in anguish.

And besides, there is a great gulf between us that neither one of us can bridge.

And the rich man said:

I beg you, Father Abraham, to let Lazarus go to my father's house and tell my five brothers about this place so they can avoid this place of torment.

Abraham said:

Your brothers have Moses and the prophets.

The tormented man said:

No, Father Abraham. If one goes to them from the dead, they will repent.

Abraham answered him:

If they do not listen to Moses and the prophets, they will not be persuaded by someone who has risen from the dead.

Flowers bloom in the desert

FAITH AND SERVICE

Jesus said to his disciples:

Temptations to sin are sure to come, but woe to him through whom they come!

It would be better if a great weight was tied around his neck, and then be thrown into the sea, rather than be the one who causes one of these little ones to stumble.

Be careful yourselves. If your brother sins, rebuke him, and if he repents, then forgive him. If he sins against you seven times and comes to you for forgiveness, you shall forgive him.

And the apostles said to Jesus:

Increase our faith.

And Jesus said:

If you had faith as a grain of mustard seed, you might say to this sycamore tree:

Lift yourself up from your roots and plant yourself in the sea, and it would obey you.

Which one of you who has a servant plowing or keeping your sheep, when he comes in from the field will invite him to sit down and eat?

Isn't it more likely that you will tell him to prepare your meal and serve you until your have finished eating, and then after that he can have his meal?

Do you thank the servant because he does the things that you command him to do?

In the same way after you have done all that is commanded, don't think you deserve a reward. All you have done is your duty.

RAISING OF LAZARUS

A friend of Jesus was sick. His name was Lazarus. He lived in Bethany with his sisters Mary and Martha. It was Martha who had anointed the Lord with ointment and **wiped his feet**† with her hair.

---

† Further reading available at the end of this chapter.

Mary and Martha sent word to Jesus that their brother Lazarus, who Jesus loved, was sick to the point of death.

When Jesus heard it, he said:

This sickness has come about so that God and his Son will be glorified.

Jesus loved Mary and Martha and their brother Lazarus.

Jesus stayed two more days where he was. Then after two days he said to his 12 disciples:

Let's go back to Judea.

The disciples said to him:

Teacher, the Jews who live in that region want to stone you, and you want to go back there?

Jesus answered:

Are there not twelve hours in the day? If a man walks in the daylight he doesn't stumble because he sees the light of this world.

But if a man walks in the night, he stumbles because the light is not in him.

Jesus said these things to his disciples after he told them that their friend Lazarus had fallen asleep:

I will go and wake him up.

His disciples said:

If he is asleep then perhaps the fever is gone.

Jesus was saying that Lazarus was dead, but the disciples thought he was saying that Lazarus was restfully sleeping.

Finally, Jesus said to his disciples:

Lazarus is dead. And I am glad for your sakes that I was not there, so that you may believe. Let's go to him.

Thomas, who is also called *Didymus*, said to his fellow-disciples:

Tomb of Lazarus in Bethany

Let's go so that we may die with him.

So when Jesus came to Bethany, to the house of Mary and Martha, he found that Lazarus had been in the tomb for four days.

Now Bethany was very near Jerusalem. Many of the Jews had come to Martha and Mary to console them over the death of their brother.

When Martha heard that Jesus was coming, she went to meet him, but Mary stayed in the house.

Martha said to Jesus:

Lord, if you had been here my brother would not have died. But even now I know that what you ask God to do, He will do.

Jesus said to her:

Your brother will rise again.

Martha said to him:

I know that he will rise again in the resurrection at the last day.

Jesus said to her:

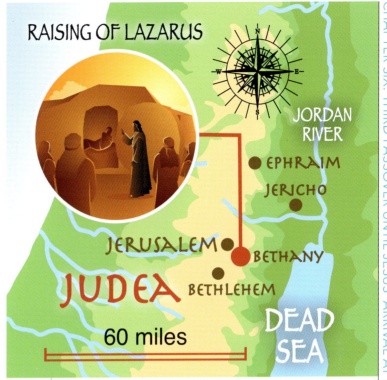

I am the resurrection and the life. He who believes in me, even if he dies, he will live, and whoever lives and believes in me will never die. Do you believe this?

Martha said to him:

Yes, Lord. I believe that you are the Christ, the Son of God, the one sent into this world from God.

After she said this she went and called Mary her sister secretly, saying:

The Teacher is here and is looking for you.

Mary got up quickly and went to Jesus.

Jesus was not yet in Bethany, but waiting at the same place that Martha had left him.

The Jews who were consoling Mary and Martha in their homes, saw Mary get up quickly and leave. They supposed that she was going to the tomb to weep, and they followed her.

When Mary came to where Jesus was, she fell at his feet and said to him:

Lord if you had been here, my brother would not have died.

Jesus saw her weeping, and he saw the Jews also who had come along with her weeping. He groaned in his spirit and was troubled and asked:

Where have you laid him?

They said to him:

Lord, come and see.

Jesus wept.

The Jews said:

Look how he loved him!

But others said:

If he could open the eyes of the blind couldn't he have prevented Lazarus from dying?

After groaning, Jesus came up to the tomb that was in a cave with a stone lying against the opening.

Martha said:

Lord, the body is decayed since it has been dead for four days.

Jesus said to her:

Didn't I tell you that if you believed you would see the glory of God?

So at Jesus' instruction they took away the stone from in front of the tomb.

Jesus lifted up his eyes and said:

Father, I thank you that you hear me. I know you always hear me, but I want the people who are here to believe that you sent me.

And then Jesus with a loud voice said:

Lazarus come out.

Lazarus came out of the tomb, his hands and feet were bound with grave-clothes, and his face was covered by a napkin.

Jesus said to them:

Unwrap him and let him go.

Rock-cut tombs in Sonhedrio, believed to be the burial site of Second Temple era judges

Many of the Jews who had come to comfort Mary and her sister Martha saw Jesus raise Lazarus from the dead and believed in him.

Others went out and told the Pharisees what Jesus had done.

THE SANHEDRIN'S DECREE

The chief priests and the Pharisees gathered a council. They asked:

What should we do? This man does many signs and miracles and if we let him continue, then everyone will believe in him. Then the Romans will come and take away our positions of authority and our nation.

But the high priest, **Caiaphas**†, said to them:

Don't you know anything at all? Don't you think it is better for one man to die than for the entire nation to perish?

Caiaphas did not realize it but he was not speaking this by himself. Because he was the high priest that year, he was actually prophesying that Jesus was going to die for the nation — and not for the nation of Israel only, but also for all the children of God who are scattered abroad.

So from that day forward the chief priests and the Pharisees began scheming how they might put Jesus to death.

Jesus, knowing this, did not walk openly among the Jews. He left for a city called Ephraim, near the wilderness. And there he stayed with his disciples.

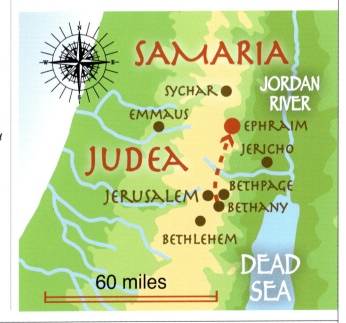

† Further reading available at the end of this chapter.

TEN LEPERS

Later on Jesus decided to return to Jerusalem. As he was passing along the borders of Samaria and Galilee he entered into a village where he was met by ten lepers.

The lepers kept their distance from Jesus but they did yell to him with a loud voice saying:

Jesus, have mercy on us.

When he saw them, he said to them:

Go and show yourselves to the priests.

And they were all cleansed.

One of the ten lepers, when he saw that he was healed, returned to Jesus and fell down on his face before him and gave him thanks and glorified God. He was a Samaritan.

Jesus answered him:

Didn't I cleanse ten of you? Where are the other nine? Why did they not return to give glory to God?

Go your way, your faith has healed you.

Later, the Pharisees approached Jesus and asked when the kingdom of God was going to come so that men could see it, since he had been promising that it was at hand for nearly three years.

Jesus answered:

The kingdom of God is not coming in the way you are looking for it to come. No one is going to come to you and say:

Look there is the kingdom of God, or come with me and let's go look at the kingdom of God.

The kingdom of God is within you.

Road through Samaria

Then he said to his 12 disciples:

It will not be very long before you will desire to see the Son of man, but you will not see him. They will say to you:

Come see him here, or come see him there.

But do not believe them or follow after them.

When the lightning flashes, it lights up the entire sky, and everyone sees it. This is the way it will be when the Son of man comes in glory.

*First, I must suffer many things and be rejected by this generation. And just like in the days of **Noah**†, they ate and drank and married right up to the day that Noah entered into the ark. And then the flood came and destroyed them all.*

*And just like the days of **Lot**†, they ate and drank, and bought and sold. They planted, and they built. But the day that **Lot**† left Sodom it rained fire and **brimstone**† from heaven and destroyed them all.*

This is what it will be like just before the Son of man is revealed.

In that day that is coming, there will be no time to gather up all your possessions or to finish the job you are doing.

Remember Lot's wife.

Whoever seeks to gain his life will lose it; but whoever loses his life will preserve it. I tell you, in that night one will be taken and another left.

Two men will be sleeping and one will be taken and another will be left.

Two women will be cooking a meal and one will be taken and the other will be left.

And they asked Jesus:

Where is this going to happen?

Jesus answered:

Everywhere there are wicked men.

Ein Karem tower, a biblical site just outside Jerusalem

PARABLE OF THE IMPORTUNATE WIDOW

Jesus then spoke a parable to the 12 disciples in order to encourage them to pray and not become weary:

† Further reading available at the end of this chapter.

There was, in a city, a judge who neither feared God or man.

And there was widow who was trying to get a settlement with someone who had stolen from her. The widow kept coming to the judge and asking for justice.

The judge finally said to himself:

> *Even though I do not fear God, or have any regard for men, I will still give her justice because if I do not she will continue to disturb me with her persistent pleas.*

If an unjust judge will render a just verdict, how much more will God avenge his elect, who make petition to him both day and night?

But remember that God is patient, and sometimes it seems like he is delaying his justice. That is because God is merciful, even to his enemies.

But when the day comes that the chance to repent ends, then justice will come suddenly and the opportunity for mercy will be over.

When the Son of man comes will he find faith on the earth?

Old City, Tower of David Museum seen at day with its stone walls

PARABLE OF THE PHARISEE AND PUBLICAN

Then Jesus spoke a parable to those who were trusting in themselves and were impressed with their own righteousness.

Jesus said:

Two men went up into the temple to pray. One was a Pharisee and the other was a tax collector.

The Pharisee stood and prayed, having himself as the object of his own prayers:

> *God, I thank you that I am not like the rest of men, swindlers, unjust, adulterers, or even tax collectors. I fast twice a week. I give my tithes faithfully.*

The tax collector, standing far away from the temple, would not even lift his eyes to heaven, but struck his chest and said:

God be merciful to me, a sinner.

I tell you that the tax collector went home justified.

The Pharisee did not.

Everyone who exalts himself will be humbled, and he that humbles himself will be exalted.

JESUS TEACHES ABOUT DIVORCE

After Jesus had finished this teaching, he left from Galilee. He came to the borders of Judea and beyond the Jordan River.

And the multitudes gathered together around him and he taught them and healed them.

And Pharisees came to Jesus and asked him if it was lawful for a man to divorce his wife for any reason.

The were testing him to try and find fault with his answer.

Jesus answered them by asking:

What did Moses command you?

They replied:

Moses required that he write a certificate of divorce and send her away.

Jesus answered:

Have you not read that God made them male and female from the beginning?

And for this reason, a man will leave his own father and mother and join himself to his wife, and the two will become one. They are no longer two, but one flesh.

A view from the streets of Jerusalem's Old City

What God has joined together let no man break apart.

They answered Jesus:

Then why did Moses command us to give a certificate of divorce, and send her away?

Jesus answered:

Moses, because of the hardness of your hearts, wrote you this commandment and tolerated you putting away your wives.

But that is not the way it was supposed to be. From the beginning of creation, God made them male and female.

Later on the disciples of Jesus came to him and asked him to explain the matter of marriage and divorce.

Jesus told them:

Whoever puts his wife away, except for sexual immorality, and marries another women, commits adultery against her.

His disciples said to him:

If that is the way it is then it is not a good idea to marry?

Jesus said to them:

I am going to tell you something that is not for everyone, but for only for those who can receive it.

There are eunuchs who were born that way, and those who have been made eunuchs by the violence of men.

*But there are also eunuchs who have made themselves **eunuch**† for the sake of the kingdom of heaven.*

He that is able to receive it, let him receive it.

JESUS BLESSES THE CHILDREN

Many others began bringing their little children to Jesus so that he would lay his hands on them and pray over them.

A boy at a flowers for export Kibbutz

† Further reading available at the end of this chapter.

When the 12 disciples saw this, they rebuked them and told them to stop.

When Jesus saw that his disciples were trying to stop the children from coming to him, he became indignant and called to his disciples and said:

Biblical era foods for sale at an Old City market

Do not stop the little children from coming to me. Don't you understand that the kingdom of heaven is made up of the childlike?

Listen carefully to this truth, Whoever does not receive the kingdom of God as a little child will never enter into the kingdom.

Then Jesus took the children in his arms and layed his hands on them and blessed them.

Jesus then began his journey again.

PERIL OF RICHES

As Jesus continued his journey a very rich ruler came running up to Jesus and kneeled before him and asked him:

Good Teacher, what good thing can I do to inherit eternal life?

Jesus said to him:

Why are you calling me good? There is none good, except God.

Why are you using the word "good?"

If you want to enter into life, keep the commandments.

The rich young ruler asked:

Which commandments?

Jesus said to him:

You know the commandments:

Do not commit adultery, Do not kill, Do not steal, Do not bear false witness, Do not defraud, Honor your father and your mother, Love your neighbor as you love yourself.

The man answered:

Teacher, I have kept all these commandments since I was a child, what am I missing?

And Jesus, when he heard it, looked at him and loved him, and said to him:

One thing is missing if you want to inherit eternal life, go sell everything that you have and distribute it to the poor and you will have treasure in heaven. And then come and follow me.

When the man heard this, he became discouraged and depressed and full of sorrow, for he was very rich and had great possessions.

Jesus saw his demeanor change and looked around at his disciples and said:

How difficult it is for a rich man to enter in the kingdom of God.

And the disciples were amazed at these words.

Jesus answered again and said:

Children, it is very hard for those who trust in riches to enter into the kingdom of God!

It is easier for a camel to go through a needle's eye, than for a rich man to enter into the kingdom of God.

The disciples were astonished and said to Jesus:

Then who can be saved?

Jesus looked at them and said:

With men this is impossible, but not with God. For all things are possible with God. The things that are impossible with man are possible with God.

Then Peter said:

We have left everything to follow you, what are we going to get out of it?

Then Jesus said to him:

Listen carefully to this truth, When I come in my glory and sit on my throne, you will sit on twelve thrones, judging the twelve tribes of Israel.

Everyone who has left houses or children or lands for my sake, and for the sake of the gospel, will receive his reward in the world to come.

Many of the last will be first, and the first will be last. For the kingdom of heaven is like a man managing his house, who goes out early in the morning to hire laborers.

And he agrees to pay these laborers fifty dollars a day, and sends them into his vineyards to work.

Later that day he sees men standing around in the marketplace with nothing to do. And he says to them, Go into my vineyard and work and I will pay you a fair wage.

After this, even later in the day, he went and found some other men who had nothing to do, and he told them to go into his vineyard and work.

At the end of the day, he paid all the workers the same amount, fifty dollars.

But those who had been working all day complained bitterly, saying:

> *These men who only worked in the vineyard for one hour are receiving the same wages as those of us who worked all day under the hot sun.*

The man replied and said:

> *Friend I have not done anything wrong. Didn't I give you what I agreed to pay you? Take what is yours and go your way and do not be angry with me.*
>
> *It is my will to give to the last, just like I have given to you. Are you going to be jealous because I am good?*
>
> *The last will be first and the first will be last.*

FORETELLING HIS PASSION

Jesus and his disciples were going up to Jerusalem. His 12 disciples, aware of the dangers awaiting Jesus, were amazed that he was returning to Jerusalem.

Jesus took his disciples aside and began to tell them what was going to happen to him when he got to Jerusalem.

He told them that he was going to be delivered over to the chief priests and that they

Restored windmill in Jerusalem's Old City

would condemn him to death. He told him that he would be mocked by the Gentiles, and **scourged**† and **crucified**†.

He told them that after they spat on him and whipped him, he would be killed.

He told them that he would rise again after three days.

He told them that all of this would fulfill all that was written by the prophets.

They did not understand anything that he told them. It was hidden from them.

After this, the mother of James and John the sons of Zebedee came and worshiped Jesus. She wanted Jesus to do something for her.

Jesus asked her:

What do you want me to do for you?

She answered:

Command that my two sons sit on your right and left side, in your kingdom.

Jesus answered:

You do not know what you are asking. Are you able to drink the cup that I am about to drink? Or be baptized with the baptism that I am going to be baptized with?

James and John said:

We are able.

Jesus said to them:

The cup that I drink you will drink someday. And someday you will be baptized with the baptism that I am going to be baptized with.

But to sit at my right and left hand, that is not for me to determine. My Father has made preparations for that and it is out of my hands.

And when the other ten disciples heard what James and John were asking they became indignant and angry with James and John.

Jesus called them together and said to them:

You know how the Gentiles lord it over you. You have seen how the world exercises authority. But this is not what it is going to be like with those who belong to me.

The one who wants to become great, let him become your servant. And the one who wants to be first, let him become the servant of all.

---

† Further reading available at the end of this chapter.

The Son of man did not come to be served, but to serve, and to give his life as a ransom for many.

BARTIMAEUS HEALED

As Jesus came near to the city of Jericho, a blind man sat by the wayside begging.

He heard the multitude and asked what all the commotion was about. He was told that Jesus of Nazareth would soon be passing by. When Jesus and his disciples came to Jericho with his disciples, and a great multitude followed him.

Archaeological site of a palace in Jericho

The blind beggar, Bartimaeus was sitting by the way side along with another blind man. And when he heard Jesus coming near, he cried out with a loud voice:

Lord, son of David, have mercy on me.

Many in the multitude rebuked Bartimaeus, telling him to be quiet, which made him yell even louder:

Lord have mercy on us!

Jesus heard Bartimaeus and stood still, commanding him to be brought forward.

And they called Bartimaeus and told him to be of good cheer because Jesus was calling for him.

Bartimaeus threw his coat on the ground and sprang to his feet and came to Jesus.

Jesus asked:

What can I do for you?

Bartimaeus said:

Lord, I want to receive my sight.

Jesus was moved with compassion and touched his eyes, and said:

Receive your sight. Your faith has made you whole.

Immediately he received his sight and began following Jesus along the way, glorifying God. All the people who saw this began to praise God.

ZACCHAEUS

Jesus entered into Jericho and began to pass through the city. There was a man named Zacchaeus. He was a chief tax collector, and he was very rich.

He wanted to see Jesus, but he could not because of the crowds and because he was a very short man.

So Zacchaeus ran and climbed a sycamore tree in order to get a glimpse of Jesus.

Jesus passed right under the tree that Zacchaeus was in and looked up. Then Jesus said:

Zacchaeus, hurry up and come down here, for today I am going to stay in your home.

The old city of Petra

Zacchaeus quickly slid down the tree and made preparations to receive Jesus into his home. And he did it with joy in his heart.

When the crowds heard and saw what Jesus was doing, they murmured, saying:

He is going to stay with a man who is a sinner.

And Zacchaeus stood and said to Jesus:

Behold, Lord, half my goods I am going to give to the poor, and if I have cheated any man, I will restore fourfold.

Jesus said to him:

Today salvation has come to your house. For the Son of man came to seek and to save that which was lost.

There was a great expectancy among the crowds that the kingdom of God was about to immediately appear.

As Jesus came close to entering Jerusalem, he told them this parable:

A nobleman went to a far country to take over a kingdom, and then to return. He called ten of his servants and gave them one hundred dollars each and told them to do business with the money until he returned.

The citizens of the town he was going to rule sent an ambassador to him saying:

We do not want you to rule over us.

And after he ruled the kingdom, he came back and commanded that the ten servants he had given the one hundred dollars to should give an account for the money they had been entrusted with. The first came and said:

- I turned your one hundred into one thousand dollars.

And the nobleman said:

Well done, you are a good servant, because you were found faithful with very little, you will now have authority over ten cities.

The second came and said:

I turned your one hundred dollars into five hundred dollars.

And the nobleman said:

Well done, you will rule over five cities.

Another servant came and said Lord:

Here is your one hundred dollars. I kept it safely in a napkin. For I feared you because you are a very austere man.

You take up what you have not laid down, and you reap where you have not sown.

The nobleman said to him:

Out of your own mouth, you judge yourself. You knew that I was an austere man, taking up things that I had not laid down and reaping where I did not sow.

Why didn't you put the one hundred dollars in the bank where it would at least draw some interest?

And he told his guards to take away the one hundred dollars from the wicked servant and give it to the good servant who had earned one thousand dollars.

And then he said to them:

Everyone who makes use of what has been given to them, they will increase.

But those who do nothing with what they have been given, even the little they have been given will be taken away.

Then he called for the enemies who sent an ambassador, to say that they did not want him to rule over them, to be brought forward and killed in front of him.

And after Jesus had told this parable he began leading the crowd up to Jerusalem.

END OF CHAPTER SIX

CHAPTER SIX
COMPANION

BRIMSTONE (page 199)
Another word for sulphur. It is highly flammable and often one of the products of a volcanic eruption.

It symbolizes agonizing judgment.

CAESAREA-PHILLIPPI (page 152)
The source of the River Jordan, located in the mountains of what is today called the Golan Heights. No village remains. There are remains of a pagan temple carved into the rocks.

The source of the river Jordan in Caesarea-Phillippi (now Golan Heights)

CAIAPHAS (page 197)
The High Priesthood of Annas and Caiaphas. Annas was the father in law of Caiaphas, and although Caiaphas was the official high priest of Israel, Annas who had been the former high priest still held power and authority. Caiaphas is the high priest who tore his clothes and declared Jesus was worthy of death.

Fragment of "The House of Caiaphas," painted by Gustave Doré

CANAANITE (page 147)
These were descendants of Canaan who was the son of Ham, the son of Noah.

They settled in the lowlands along the Mediterranean coast near where the present-day nation of Israel is located.

Tyre and Sidon were two Canaanite cities. They were known for being seafaring traders and merchants. Each village had a different name for its own god, but generally Canaanites worshipped the sun-god who was known as "Baal."

Baal, right arm raised. Bronze figurine, Louvre Museum

They were constant enemies of Israel. Simon was referred to as a Canaanite, not because he was from Canaan, but because he belonged to a specific sect of the zealots who were called "Cananaens."

Zealots were Jews who wanted to overthrow the occupying Roman army by armed revolt.

CRUCIFIXION (page 206)
Method of execution often used by the Romans to make an example of criminals.

The victim was usually scourged by whips with pieces of metal or bone on the ends that would bruise then rip the flesh.

They would then have their wrists and feet nailed to a cross.

The pectoral muscles become paralyzed and the pressure on their chest allows breath to come in, but the only way to exhale is to push up on their feet.

Soon, the victims become too weak and suffocate, but sometimes it could take many hours.

When Jesus was crucified, he suffered physically and died to pay the penalty for our sins. He also suffered spiritually by taking the sins of the world on himself and being separated from God for a while.

Even though the Jews accused him, and the Romans were in charge of carrying out the crucifixion, he gave up his life willingly.

DROPSY (page 184)
A symptom of an infection that results in swelling of the stomach and extremities. The only time it is mentioned in the Bible is Luke 14:2.

EUNUCH (page 202)

A confidential court official, usually one who was castrated.

In **Matthew 19:12,** Jesus was talking about men who voluntarily abstain from marriage so they can devote their energies to serving God.

The implication here and in other places in the Bible is that some men are called to this but marriage is also an honorable choice.

GREEK (page 148)

The Greeks mentioned in **John 12:20** were probably Gentiles who had been worshiping the one God of Israel.

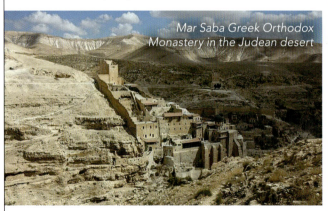
Mar Saba Greek Orthodox Monastery in the Judean desert

They had a strong desire to interact with Jesus because they took the time to seek him out.

They also showed that they honored him because they asked permission from Philip, his disciple, to speak to him, and were very respectful when they addressed Philip.

JERICHO (page 178)

Located in the Syrian-African Rift Valley, at the northern end of the Dead Sea, this is one of the oldest cities in the world in the lowest place on earth.

LEVITE (page 179)

Descendants of Levi who were responsible for maintaining the sanctuary and assisting the priests.

When the Jews were in the wilderness about 1,400 years before Christ, this meant setting up, dismantling and loading up the pieces of the tabernacle every time they moved. (The tabernacle was a tent sanctuary.)

When a permanent temple was built the Levites took care of the building and assisted the priests. They were exempt from military service.

LOT (page 199)

Nephew of Abraham. Lot came with Abraham when he came into the region of Canaan, which includes present day Israel.

When their herds of animals got too big, they had to split up. Abraham gave Lot first choice of where he wanted to live.

Lot chose the plains where Sodom was located. Before God destroyed Sodom, he sent angels to warn Lot. He and his family escaped, but contrary to what the angels had instructed them, Lot's wife looked back and immediately turned into a pillar of salt.

MOUNT OF OLIVES (page 166)

A mountain ridge east of Jerusalem, separated from the city by the Kidron valley.

It gets its name from the olive trees that grow there and the fact that it stands about 200 feet above Jerusalem.

Mount of Olives in the modern Jerusalem

It was one of Jesus' favorite places. He would often walk there on a road that went to Bethany.

He went to pray there the night before he allowed himself to be crucified, and Judas knew where to find him. It is also prophesied that Jesus will return there *(Zechariah 14:3-5)*.

NOAH (page 199)

Old Testament figure who lived after Adam and before Abraham, probably about 2500 years before Christ.

In Noah's time, people became so wicked that God sent a flood to kill them all. God warned Noah of the flood, and he believed God even though his neighbors made fun of him for building a huge boat in the middle of the desert.

The whole earth was covered with water. When it began subsiding, Noah and his wife and his extended family came upon dry land.

God made the rainbow as a promise to Noah and his descendants that he would never send another worldwide flood.

Noah's Ark

SANCTIFIED (page 183)

Set apart for a special purpose. In *John 17:16-18* Jesus is saying that His disciples will be in the world, but separated from it as the word of God, which is Scripture and the voice of the Holy Spirit, influences how they think and live.

SCOURGED (page 206)
Whipping done with pieces of bone or metal attached to the ends of the leather strips. Roman soldiers who did this often would lay bare the victim's bones, veins, and internal organs and leave them just short of death.

TORMENTORS (page 161)
The same word in Greek can be translated jailer or tormentor. Jailer would be the modern choice for this passage.

TRADITION OF THE ELDERS (page 145)
Oral and written teaching of rabbis *(religious teachers)* handed down from generation to generation.

By the time Jesus lived, the Torah had been in existence for about 1,400 years, so there were many additional teachings which had been collected.

Most of these traditions were attempts to determine how the Law which God had given them should be applied to specific situations.

Sometimes it was helpful, and sometimes it influenced people to be more concerned about the letter of the law rather than the spirit of the law. That's what Jesus was talking about in *Matthew 5:17-48.*

STONING (page 166)
The Jewish law prescribed stoning as the punishment for certain offenses. The convicted person would be taken to a place outside of town and people would throw rocks at him until he died.

It is interesting that one of the offenses for which people would be stoned is blasphemy. The Jewish leaders gave their reason for killing Jesus as blasphemy, but since the Romans were in charge, Jesus was crucified instead.

Later, scholars realized that if Jesus had been stoned, he would not have fulfilled many of the many of the prophecies of how he would die, such as *Psalm 22:13-18.*

VINEGAR, MYRRH, GALL (page 179)
Vinegar mixed with myrrh or gall- The vinegar mentioned here was a common sour wine used daily by the Roman soldiers.

Myrrh and gall both refer to a bitter-tasting substance that is a mild analgesic pain-reliever.

It was offered to people who were crucified to relieve their pain. Jesus chose to suffer the pain instead.

It is interesting that myrrh is one of the gifts the magi presented to Jesus when he was a small child.

WASHING FEET, AND ANOINTING WITH OIL
(page 193)

Washing feet was commonly done by servants for guests entering a wealthy person's house.

Most people wore sandals, and the roads were dusty so when travelers arrived, someone would wash their feet.

Anointing usually involved pouring oil on someone's head or body as a sign of being set apart to be a prophet, priest or king.

People would also put oil on their bodies to refresh themselves or for medicinal purposes. It was also use to embalm dead bodies. When the woman anointed Jesus' feet, she used costly perfume along with her tears and hair. This was done in light of Jesus impending death on the cross. It can also be seen as a symbol of his being set apart as prophet, priest and king.

THE STORY OF JESUS

CHAPTER SEVEN

LAST WEEK OF JESUS' MINISTRY

JESUS ARRIVES AT BETHANY

The Passover of the Jews was very near. Many went to Jerusalem before the Passover in order to purify themselves.

The people were looking for Jesus and wondering out loud if he would come to the feast.

They knew that the religious leaders were actively looking for the opportunity to arrest him.

Six days before the Passover, Jesus arrived in Bethany.

Bethany was where Jesus had raised Lazarus from the dead and was very near Jerusalem.

When Jesus was in Bethany, they made a supper for him in the house of Simon the leper. Martha served the dinner, and Lazarus, whom Jesus raised from the dead, was there.

While Jesus was sitting for the meal, Mary Magdelene carried an alabaster jar of exceedingly costly perfume and broke it and poured it over the head of Jesus.

She then anointed his feet with the expensive perfume and wiped it with her hair. This was the second time that Mary had done this.

The house was filled with the smell of the ointment.

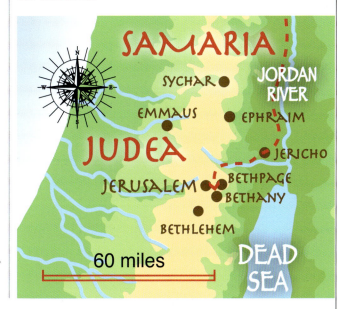

THE STORY OF JESUS

But Judas Iscariot, one of the 12 disciples and the one who would betray Jesus, said:

Why wasn't this ointment sold for the great amount of money it would bring, and the money given to the poor?

Others at the party began to criticize Mary.

Jesus heard this said:

Leave her alone. She is pouring this ointment upon my body in preparation for my burial.

The poor you have with you always, and you can do good to them whenever you want.

The truth is that wherever the good news is preached, what Mary has done today will be spoken about in memorial to her.

The common people, meanwhile, learned where Jesus was and they came to see him and Lazarus.

But the chief priests were conspiring to put Lazarus to death.

They hated Lazarus and wanted to destroy him. Because of him, many had believed in Jesus.

JESUS' TRIUMPHANT ENTRY

The next day, as Jesus came near to Bethphage and Bethany at the Mount of Olives, he sent two of his disciples on a mission.

He told them to go in a nearby village where they would find a donkey:

If anyone asks what you are doing with the donkey, just tell them that the Lord has need of him and will send him back very shortly.

This happened as was prophesied:

Tell the daughter of Zion (poetical name for the city of Jerusalem):

Look, your King comes to you, meek, and riding upon a donkey, and upon a colt, the foal of a donkey.

The two disciples left and did as Jesus had commanded.

They brought the animals to Jesus and put their coats on the back of the colt, where Jesus sat.

A multitude came to the feast. When they heard that Jesus was coming to Jerusalem, they took the branches from palm trees and went to meet him.

When they saw Jesus coming, they began to cry out:

Hosanna, Blessed is he who comes in the name of the Lord, even the king of Israel.

The Pharisees, seeing this, said among themselves:

We cannot stop this man. The world has gone after him.

As Jesus went to Jerusalem riding on the back of the colt of a donkey, people spread their garments and branches in his path.

As he approached the foot of the Mount of Olives, all his disciples rejoiced and praised God with a loud voice for all the mighty works which they had seen.

The multitude cried:

Hosanna to the Son of David. Blessed is the King who comes in the name of the Lord. Peace in heaven, and glory in the highest.

But some of the Pharisees who were in the multitude came to Jesus and told him to rebuke his disciples.

Jesus said to them:

I tell you that if they keep silent, the stones will cry out.

When Jesus came near Jerusalem, he wept over it, saying:

If you had only known what this day might have meant. But now it is hidden from your eyes.

Then Jesus said:

The day is coming when they will encircle you with embankments and keep you surrounded from every side.

Jerusalem will be dashed to the ground, and her children with her.

They will not leave one stone upon another because you didn't realize that you have been given a special period of grace.

Jesus entered the temple of God. The blind came into the temple and he restored their sight.

But when the chief priest and scribes saw the wonderful things that he did, and they heard the children in the temple who were crying, Hosanna to the Son of David; they were displeased.

They said to Jesus:

Don't you hear what they are saying?

Jesus answered:

Haven't you read, Out of the mouth of babes and nursing infants you have prepared praise?

It was sunset. Jesus inspected the temple and left for Bethany, where he and his 12 disciples would spend the night.

THE TEMPLE CLEANSED

The following morning, as he was returning to Jerusalem, Jesus saw a fig tree by the side of the road.

The tree had leaves, which suggested that it should also have fruit. When fig trees are barren, they have no leaves.

All but one variety of fig trees were out of season, making the prospect of finding a fig all the more delicious.

Jesus went to the tree and inspected it for fruit. When Jesus found nothing but leaves, he cursed the tree and said:

No one will ever again eat fruit from this tree.

The fig tree immediately withered away.

After they arrived in Jerusalem, Jesus entered into the temple and began turning over the tables on all the **moneychangers**† and those selling doves for sacrifice.

Notre Dame Hostel opposite Jerusalem's New Gate

† Further reading available at the end of this chapter.

Ripe fig tree in Israel

Jesus would not allow anyone to carry goods through the temple.

Jesus told them:

Isn't it written that my house will be called a house of prayer for all the nations? Why are you making it a den of robbers?

The chief priest and scribes heard what Jesus said and they wanted to destroy him, but they feared him.

Jesus began daily teaching in the temple. But the religious leaders and men in authority began to plot ways to kill him.

The common people hung on each word that Jesus said.

FIG TREE WITHERED

Every day Jesus went to the temple to teach and every night he returned to the Mount of Olives, where he slept.

People came early in the morning to hear him.

As the disciples were going into Jerusalem with Jesus to listen to him teach in the temple they passed the fig tree that Jesus had cursed. It was dead, both root and branch.

When the disciples saw it they marveled and asked:

How did the fig tree wither and die so quickly?

Peter remembered that Jesus had cursed the fig tree, and told the other disciples that this was the reason it had withered.

Jesus said:

Have faith in God. If you have faith and do not doubt, you could not only do what has been done to this fig tree, but you could say to this mountain, "Be taken up and cast into the sea."

If you believe it in your heart and do not doubt, what you say will be done. Ask believing in prayer and you will have it.

Whenever you stand praying, forgive those that you have something against so that your heavenly father will forgive your sins.

THIRD GROUP OF PARABLES

On one of the days that Jesus came to Jerusalem and was preaching and teaching, the chief priests and scribes came to him and said:

Tell us, by what authority do you do these things? Who gave you this authority?

Jesus answered by way of asking:

Where did John the Baptist get his authority to baptize? Was it from heaven, or from men? Answer me.

The chief priests and scribes reasoned among themselves and said:

If we say that John the Baptist got his authority from heaven, then he will ask us why we did not believe John's testimony about Jesus.

But if we say that John got his authority from men, then the people will turn on us because they believe that John the Baptist was a prophet sent by God.

So they finally said:

We do not know.

Jesus said to them:

Neither will I tell you by what authority I do these things.

Tower of David Museum in Jerusalem's Old City

THE TWO SONS

Then Jesus asked those who were standing nearby:

Tell me what you think of this story:

A man had two sons. He told the first son to go work all day in the vineyard. The son said:

> *I will not!*

But afterward he changed his mind and spent the day working in the vineyard.

Citrus orchard in Israel

The man also told his second son to go and work in the vineyard. The son said that he would, but he didn't.

Which one of these two did the will of the father?

They answered him:

The first.

Jesus said to them:

The truth is that the tax collectors and the harlots will go into the kingdom rather then you.

John came to you in the way of righteousness, and you did not believe him. Even when you saw his authority you did not repent and believe.

THE WICKED HUSBANDMEN

Then Jesus began to speak to the people, if not the rulers, in parables:

> *Hear another parable:*
>
> *There was a man who was the head of a household who planted a vineyard and put a hedge around it, dug a pit for the wine press and built a tower. He leased it out to a tenant. He left and went into another country where he stayed for a long time.*
>
> *When the season was right, he sent one of his servants to collect the rent.*
>
> *Instead of paying him, the tenants beat the servant and sent him away empty-handed.*
>
> *He then sent another servant, who the tenants treated even worse than the first servant.*

He sent a third servant, who the tenants killed.

The man sent more servants, but every servant the man sent was either killed, stoned or beaten by the tenants.

Finally, the lord of the vineyard sent his son. Surely they will respect the son of the lord of the vineyard.

When the tenants saw the son coming, they reasoned that if they killed the son they could steal his inheritance and take the vineyard for themselves.

So they took the lord's son, threw him out of the vineyard and killed him.

Jesus asked his listeners:

When the lord of the vineyard comes, what will he do to the tenants?

Some of the people answered:

He will utterly destroy them and all who serve him and lease the vineyard out to another.

Others said:

God forbid!

Jesus looked at them and said:

What is written? Have you never heard the Scripture:

The stone which the builders rejected was made the head cornerstone. This was from the Lord, and it is marvelous in our eyes.

I tell you, the kingdom of God will be taken from you and given to a nation that produces fruit. Everyone who falls on this stone will be broken in pieces and anyone the stone falls on will be pulverized into dust.

When the Pharisees heard Jesus say this, they tried to arrest him. They understood

Jerusalem City Museum. Roman mosaic

that he had told the parable as a way of turning the people against them.

But the fear of the crowd, who thought Jesus was a prophet, kept the Pharisees from carrying out their plans to arrest Jesus.

The religious leaders left Jesus and went away.

Stone arches of Jerusalem's Triple Gate

THE MARRIAGE OF THE KING'S SON

Jesus told them another parable:

The kingdom of heaven is like a marriage feast that a king made for his son.

He sent his servant out to call all of those who had received an invitation, to tell them that it was time to come to the feast.

But the invited guests made light of it, and they ridiculed the servants and beat them and killed them.

The king became very angry and sent out his army to destroy the murderers and burn down their cities.

He told his servants that the marriage feast is ready, but those who were invited were not worthy to come. He said:

>*Go into the highways and the byways and tell everyone you find to come and be my guest at the marriage feast.*

>*The servants went out, and they found both good and bad and all were invited and came to the wedding feast.*

>*But when the king entered into the wedding hall, he saw one guest who did not have on a wedding garment. He said to him:*

>>*Friend, how did you get here without a wedding garment?*

The man was speechless.

The king said to his servants, Bind him hand and foot and cast him into the outer darkness where there is weeping and gnashing of teeth.

For many are called, but few are chosen.

JEWISH RULERS SEEK TO ENSNARE JESUS

The Pharisees began to plot how they might trap Jesus with his own words.

They sent out some of the younger Pharisees, thinking Jesus would be more likely to answer their questions because they looked like students.

They came and found Jesus and said to him:

I know you teach only what is true and pleasing to God. Tell us then, is it lawful for us to give tribute to Caesar, or not?

Jesus knew they were being wicked and crafty. He knew the hypocrisy that was in their heart and he said to them:

Julius Caesar statue

Why are you trying to put me on trial, you hypocrites? Show me the tribute money. Bring me a coin.

Once Jesus had the coin, he asked:

Whose image and name is on the coin?

The Pharisees answered:

Caesar.

Jesus said:

Give to Caesar the things that belong to Caesar and give to God the things that belong to God.

The Pharisees were not able to find any fault with that and marveled greatly at his answer. They became silent and left.

SADDUCEES AND THE RESURRECTION

One day, some of the Sadducees *(Sadducees do not believe in the resurrection)* came to Jesus and said:

Teacher, Moses wrote that if a man's brother dies and has no children that the brother should take his wife and have children together.

If the second brother dies, then the third brother should take his wife and have children.

If there were seven brothers and each died without having any children by the same

First Temple-period walls being excavated underneath the Cardo in the Jewish Quarter of the Old City

wife and then finally the wife dies, whose wife will she be after the resurrection?

Jesus answered:

You have made a mistake. You do not know the Scriptures, nor do you know the power of God.

The sons of this world marry and take wives. But those who are worthy to be in the heavenly kingdom, once they rise from the dead in the resurrection, will not marry or take wives.

They cannot die anymore, and they will be like the angels.

As far as the resurrection of the dead, Moses even showed that the dead are raised when at the burning bush he called the Lord, the God of Abraham, Isaac and Jacob.

Haven't you read the book of Moses?

God is not the God of the dead; he is the God of the living. Your way of thinking is flawed.

When the multitude heard Jesus say this, they were astonished. Some of the scribes said to Jesus:

You have answered well.

THE GREAT COMMANDMENT

When the Pharisees heard that Jesus had silenced the Sadducees, they had a meeting. One of them, a lawyer, went to Jesus with a question.

He asked:

Teacher, which is the greatest commandment in the law?

Jesus said:

The first is, Hear, O Israel, the Lord our God is one:

You shall love the Lord your God with all your heart, and with all of your soul and with all of your mind and with all of your strength.

This the first and greatest commandment. The second is connected to it:

You shall love your neighbor as you love yourself.

There are no other commandments greater than these. On these two commandments, the entire law and all the prophets rest.

The scribe said:

Teacher, you have answered well. To love the Lord with all your heart, your understanding and your strength — and to love your neighbor as yourself — is more important than all the burnt offerings and sacrifices.

When Jesus heard the lawyer's answer, he said:

You are not far from the kingdom of God. After that, no one dared to ask Jesus any more questions.

JESUS' QUESTION

Later, the Pharisees gathered as Jesus taught in the temple, and he asked them a question.

Jesus asked:

What do you think about the Christ? Whose son is he?

They answered:

He is the Son of David.

Grave-site on Mount of Olives

Stone wall in Jerusalem

He said to them:

Why do you call him the son of David when David himself, under the influence of the Holy Spirit, calls him Lord? For David himself said:

The Lord said unto my Lord, Sit at my right hand until I put your enemies under your feet.

If David himself called him Lord, how is he his son?

No one was able to answer Jesus.

No one dared from that time forward to ask Jesus any more questions.

The common people heard Jesus gladly.

DENUNCIATION OF SCRIBES AND PHARISEES

Then Jesus spoke to all his disciples and to the multitudes. He spoke so that everyone could hear what he had to say:

Beware of the scribes and the Pharisees. When they speak for Moses, do as they say, but do not do what they do.

They bind heavy burdens too heavy to carry and lay them on men's shoulders, while they themselves will not lift a finger to keep the very commandments that they ask others to do.

They do their works to be seen by men. They like to be seen keeping the law and make themselves conspicuous whenever they do a good work.

They love to wear the clothing of rulers and kings, and they love to sit in the seats of honor at all events. They love the greetings they receive in the marketplace and they love to be called Master.

They take advantage of the widows and figure out ways to profit from the duties they have. They make a pretense of long prayers.

These will receive greater condemnation.

But do not desire to be called Teacher, for only one is your teacher.

Roman ruins in Israel

Do not call any man your father except your earthly father and your Father who is in heaven.

Do not let them call you Master, for only one is your master. That is Christ.

He who would be the greatest among you let him be the servant of all. Whoever exalts himself will be humbled and whoever humbles himself will be exalted.

Woe to you, scribes and Pharisees. You shut the doors to the kingdom to others and do not even try to enter into the kingdom yourself.

Woe to you, scribes and Pharisees. You are hypocrites! For you go sailing around the world to make one convert, and when you make a convert you turn him into twice the son of hell that you are yourselves.

You are the blind leading the blind.

You say:

If anyone swears an oath by the temple, it means nothing.

But if you swear an oath by the gold in the temple then you are a under obligation to keep the oath.

You fools and blind men. Which is greater? The gold? Or the temple that sanctifies the gold?

All oaths are binding no matter what you swear the oath by, because it all belongs to God.

Woe to you, scribes and Pharisees. You are hypocrites! You tithe the outward things, but you leave out the important things like justice and mercy and faith.

You strain a gnat, and yet you will willingly swallow a camel!

Woe to you, scribes and Pharisees. You are hypocrites! You clean the outside of the cup and the platter, but within you are full of extortion and self-indulgence.

You blind Pharisees, clean the inside of the cup and platter, and the outside will become clean also.

Woe to you, scribes and Pharisees. You are hypocrites! You are like whitewashed tombs, which outwardly appear beautiful, but inwardly are full of dead men's bones and all uncleanness.

You appear outwardly to be righteous, but inwardly you are full of hypocrisy and wickedness.

Woe to you, scribes and Pharisees. You are hypocrites! You decorate the tombs of the prophets and yet your fathers are the ones who killed the prophets.

By your own testimonies you also would have killed the prophets.

How are you going to escape the judgment of hell?

Jerusalem, Jerusalem, how often I would have gathered your children together, even as a hen gathers her chicks under her wing, but you would not stand for it.

Look, your house is going to be left desolate. For I say to you, you will not see me again, until the day you say:

Blessed is he who comes in the name of the Lord.

Pieces of Roman columns and ruins

THE WIDOW'S MITES

Jesus sat down in the temple area near the treasury. He watched as the people cast their gifts into the treasury. He watched the rich give valuable gifts.

Then Jesus saw a widow put two cents into the treasury.

When Jesus saw this, he called his disciples together and said:

I tell you the truth. This poor widow has put more into the treasury than everyone else. Everyone else gave out of their abundance, but she has given out of her poverty. She has given all she had.

HE SHALL DRAW ALL MEN TO HIM

There were Greek converts who had come up to the feast to worship. They came to Philip, who was from Bethsaida of Galilee, and asked to see Jesus.

Philip went and told Andrew, and together they went and told Jesus.

Jesus answered:

The hour has come for the Son of man to be glorified.

Listen carefully to the truth I am about to tell you, for if a grain of wheat does not fall into the ground, it remains like it is; but if the wheat falls to the earth and dies, it bears much fruit.

He who loves his life will lose it, and he who loses his life in this world will keep it for eternal life.

If anyone serves me, let him follow me. Where I am, there the servant will be also. If any man serves me, the Father will honor him.

What should I say? Save me from this hour?

But this is why I came into the world.

Rather, Father, glorify your name.

After Jesus said this, there was a voice out of heaven saying:

I have both glorified it, and I will glorify it again.

The multitude that was standing near Jesus heard it and said that it had thundered.

Others said an angel had spoken to him.

Jesus answered them:

This voice has come for your sakes not mine.

Now is judgment come to the world.

Now shall the prince of this world be cast out.

Then Jesus said:

If I am lifted up from the earth, I will draw all men to myself. He said this to signify what sort of death he should die.

The multitude answered him:

We have heard that the Christ abides forever, so why are you saying:

The Son of man must be lifted up?

Who is the Son of man?

Jesus said to them:

The light is going to be with you for only a little while longer. Walk while you have light, so that the darkness does not overtake you.

While you have the light, believe in the light, that you may become sons of light.

After speaking these things Jesus left them and hid himself from them.

Even though he had made many signs and performed miracles among them, they still did not believe in him. This was a fulfillment of the words of the prophet Isaiah who said:

Who has believed our testimony? Who has had the mighty works of God revealed to him?

This was the reason they could not believe. As Isaiah said:

He has blinded their eyes, and he has hardened their hearts.

Some of the Pharisees believed in Jesus but were afraid to confess it publicly because they feared that they would be expelled from the synagogue.

They loved the glory that came from man more than they loved the glory that came from God.

Jesus cried out and said:

He who believes in me does not believe in me only, but also in the one who has sent me. I am come as light into the world so that whoever believes in me will not live in darkness.

If any man hears my words and does not keep them, I do not judge him, for I came not to judge the world but to save the world. The person who rejects me and does not receive my sayings, he has something that judges him. The word that I speak will judge him in the last day.

Nebi Musa, Greek Orthodox Monastery in Israel, air view

THE STORY OF JESUS

For I did not speak from myself; but the Father who sent me told me what to say and what to speak. I know that his commandment is life eternal. The words that I speak are the words he has told me to speak.

DESTRUCTION OF JERUSALEM FORETOLD

Jesus went out from the temple for the last time. He would never return. As he was going by the temple buildings, one of the disciples came to Jesus and said:

Look at the majesty of these buildings. The stone work is marvelous and the adornments are spectacular.

Jesus said:

You see these buildings? The truth is that in the days to come there will not be one stone left upon another. It will all be thrown down.

Later, as Jesus sat on the Mount of Olives, on the side near the temple, the disciples Peter, James, John and Andrew came to Jesus privately and said:

Teacher, tell us when will these things happen? What will be the sign of your coming, and of the end of the world?

Jesus said:

Beware that no one leads you astray: For many will come using my name and will tell you that the time to set up the eternal kingdom has arrived. Do not follow after them.

You will hear of wars and disturbances, and rumors of wars. Do not let this trouble you or make you afraid.

These things must happen before I come, but the end is not yet.

Nation will rise up against nation, and kingdom against kingdom.

There will be earthquakes all over the world, and all over the world there will be famines and earthquakes; and there will be terrors and great signs from heaven.

All these are just the beginning of birth pains.

But before all these things happen, they will lay hands on you and persecute you, they will deliver you up to the synagogues and prisons, and bring you before kings and governors for my name's sake.

They will deliver you up to councils and to tribulation, and they will kill you. You will be beaten in the synagogues and hated of all nations for my name's sake.

You will stand before kings and give testimony for my name's sake.

The Gospel must first be preached to all the nations. When they lead you to judgment and deliver you up, do not be anxious ahead of time about what you will say.

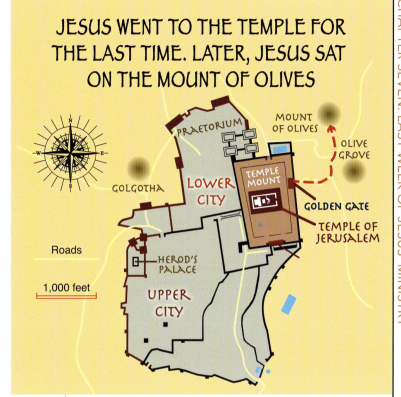

JESUS WENT TO THE TEMPLE FOR THE LAST TIME. LATER, JESUS SAT ON THE MOUNT OF OLIVES

Settle it in your hearts not to meditate beforehand on how to answer. I will give you wise words to say that your adversaries will not be able to withstand.

Whatever is given to you in that hour to say, you can say it, but it is not you who speaks, it is the Holy Spirit.

Many will stumble and betray you, and hate you. Many false prophets will rise and lead many astray.

Because iniquity will come to its full fruition, the love of many will grow cold. Even parents will deliver up their own sons and daughters and friends.

Brother will deliver up brother to death, and children will rise up against their parents and cause them to be put to death.

You will be hated of all men for my namesake.

But he who endures to the end will be saved. In your patience you will win your souls.

This Gospel of the kingdom shall be preached in the whole world for a testimony to all the nations; and then the end will come.

But when you see Jerusalem encompassed with armies, then know that her desolation is at hand.

When you see the abomination of desolation, which was spoken of through Daniel the prophet standing in the holy place where he should not be, then let those in Judea flee to the mountains.

Don't let those who are in the middle of Jerusalem depart; don't let those who are in the country enter into Jerusalem.

Don't waste your time trying to collect your property or goods for these are the days of vengeance, so that all that is written may be fulfilled.

Woe to those who are pregnant and to those with small children. There is going to be great distress upon the land and wrath to this people.

They will fall by the edge of the sword, and will be led captive into all nations. Jerusalem will be trodden down by the Gentiles.

Pray that your flight not be in the winter, or on the Sabbath.

For in those days there will be great tribulation, such as there has not been since the beginning of the world.

Unless those days were shortened no human would have been saved. But for the sake of the elect, the ones God has chosen, he has shortened those days.

If any man says to you:

> *Go here to see the Christ.*

Do not believe him. For there will arise false Christs and false prophets, and they will show great signs and wonders so as to lead the elect astray, if possible.

Be warned ahead of time, I have told you all these things so that you will not be deceived. If they tell you:

Look, he is in the wilderness.

Do not go looking for him.

Or if they say:

Look, he is in the inner chambers.

Do not believe it.

For as the lightning comes out of the east, and is seen in the west; so it will be with the coming of the Son of man.

THE SECOND COMING OF CHRIST

Jesus said:

But in those days the sun will become dark, and the moon will not give her light, and the stars will be shaken, and the powers of the heaven will be shaken.

And there will be signs in the sun and moon and stars, and upon the earth distress of nations, and there will be great agitation in the oceans that will cause men to be perplexed.

Men will faint with fear because of the things coming on the world, for the powers of the heaven will be shaken.

And then will appear the sign of the Son of man in heaven, and all the tribes of the earth will mourn.

And then they will see the Son of man coming in the clouds of heaven with great power and glory.

He will send out his angels with the great sound of the trumpet, and they will gather together his elect from everywhere in the universe.

Distant view of Jerusalem's Old City wall

But when these things begin to come to pass, look up, and lift your head, because your redemption is coming near.

And he spoke a parable to them.

Learn the parable of the fig tree. When her branches become tender and puts out leaves, you know that summer is near.

In the same way, when you see all these things coming to pass, know that the kingdom of God is near, even knocking at the door.

Almond tree in the Judean Hills

This is the truth you need to understand. This generation will not pass away until all these things are fulfilled.

Heaven and earth will pass away, but my words will not pass away.

But the day and the hour this is going to happen, only the Father knows.

It will be like the days of Noah when the Son of man comes.

In those days there was eating and drinking and marrying until Noah entered into the ark. No one knew what was happening until the flood came and swept them away.

It will be like this when the Son of man comes.

Two men will be in the field, one will be taken and the other will be left behind.

Two women will be grinding at the mill; one will be taken and the other will be left.

Watch with anticipation, because you do not know the day your Lord is going to come.

If the head of the house knew when the thief was going to arrive, he would have been prepared for his coming and prevented his house from being broken into. Be ready, for his coming will be unexpected.

Beware that you don't let your hearts become filled with the concerns and cares of this world, or become careless in how you live your life, the day will come like a net enclosing a flock of birds. And it will come on everyone.

Blessed is the wise and faithful servant, whom his Lord will find doing his business when he comes.

An evil servant says in his heart: My Lord is going to be late.

And he begins to misuse his position and mistreat those under him, and lives an evil life full of self indulgence.

When the master does come, that servant will have his position and authority given to someone else. And he will go where all the hypocrites go, where there will be gnashing of teeth and weeping without end.

Watch and pray so that you might escape all these things and stand before the Son of man. Only the godly are able to stand in his presence.

Watch and pray for you do not know when the Lord is going to come.

THE FINAL JUDGMENT

Jesus said:

The kingdom of heaven will be like ten virgins who went out to meet the bridegroom.

Five of them where foolish and five of them were wise.

Alley of a neighboorhood near Yemin Moshe Park

The foolish virgins took lamps without oil in them. The wise virgins took plenty of oil.

While the bridegroom delayed his coming all the virgins nodded off and went to sleep.

At midnight the cry went out in the land:

> *Look the bridegroom! Come out and meet him.*

All the virgins arose and trimmed their lamps. But the foolish virgins said to the wise:

The tower of David near the modern city life of Jerusalem

Give us your oil, our lamps are going out.

The wise virgins responded:

But then there may not be enough for us; go and buy some more oil for yourselves.

While the foolish virgins were out trying to find oil, the bridegroom came and the wedding party entered the house and the doors were shut and locked.

After a little time, the five foolish virgins arrived and knocked on the door:

Lord, Lord open to us.

But the Lord answered and said:

The truth is that I do not know you.

Be watchful because you do not know the day or the hour of your Lord's coming.

It is like when a man goes to another country, but before he goes, he calls his servants together and gives them **talents**†, *one five, another two and yet another one, in order to invest and make a profit while he is gone.*

The one given five talents traded and made five more talents.

The one given two talents traded and made two more.

But the one given one talent hid the Lord's money in the earth.

Then one day the Lord returned and called his three servants together for a reckoning with them.

† Further reading available at the end of this chapter.

THE STORY OF JESUS

He received back the five talents and then another five from the first servant:

Well done you good and faithful servant, You have been faithful with a little now I will put you in charge of a lot. Enter into the joy of your Lord.

He received back the two talents and then another two from the second servant:

Well done you good and faithful servant. You have been faithful over a few things; now I will put you over many things. Enter into the joy of your Lord.

He then received back the one talent from the third servant, but no more. The third servant said:

I knew that you were a hard man, reaping where you did not sow and gathering where you did not scatter. I was afraid, and so I went and hid the talent in the ground.

The Lord answered:

You wicked and lazy servant, you knew that I reaped where I did not sow and gathered where I had not scattered, you should have put the talent into the bank to make interest.

Take this wicked servant away and give what he had to the first servant who was has the ten talents.

For the one who has will be given more and he will have an abundance.

But the one who does not have, even the little he has will be taken away.

He cast the unprofitable servant into outer darkness, where there was weeping and gnashing of teeth.

When the Son of man comes in his glory, and all the angels with him, he will sit on the throne of glory and gather the nations before him.

He will separate them one from another, like a shepherd separates the sheep from the goats.

He will put the sheep on one side and the goats on the other side.

Then the King will say to the ones on his right side:

Come, you who are blessed by my Father, inherit the kingdom prepared for you since the beginning of the world.

I was hungry, and you gave me something to eat.

I was thirsty, and you gave me something to drink.

I was a stranger, and you took me in.

I was naked, and you clothed me.

I was sick, and you visited me.

I was in prison, and you came to me.

Then the righteous will answer him, saying:

Lord, when were you hungry and we fed you? Or thirsty and we gave you drink?

When did we see you as a stranger and take you in?

Or naked and clothe you?

And when did we see you sick or in prison and come to you?

The King answered:

Here is a truth that you really need to understand, As you did it to the least of my brothers, you did it to me.

Then the King will say to the ones on his left hand:

Depart from me, you cursed ones, enter into the fire which is prepared for the devil and his angels.

I was hungry, and you gave me nothing to eat.

I was thirsty, and you gave me nothing to drink. I was a stranger, and you didn't take me in.

I was naked, and you didn't clothe me.

I was sick, and you didn't visit me.

I was in prison, and you didn't come to me.

Here is a truth that you tragically missed. As you didn't do it to the least of my brothers, you didn't do it to me.

The wicked will go away into eternal punishment. But the righteous will go into eternal life.

JUDAS BARGAINS FOR JESUS' DEATH

Then Jesus said to his disciples:

You know that in two days it will be Passover, and the Son of man is going to be delivered up to be crucified.

The chief priests and elders gathered together to hold court with the high priest Caiaphas.

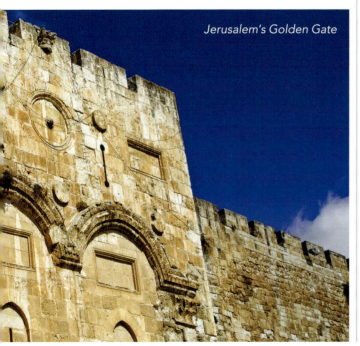
Jerusalem's Golden Gate

And they began planning how they would arrest Jesus without creating a crisis with the people, and then put him to death.

They feared the people.

Satan entered into Judas Iscariot, who was one of the twelve disciples.

Judas went to meet with the chief priests and captains to discuss how he might deliver Jesus up to them.

Judas asked:

What will you pay me to deliver Jesus up to you?

When the chief priests heard that Judas was willing to give up Jesus, they were glad. They agreed to pay Judas thirty pieces of silver.

Judas agreed, and from that time on he looked for an opportunity to deliver Jesus up to the Jewish leaders, when there were no crowds around.

PREPARATION FOR PASSOVER

The days of unleavened bread came. It was the day that the Passover lamb must be sacrificed.

The disciples came to Jesus and said:

Where will we go to eat the Passover meal?

Jesus sent Peter and John to make ready the Passover meal.

He said to them:

Go into the city, and when you have entered you will meet a man who is carrying a pitcher of water. Follow him into the house that he enters.

And when they ask you why you are there, tell them that the Teacher says:

My time is at hand. Where will I eat the Passover with my disciples?

And he will show you a large upper room that is furnished and ready. Go to the upper room and make things ready for us.

The disciples went into the city and found the man who Jesus described, and made ready the Passover.

When the evening came, Jesus and the twelve disciples came to the upper room.

Jesus sat down with his twelve disciples. He said to them:

I desire to eat this Passover with you before I begin my suffering.

And Jesus received the cup and gave thanks and said:

Take this cup and distribute it among yourselves. For I say to you:

I will not drink from the fruit of the vine again until the kingdom of God shall come.

An argument started among them as to which one of them was going to be considered greatest in the coming kingdom.

They misunderstood Jesus and thought that he was just about to set up his earthly kingdom.

Jesus said to them:

The kings of the Gentiles have lordship over others, and those who have authority over others are called Benefactors.

But it will not be that way with you.

He that is greater among you let him take the place of the youngest; and the one who is chief among you, let him be the one who serves.

Who is greater, the one who is served the meal or the one who serves it? Isn't it the one who sits at the meal?

But I am in the midst of you, as one who serves.

You have continued with me in my trials. And I will have appointments for you in the kingdom, just as the Father has appointed me, that you may eat and drink at my table in the kingdom; and you will sit on thrones judging the twelve tribes of Israel.

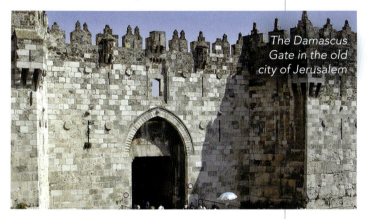
The Damascus Gate in the old city of Jerusalem

THE PASSOVER MEAL

Before the feast of the Passover, Jesus knew that his hour had come that he should leave this world and go to the Father.

Now, Jesus loved his own who were in the world and he loved them to the end.

And during the supper Jesus knew that Satan had already entered Judas Iscariot and that he was plotting to betray him.

Jesus rose up from the supper and laid his garments aside and put a towel around his waist. Then he poured water into the basin and began to wash the disciples' feet, and to wipe them with the towel that girded his waist.

When he came to Peter, Peter asked:

Lord, are you planning to wash my feet?

Jesus answered him:

You do not understand what I am doing, but you will later.

Peter said to Jesus:

You will never wash my feet.

Jesus answered him:

If I do not wash your feet, then you have nothing to do with me.

Peter said to the Lord:

Then do not just wash my feet, but wash my head and my hands as well as my feet.

Jesus said to Peter:

He who is bathed does not need anything washed but his feet. But is clean completely, and you are clean.

But not all of you are clean.

So Jesus washed their feet and then put his garment back on and returned to the table and sat with them.

And then Jesus said to them:

Do you understand what I have just done to you?

You call me Lord and Teacher, and just as I have washed your feet you should also wash each others feet. I have given you an example of how you are to treat each other, just as I have done to you.

I want to tell you and important truth that you really need to understand. I tell you that a servant is not greater than his Lord, nor is the one who is sent greater than the one who sent him.

If you understand these things, then you are blessed when you do them.

I do not speak to all of you. I know the ones I have chosen.

But in order that scripture be fulfilled, He who eats my bread lifts up his heel against me.

I am telling you this before it happens so that when it does happen, you will believe that I am he.

The truth you really need to understand and pay attention to is that anyone who receives me also receives the one who sent me.

First Temple period excavation in Jerusalem

JUDAS' BETRAYAL FORETOLD

After Jesus said this as he was eating, he became troubled in his spirit and testified:

Truly, truly, I tell you that one of you will betray me, someone who is eating with me right now.

The disciples looked at one another, upset and wondering who he was talking about.

They became very agitated and sorrowful. Each one asked the Lord:

Is it me?

And he answered and said to them:

It is one of the twelve, He who dips his hand with me in the dish, the same is the one who will betray me.

I am going to do what the Father has sent me to do, as it is written in scripture, but woe to the man who betrays the Son of man.

It would be better if he had not been born.

One of the disciples, the one who Jesus loved very much, was reclining on Jesus' bosom. Peter beckoned to him, and told him to ask the Lord who it was that was going to betray him.

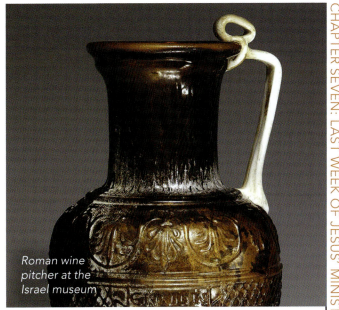

Roman wine pitcher at the Israel museum

And the disciple leaned back and asked the Lord:

Who is it?

Jesus answered:

It is the one I will give this bread to when I have dipped it. So Jesus dipped the bread and gave it to Judas Iscariot.

Judas answered the Lord and said:

Is it I, Teacher?

Jesus said to him:

It is as you say.

And Satan immediately entered into Judas.

THE STORY OF JESUS

And Jesus said to Judas:

Go quickly and do what you are going to do.

Nobody knew what Jesus meant when he told Judas this. They supposed that Judas, who was in charge of the purse, was being sent on a mission to buy something needed for the rest of the feast.

Judas went out into the night.

After Judas was gone, Jesus said:

Now the Son of man is glorified, and God is glorified in him.

Little children, I am only going to be with you a little while longer. You will seek me, but as I said to the Jews, you will not find me or be able to go where I am going.

I give you a new commandment — that you love one another just as I have loved you, so love each other. This is the way that men will know that you are my disciples, if you have love for one another.

Then Jesus said:

This night all will be offended in me, just as it is written, I will smite the shepherd and the sheep will be scattered abroad.

But after I am raised up, I will go before you into Galilee.

Simon Peter said to him:

Lord, wherever you go I will follow you. I will lay down my life for you.

Jesus answered Peter:

Will you lay down your life for me? Simon, Simon, behold Satan has asked for you that he might sift you like wheat.

But I have prayed for you that your faith does not fail. Here is what I want you to do. Once you have repented, establish your brothers.

Peter protested:

Lord I am ready to go to prison for you. I am willing to die for you. If all fall away because of you, I will never fall away.

Jesus said to Peter:

The truth you need to understand is that before the rooster crows tomorrow morning you will have denied me three times.

Peter became agitated and vehemently said that even if he would die, he would not deny him. The other disciples joined in and said the same thing.

Jesus said to them:

When I sent you out without purse and without wallet or shoes, did you lack anything?

They answered:

Nothing.

And he said to them:

But now, he who has money, let him take it and sell it and buy a sword. For I say to you, that what is written will be fulfilled in me:

And he was counted with the transgressors.

For these things written about me are being fulfilled.

And they said:

Lord, we have two swords, it that enough?

THE LORD'S SUPPER INSTITUTED

As they were eating, it was the same night that the Lord was betrayed, and he took the bread and after he had given thanks, he broke it and gave it to his disciples and said:

Take, eat. This is my body which is given for you. Do this in remembrance of me.

And he took the cup in a similar manner after the supper, and he gave thanks and said to them:

Drink all of it, for this is my blood of the covenant which is poured out for many for the forgiveness of sins.

Do this in remembrance of me, for as often as you eat this bread, and drink the cup, you proclaim the Lord's death until he comes again.

But I will not drink anymore of the fruit of the vine, until that day when I drink it new with you in my Father's kingdom.

And they all drank of it.

FAREWELL DISCOURSE TO DISCIPLES

Jesus said:

Don't let your hearts be troubled. Believe in God and believe also in me. In my Father's house there are many mansions. If it were not so, I would have told you.

I go to prepare a place for you. And if I go and prepare a place for you. I will come again, and will receive you to myself so that where I am you will also be.

And where I go, you know the way.

Thomas said to the Lord:

We do not know where you are going and how can we know the way?

Jesus said to him:

I am the way, and the truth and the life, no one comes to the Father, except through me.

If you knew me, you would know that my Father has sent me. And from now on you do know him, and have seen him.

Phillip answered and said:

Show us the Father and that will be enough for us.

Jesus said to them:

Have I been with you all this time and you do not recognize me or know who I am? How can you say, Show us the Father?

Don't you believe that I am in the Father and the Father is in me?

The words which I speak to you are not my own, they are the words of the Father who is in me. Believe me that I am in the Father,

and the Father is in me, or else believe for the sake of the works that I have done.

This is the truth you really need to understand. He who believes in me will also do the works that I do.

Greater works than these he will do, because I go to the Father. And whatever you ask in my name, the Father will do it for you, so that the Father may be glorified in the Son. Ask anything in my name and I will do it.

And I will pray to the Father, and he will give you another Comforter, that he may be with you forever. He is the Spirit of truth, whom the world cannot receive, for it cannot see him or know him. He will abide in you, and will live in you.

Inside the Church of All Nations in Jerusalem

I will not leave you as orphans: I will come to you. In a little while the world will see me no more, but you will see me. Because I live, you will live also.

In that day (Pentecost or the period that began on that day), you will know that I am in my Father, and you are in me, and I am in you.

He who has my commandments and keeps them, he is the one who loves me. He who loves me will be loved by my Father, and I will love him and reveal myself to him.

Judas (not Judas Iscariot, who had left) said to the Lord:

What is going to happen, that you will manifest yourself to us, and not to the world?

Jesus answered and said to him:

If a man loves me, he will keep my word, and my Father will love him, and we will come to him and make our home in him.

The person who does not love me or keep my words, is also not keeping the words of the Father who sent me.

I am telling you these things while I am still with you. But the Comforter, the Holy

Spirit, who the Father will send in my name, will teach you all things.

The Holy Spirit will bring to your memory all the things that I have said to you.

Peace I leave with you; my peace I give to you, not as the world gives peace. Do not let your hearts be troubled, neither let them be fearful.

You have heard how I said to you, I go away, and I come to you. If you loved me, you would rejoice, because I am going back to my Father, for the Father is greater than I.

I have told you all of these things so that when they happen you will remember that I have told you, and you will believe.

I am not going to be speaking much with you from now on, for the prince of this world is coming and he has no right or reason to exercise power over me.

But in order that the world may know that I love the Father, and am doing as the Father has commanded, I will willingly give my life up.

Then Jesus said:

Arise, let us go.

(Some believe that what Jesus taught next happened as they left the upper room and walked to Gethsemane. But it is more likely that these words were spoken while they were preparing to leave.)

Passover Seder plate with wine and matzot

I am the true vine and my Father is the gardener. Every branch in me that does not produce fruit is cut off and taken away. Every branch that produces fruit, he prunes so that it will bear more fruit.

You are already clean because of the word that I have spoken to you.

Abide in me and I will abide in you. A branch cannot produce fruit by itself. It must be attached to the vine. You cannot produce fruit unless you abide in me.

I am the vine and you are the branches. He who abides in me, and I in him, produces much fruit. Apart from me you can't do anything.

If a man does not abide in me, he is thrown away like a branch, becomes withered and they will gather the withered branches up and cast them into the fire where they will be burned.

*If you had known me, you would have known my Father also. From now on you know him and have seen him.
My Father is glorified if you produce much fruit, revealing yourself to be my disciples.*

Just like the Father loves me, I will love you. Abide in my love. If you keep my commandments, you will abide in my love, just like I have kept my Father's commandments and abide in his love.

I have told you these things so that my joy will be in you and your joy will be made full.

This is my commandment, Love one another, just as I have loved you. Greater love has no man than this, that a man lay down his life for his friends.

You are my friends if you do the things that I command you. I will no longer call you my servants because a servant does not know what his Lord does. But I have called you friends, for all the things that I heard from the Father, I have revealed to you.

You did not choose me, but I chose you and appointed you that you should go and produce fruit, and that your fruit would last. Whatever you ask of the Father in my name, he will give it to you.

All these things I command you to do, so that you will have love for one another. If the world hates you, know that it has also hated me before it hated you.

If you were of the world, the world would love you, because the world loves its own. But you are not of this world, for I have chosen you out of the world; therefore the world hates you.

Remember the words that I said to you. A servant is not greater than his Lord. If they persecuted me, they will also persecute you.

If I had not come and spoken to them, they would have had no sin. But now they have no excuse for their sin. He who hates me hates the Father. This is happening so that the scriptures will be fulfilled that say:

They hated me without cause.

When the Comforter has come, who I will send from the Father, that is, the Spirit of Truth, he will bear witness of me. You also will bear witness of me because you have been with me from the beginning.

I have spoken these things to you so that you do not stumble. They will persecute you, and the time is coming when they will kill you and think they are doing God a service.

They will do these things because they do not know the Father, or me. But I have told you these things so that you will remember them when I am gone.

I am going to go to be with the one who sent me. And none of you are asking me:

> *Where are you going?*

Because I have told you that I am leaving, you have become sorrowful.

But I tell you the truth, it is expedient for you that I go away. If I do not go away, the Comforter will not come to you. But if I do go, I will send him to you.

When the Comforter comes, he will convict the world of sin and of righteousness and of judgment, because they do not believe in me.

Of righteousness because I go to the Father, and you will see me no more.

I have many more things to tell you, but you cannot understand them now.

But when the Holy Spirit comes, the Spirit of Truth, he will guide you in all truth.

He will not speak about himself, he will speak the things that he hears, and will tell you things that are to come. He will glorify me because he will take what is mine and declare it to you.

Whatever the Father has is mine. That is why I said:

> *He will take what is mine and declare it to you.*

I am only going to be with you a little while longer, and then you will see me no more.

Some of the disciples said to one another:

Bedouins making bread

What is this that he keeps saying to us:

A little while and we will see him no more, and then a little while and you will see me, because I go to the Father.

What is this, little while? We do not understand what he is saying.

Jesus perceived what they wanted to ask him and said:

Why are you asking yourself about the "little while and you will not see men and then a little while and you will see me?"

I am going to tell you a truth that you need to grasp and understand. You will weep and lament, but the world will rejoice: You will be very sorrowful, but your sorrow will be turned to joy.

When a woman is about to give birth, she is in pain and sorrow, but once the child is born, she is full of joy and no longer remembers her anguish.

You have sorrow now, but you will see me again and your heart will be filled with a joy that can never be taken away.

When the Spirit comes, he will make all things clear to you.

And remember the important truth that I keep telling you. If you ask anything of

THE STORY OF JESUS

my Father, he will give it to you in my name. Until now you have asked nothing in my name, but ask and you will receive, that your joy may be full.

I have spoken these things to you in the dark, saying, the hour is coming when I will not speak to you in dark sayings, but will tell you plainly about the Father.

In that day, you will ask in my name, and I will pray to the Father for you. The Father loves you because you love me, and have believed that I came from the Father.

I came from the Father to the world and now I am going to leave the world and return to the Father.

His disciples said:

Now he is speaking plainly and not in dark sayings. Now we know that you know all things, and do not need any man to help you, and we believe that you came from God.

Jesus answered:

Do you believe now? Look, the hour is coming, in fact it is here, when you will all be scattered, everyman for himself, and you will leave me alone: And yet I am not alone, because the Father is with me. I have told you these things in order for you to have peace. In the world you will have tribulation, but be of good cheer for I have overcome the world.

THE LORD'S PRAYER

These are the words that Jesus spoke as he lifted up his eyes to heaven and said:

Father, the hour has come. Glorify your Son, so that the Son may glorify you. Even as you have given me authority over all people, so that all the ones you have given me, I should give eternal life.

And this is eternal life, that they should know you, the only true God, and the one you sent.

I glorified you on earth, and have accomplished the work that you gave me to do. And now Father, glorify me with your own glory which you had before the world existed.

Model of Herod's Second Temple at Holy Land Hotel in Jerusalem

I manifested your name to the men you gave me out of this world. They belong to you, and you gave them to me.

They have kept your word. Now they know that all things you have given me, are from you. The words that you gave me, I have given to them. And they have received them, and they know that the truth came from you and they believe that you sent me.

I pray for them. I do not pray for the world, but for those that you have given me, for they are yours.

I am not going to be in the world anymore, but I am coming to be with you.

They are in the world.

Holy Father, keep them in your name which you gave me, that they may be one, even as we are one.

While I was with them I kept them in your name, I guarded them and not one of them has perished, except the son of perishing, in order that the scriptures might be fulfilled.

But now I am coming to you, and I am speaking these things in the world so that they may have my joy made full in themselves.

I have given them your word, and the world has hated them, because they are not of this world, even as I am not of the world.

I do not pray that you would take them from the world, but that you would keep them from the evil one.

They are not of the world, even as I am not of the world. Sanctify them with your truth. Your word is truth.

Just as you sent me into the world, I have sent them into the world. And for their sakes I sanctify myself, so that they will also be sanctified in truth.

I not only pray for these, but also I pray for all those who will believe in me through their word: that they may all be one, even as you Father are in me, and I am in you. I pray that they may be in us, that the world may believe that you sent me.

And the glory which you have given to me, I have given to them, that they may be one even as we are one.

I in them and you in me, so they may be perfected into one. So that the world will know that you sent me and love them, even as you love me.

Father, I desire that the ones you have

given to me be with me where I am, that they may behold my glory, which you have given to me. For you loved me before the foundation of the world.

Oh righteous Father, the world did not know you, but I know you. And those who you have given me, they know that you sent me. I have made your name known to them, and will make it known, so that the love that you love me with may be in them, and I in them.

GOING TO GETHSEMANE

When Jesus had spoken these words they went out *(from the upper room)* and went over the brook of Kidron, into the Mount of Olives.

He and his disciples entered into a garden and came to a place called Gethsemane. And when they had come to this place he sat the disciples down and asked them to pray. He told them to pray that they would not fall into temptation.

Then he took Peter, and the two sons of Zebedee, James and John, and moved about a stones throw from the other disciples, and he began to be greatly amazed and sorrowful and very troubled.

He kneeled down and fell on his face, and prayed that if is were possible that the hour might pass away from him. He said:

Abba, my Father, if it is possible, let this cup pass away from me. All things are possible with you. If you are willing, remove this cup from me. Nevertheless, not what I want, but what you want. Not my will, but your will be done.

And there appeared unto him and angel from heaven, strengthening him. And being in an agony, he prayed more earnestly, and his sweat became, as it were, great drops of blood falling down on the ground.

And when he rose up from his prayer, he came to where his disciples were and found them sleeping.

Jesus said to them:

Why are you sleeping? Rise up and pray that you do not enter into temptation.

Ancient olive trees in the Garden of Gethsemane

Watch and pray, the spirit is willing, but the flesh is weak.

And Jesus went the second time to pray, saying the same words he had said before:

My Father, if this cannot pass away, unless I drink it, your will be done.

And Jesus came again and found them sleeping, for their eyes were very heavy. And they did not know what to say to Jesus.

Jesus left the third time to pray. And he prayed as he had the first two times, and when he returned to the disciples, they were asleep.

Jesus said to the disciples:

So far as I am concerned you can continue to sleep for now. Take your rest, for the time for you to be of comfort and assistance has passed.

But as far as you are concerned, look, the hour has come and the Son of man is about to be betrayed into the hands of sinners. Get up and let's be going. Look, the one who is going to betray me is here.

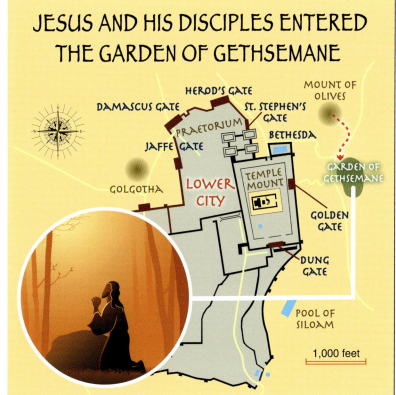

JESUS BETRAYED, ARRESTED, AND FORSAKEN

Now Judas, who betrayed Jesus, knew the place where Jesus and his disciples met. Judas and a band of soldiers and officers from the chief priests and Pharisees came with lanterns, torches and weapons.

Jesus knew all the things that were going to happen to him.

He went up to Judas and his band of soldiers and said to them:

Who are you looking for?

They answered him:

Jesus of Nazareth.

Jesus said to them:

I am he.

When Jesus spoke, Judas and the band of soldiers fell backward on to the ground.

Again Jesus asked:

Who do you seek?

They answered:

Jesus of Nazareth.

When Jesus spoke, they again fell backward on to the ground.

Again he asked them:

Who are you looking for?

And again they said:

Jesus of Nazareth.

Jesus answered:

I told you that I am he, if it is me you are looking for, then let my disciples go on their way.

This was so that the word might be fulfilled which he spoke:

Of those you have given me, I have not lost one.

Now the one who betrayed Jesus had given them a token saying:

Whoever I kiss, that is Jesus.

Jesus said to Judas:

Are you going to betray the Son of man with a kiss?

Carved Roman columns in Jerusalem

Judas came to Jesus and kissed him.

Jesus said to him:

Friend, do what you have come for.

Then they came and took hold of Jesus, and arrested him. And while they were surrounding Jesus, one of Jesus' disciples said:

Lord shall we strike them with a sword?

Simon took the sword that he had and struck the servant of the high priest, and cut off his ear.

But Jesus answered and said to them:

Do not interfere with those arresting me.

Then Jesus touched the servant's ear, and it was healed. The servant's name was Malchus.

Then Jesus said to Peter:

Put your sword in its sheath. Those who take the sword will perish by the sword. The cup which the Father has given me, shall I not drink it?

Don't you realize that I could even now ask the Father and he would send twelve legions of angels? But then how would the scriptures be fulfilled? This is how it must be.

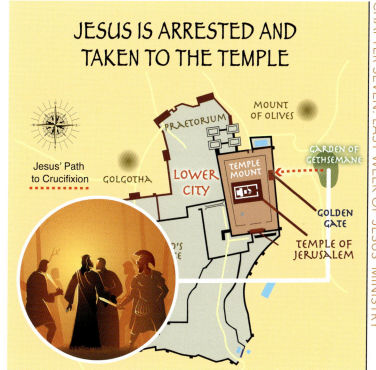

JESUS IS ARRESTED AND TAKEN TO THE TEMPLE

As Jesus was taken to the temple, the multitudes and the chief priests and the captains of the temple all came against Jesus. Jesus said:

Are you coming against me like you would a robber, with swords and clubs to seize me? When I sat daily with you in the temple teaching, you didn't stretch out your hands against me or arrest me.

But this is your hour, and the hour for the power of darkness.

This is all happened so that the scriptures and the prophets would be fulfilled.

Then all the disciples left Jesus and fled. One of the friends of Jesus and the disciples, thought to be Mark, followed Jesus with just a linen cloth covering him, and they took hold of him, but he fled naked leaving them holding the linen cloth.

EXAMINATION BY ANNAS

So the band and the chief captain and the officers of the Jews seized Jesus and bound him and lead him to Annas, who was the father in law of Caiaphas, the high priest that year.

Church of all National (Basilica of the Agony) in the Garden of Gethsemane

Caiaphas was the one who had given counsel to the Jews, that it was better that one man should die for the people.

The high priest *(Annas had been the high priest previous to Caiaphas, and was still called a high priest)* asked Jesus about his disciples and his teaching.

Jesus answered him:

I have spoken openly to the world, teaching in the synagogues where all the Jews come together. I have not taught anything in secret. Why are you asking me this? Ask those who heard me what I taught, they know the things I said.

And when Jesus said this, the officer standing by struck Jesus with his hand, saying:

Is that the way you answer the high priest?

Jesus answered him:

If I have spoken evil, bear witness of the evil. But if I have answered well, then why did you strike me?

CAIAPHAS AND THE SANHEDRIN

Annas sent Jesus, bound, to Caiaphas, the high priest. And all the chief priests and elders and scribes came together in the house of Caiaphas.

Now the chief priests and the whole council looked for false witnesses against Jesus so that they could put him to death. Many false witnesses came, but none agreed, and they could find nothing wrong with Jesus.

One said:

Jesus said that he could destroy the temple of God that is made with hands, and build another not made with hands in three days.

But none of the witnesses agreed.

And finally the high priest stood up in the midst of Jesus and said to him:

Aren't you going to answer any of the charges that these witnesses are bringing against you?

Jesus was silent and did not answer. Again, the high priest asked him:

Are you the Christ, the Son of the Blessed? I adjure you by the living God, tell us whether or not you are the Christ, the Son of God.

Jesus said to the high priest:

You have said I am. Nevertheless I say to you, in the future you will see the Son of man sitting at the right hand of Power, and coming in the clouds of heaven.

The high priest tore his clothes and said:

He has spoken blasphemy. What further witnesses do we need? You have heard his blasphemy. What do you think?

The others answered:

He is worthy of death.

And they all condemned him to be worthy of death.

The men who held Jesus mocked him and beat him. And some began to spit on him and to cover his face and ask:

Who struck you?

They hit him with their hands and did many other reviling things to him.

PETER DENIES THE LORD

Simon Peter had followed Jesus and so did another disciple. Now that disciple was known to the high priest's household, and they entered into the court of the high priest.

Nebi Samuel excavation site in Jerusalem

Peter followed along and was standing at the door outside the court of the high priest. The other disciple went and spoke to the woman who kept the door, and she let Peter inside.

The maid, who kept the door said to Peter:

Aren't you one of Jesus' disciples?

Peter replied:

I am not.

And Peter entered in.

Now the servants and the officers were standing by a fire of coals that they had going, warming themselves because it was cold.

Peter sat with them and as he was sitting there warming himself by the light of the fire, another servant girl came by and looked directly at Peter and said:

You were with Jesus the Galilean.

Peter denied it before all of them, saying:

I don't know what you are talking about. Woman, I do not know him.

Those who were with Peter by the fire said to him:

Aren't you one of his disciples?

Peter said:

I am not!

Then he went out into the porch, and the rooster crowed.

After a little while longer another said:

I am sure this man was with Jesus, for he is a Galilean.

But Peter said:

Man, I don't know what you are talking about.

And again they came to Peter and said:

Your accent gives you away; you're a Galilean and a disciple of Jesus.

And the rooster crowed the second time.

Then Peter began to curse and to swear:

I don't know this man who you are talking about.

And as soon as he said it while he was still speaking, they brought the Lord out of the house and he turned and looked at Peter.

Then Peter remembered how the Lord had told him that before the rooster crows twice you will deny me three times.

And Peter left, and as he thought about what he had done, he wept bitterly.

JESUS FORMALLY CONDEMNED

Now when the morning came, the assembly of the elders gathered together, both chief priests and scribes, and they led Jesus to the council:

If you are the Christ, tell us.

Jesus said to them:

If I tell you, you will not believe.

But in the future the Son of man will be seated at the right hand of the power of God.

And they said:

Are you the Son of God?

And Jesus said:

Jerusalem's Jewish Quarter at sunset

You say it because I am.

And they said:

We do not need any witnesses; we have heard it out of his own mouth.

And the whole company of them rose up and bound Jesus and led him away from Caiaphas into the **Praetorium**† and brought him before Pilate, the governor.

It was early in the morning.

JESUS BEFORE PILATE

The Jews would not enter into the Praetorium, because they believed it would defile them and disqualify them from keeping the Passover.

So Pontius Pilate went out to them and said:

What accusation do you bring against this man?

They answered:

If this man was not an evildoer, we would not have brought him to you.

Pilate said to them:

Take him and judge him yourself according to your law.

The Jews said to Pilate:

It is not lawful for us to put a man to death.

This happened so that the word of Jesus might be fulfilled. He had spoken of the manner of death by which he would die.

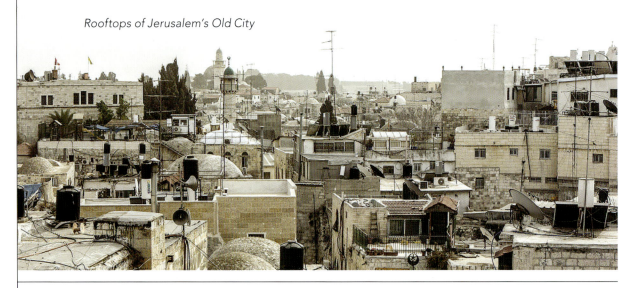

Rooftops of Jerusalem's Old City

† Further reading available at the end of this chapter.

And they began to accuse him, saying:

*We found this man perverting our nation and forbidding us to give tribute to **Caesar**†, and saying that he is the Christ, a king.*

Pilate entered into the Praetorium and called Jesus. Jesus stood before the governor who asked him:

Are you the King of the Jews?

Jesus answered:

Are you saying this yourself or did others tell you about me?

Pilate answered:

Am I also a Jew? Your own nation and your chief priests have delivered you up to me. What have you done?

Jesus answered:

My kingdom is not of this world. If my kingdom was of this world, then my servants would fight to keep me from being delivered up to the Jews.

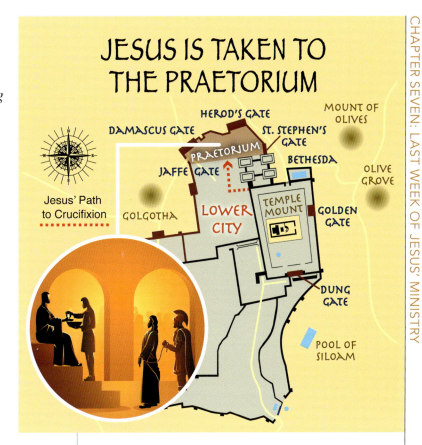

Pilate said to him:

Are you a king then?

Jesus answered:

You say that I am a king, for this purpose I have been born and for this purpose I have come into the world, that I should bear witness to the truth. Every one who is of the truth hears my voice.

Pilate said to him:

What is truth?

† Further reading available at the end of this chapter.

And after he said this, he went out to the Jews and said to the chief priests and the crowds:

I find no fault in this man, no crime in him.

Then the chief priests accused Jesus of many things. Jesus did not answer back.

Pilate again asked Jesus:

Listen to all the things they are accusing you of. Don't you have anything to say for yourself?

Jesus would not say a word, and Pilate was amazed.

But the chief priests became even more urgent, saying:

He stirs up the people, teaching throughout all Judea, from Galilee to Jerusalem.

JESUS BEFORE HEROD ANTIPAS

When Pilate heard this he asked:

Is Jesus a Galilean?

He knew that this was Herod Antipas' jurisdiction. When the answer came back, *yes*, Pilate sent Jesus to Herod who was in Jerusalem for the festival.

Now when Herod saw Jesus, he was very glad, for he had been wanting to see Jesus for a long time. Herod had heard about all the mighty works that Jesus did, and hoped to see a miracle.

Herod questioned Jesus at length, but Jesus would not answer him.

The chief priests and the scribes also stood before Herod accusing Jesus vehemently.

Old back street in Jerusalem

Herod and his soldiers began mocking Jesus and clothing him in gorgeous apparel, but finding nothing wrong with him, they returned him to Pilate.

Pilate and Herod, who had been bitter enemies, became friends that day.

PILATE SENTENCES JESUS

Now it was the custom at the feast of Passover that the authorities would release a prisoner. And there was one notable prisoner, a murderer and a rebel against Rome named Barabbas.

And the multitude went up to Pilate and began demanding their annual gift of a released prisoner. Pilate saw this as an opportunity to escape his difficulties over Jesus.

When they had gathered together, Pilate asked them:

Would you like me to release Jesus, the King of the Jews? I have examined him and I can find no fault in him.

Herod cannot find anything wrong with him either. According to your custom, I will chastise Jesus and then release him.

Or I can release Barabbas. Which would you like me to release to you, Barabbas, a murderer and a rebel or Jesus?

But they cried out all together, saying:

Away with this man, release Barabbas.

While Pilate was sitting in the judgment seat, a message came from his wife. The message said:

I have had terrible dreams regarding this man Jesus, you must release him and have nothing further to do with him.

The chief priests and the elders stirred up the multitude so that they should demand the release of Barabbas and destroy Jesus.

They cried out again saying:

Not this man, but Barabbas.

Pilate spoke to them again trying to persuade them that he should release Jesus.

The crowds would hear none of it and began shouting:

Crucify, crucify him.

They all said:

Let him be crucified.

Pilate tried the third time, asking them:

What evil has this man done? I can find nothing in him that deserves death: I will chastise him and release him.

But the crowds just became more agitated, saying:

Christ and Pilate, painted by Nikolai Ge

Crucify him. Let him be crucified.

Then Pilate took Jesus and scourged him.

And the soldiers forced a crown of thorns on his head and put a purple robe around his neck. They came to him and said:

Hail, King of the Jews!

And they struck him with their hands.

Pilate hoped that the crowd would be satisfied with the humiliation and punishment of Jesus.

He had Jesus brought out in front of the people wearing a crown of thorns and a purple robe.

Pilate said to them:

Behold, the man!

When the chief priests and the officers saw him they cried out:

Crucify him, crucify him.

Pilate said:

Take him and crucify him yourselves, for I can find no crime in him.

The Jews answered him:

We have a law that he should die because he made himself out to be the Son of God.

When Pilate heard this he was even more afraid and went into the Praetorium again, taking Jesus with him.

He questioned Jesus:

Where did you come from?

But Jesus did not give him and answer.

Pilate said to him:

Don't you know that I have the power to release you or to crucify you?

Jesus answered:

You would have no power against me, except it was given to you from above. Therefore, he who delivered me up to you has the greater sin.

Hearing this, Pilate sought even more to release Jesus.

But the Jews cried out saying:

If you release him, then you are no friend of Caesar's. Everyone who makes himself a king is in opposition to Caesar.

When Pilate heard these words he brought Jesus out and sat him down on the judgment seat at a place called The Pavement, *(in Hebrew it was called, Gabbatha).*

It was the Preparation of the Passover, about the sixth hour. And he said to the Jews:

Behold your King.

They cried:

Away with him, away with him. Crucify him!

Pilate asked:

Shall I crucify your King?

The chief priests cried out:

We have no king but Caesar.

Finally, Pilate gave up. The harder he tried to release Jesus the more agitated the crowd became in their determination to have Christ crucified.

Pilate took water and washed his hands before the people. He said:

I am innocent of the blood of this righteous man. And the people answered and said, His blood be on us, and on our children.

Pilate then released Barabbas and turned Jesus over to them, to be crucified.

The soldiers of Pilate led Jesus away to the Praetorium court where they gathered other soldiers.

And when they had gathered a band of soldiers together, they stripped Jesus and clothed him again in purple robes, and again they placed the crown of thorns on his head and began mocking him.

They kneeled down to him and saluted him, saying:

Hail, King of the Jews!

And they spat on him and struck his head with a stick, and bowed their knees as if they were worshipping him.

Judean Hills green in spring, rock fences divide the fields

SUICIDE OF JUDAS

Judas, who had betrayed Jesus, saw that Jesus had been condemned. He changed his mind and brought back the thirty pieces of silver to the chief priests and elders, and said:

I have sinned; I betrayed innocent blood.

But they said to him:

What does that have to do with us?

Judas cast down the thirty pieces of silver and went away and hanged himself. And then his body fell to the ground and his bowels burst and gushed out.

The chief priests took the silver and said:

It is not lawful to put this money into the treasury, since it is blood money.

They met together and decided to buy a potter's field, in which to bury foreigners.

When they did this, they fulfilled the prophecy of Jeremiah who said:

And they took the thirty pieces of silver, the price of him, whom some of the children of Israel had set, and they bought a potter's field, as the Lord appointed me.

This field became known to all those that lived in Jerusalem as Akeldama, which means the field of blood.

ON THE WAY TO THE CROSS

And after the Roman soldiers had mocked Jesus, they took off his purple robe and put his own garments back on. They led him out to be crucified, and he went, carrying his own **cross**† for himself.

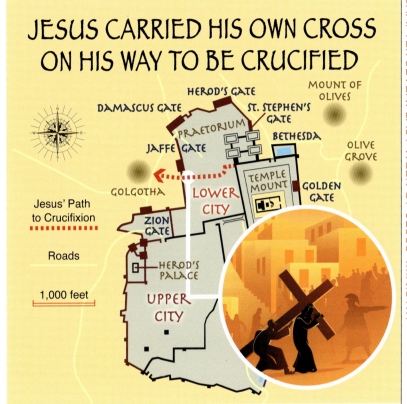

As they made their way to the place where Jesus was to be crucified, the Roman soldiers found a man named Simon of Cyrene (the father of Alexander and Rufus) and compelled him to carry the cross of Jesus.

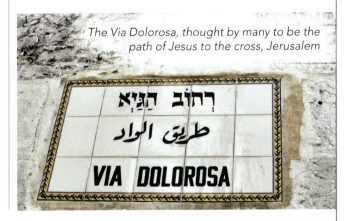

The Via Dolorosa, thought by many to be the path of Jesus to the cross, Jerusalem

† Further reading available at the end of this chapter.

THE STORY OF JESUS

And a great multitude followed and all the woman wailed and lamented.

Jesus turned to them and said:

Daughters of Jerusalem, do not weep for me, weep for yourself and for your children. The day is coming when they will say, Blessed are the barren and the wombs that never bore children.

Then they will say to mountains, Fall on us, and to the hills, Cover us. For if they do these things when the tree is green, what will they do when it is dry?

There were two others who were criminals being put to death at the same time as Jesus. And they brought them to the place which is called in Hebrew, Golgotha. This means *the place of the skull*.

And when they had come to the place, they offered Jesus wine to drink, mingled with gall. When Jesus tasted it, he would not drink it.

JESUS CRUCIFIED

It was the third hour and they crucified him.

There were two others, both robbers and criminals, one on the right side and one of the left side of Jesus.

Jesus hung on a cross in the middle.

And Jesus said:

Father, forgive them for they do not know what they are doing.

The soldiers had taken Jesus' garments and divided them between the four of them. When they came to his coat, which was woven from top to bottom and had no seams, they said:

Let's not tear it apart, but cast lots to see which one of us will keep it.

When they did this, they fulfilled the scripture that said:

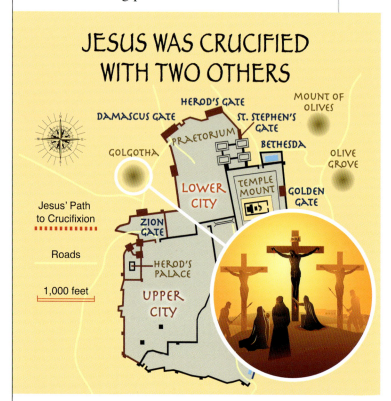

JESUS WAS CRUCIFIED WITH TWO OTHERS

They parted my garments among them, and upon my vesture did they cast lots.

Pilate wrote a title that he put above the cross. It said:

THIS IS JESUS OF NAZARETH, THE KING OF THE JEWS.

It was written in Hebrew, Latin and Greek. And all the Jews who were in the city near the place where Jesus was crucified read the title.

The chief priests and the Jews of Jerusalem went to Pilate and said:

Do not write that he is the King of the Jews, but write that he says he is the king of the Jews.

Pilate answered:

I have written what I have written.

The people stood looking, and as they passed by they wagged their heads, saying:

Ha! Here is the one that is going to destroy the temple and raise it up in three days. Save yourself if you are the Son of God, and come down from the cross.

In like manner, the chief priests and the rulers scoffed and mocked him along with the scribes and the elders saying:

He saved others, but he cannot save himself. If this is the Christ of God, his chosen, let him come down from the cross and we will see it and believe in him. He trusted God, let God deliver him if he wants to, for he said:

I am the Son of God.

If you are the King of the Jews, save yourself.

The robbers who were being crucified with Jesus also reproached him. One of the criminals railed at him saying:

Are you not the Christ? Save yourself and us.

The other robber who was also being crucified with Jesus said to his fellow criminal:

Don't you fear God, seeing that you are under the same condemnation? And we deserve this punishment for the things that we have done, but this man has done nothing wrong.

And then he said to Jesus:

Remember me when you come into your kingdom.

And Jesus said to him:

The truth is, today you will be with me in Paradise.

The mother of Jesus and her sister, along with Mary the wife of Clopas and Mary Magdalene were standing by the cross.

When Jesus saw his mother and the disciple whom he loved standing by, he said to his mother:

Woman, look, your son!

And he said to the disciple:

Behold, here is your mother!

Crosses carved into a stone in Jerusalem

From that hour on, the disciple took Mary into his own home.

THREE HOURS OF DARKNESS

Now it was about the sixth hour when darkness came over the whole land, and it lasted until the ninth hour.

Jesus is thought to have passed under this arks on the way to be crucified

About the ninth hour, Jesus cried with a loud voice saying:

Eli, Eli, lama sabachthani?

Which translated means:

My God, my God, why have you forsaken me?

And some who stood by, when they heard it said:

He is calling for Elijah.

After this, Jesus knew that all things were finished and that the scriptures had been accomplished. He said:

I thirst.

There was a vessel full of vinegar, and one of them ran and took a sponge and filled it with vinegar and put it on a hyssop reed and brought it to Jesus' mouth.

The rest of those standing around the cross said:

Let's see if Elijah comes to save him.

And when Jesus had received the vinegar, he cried again with a loud voice and said:

It is finished. Into your hands I commend my spirit.

And having said these words, he bowed his head and gave up his spirit.

And immediately the veil of the temple was torn into two pieces, in the middle from top to bottom.

And the earth shook and the rocks cracked in pieces, and the tombs were opened and many bodies of the saints who had died were raised, and they came out of

THE STORY OF JESUS

the tombs and walked into Jerusalem and appeared to many.

When the centurion, who stood watching Jesus saw him give up his spirit, and felt and saw the earthquake, and everything else that was happening, he was fearful. He glorified God, saying:

Certainly this was a righteous man.
This was the Son of God.

And the crowd that came together to view the sight of Jesus dead on the cross, went home beating their breasts in sorrow.

And all Jesus' acquaintances were there at the cross, and many women who had followed Jesus from Galilee, including Mary Magdalene, and Mary the mother of James and Joses and Salome. They had ministered to Jesus and the disciples.

JESUS FOUND TO BE DEAD

Because the Sabbath of the Passover week was approaching and the Jews did not want any bodies hanging on the cross on that Sabbath, they asked Pilate to **break their legs**† and dispose of the bodies.

The soldiers came and broke the legs of the first criminal, but when he came to Jesus he saw that he was already dead. So they did not break his legs. But to be sure that Jesus was dead they took a spear and pierced his side. Blood and water poured from his wound.

This fulfilled the scripture that said:

Not a bone of his body will be broken.
And again, They will look on him who they pierced.

Joseph of Arimathaea, who was a rich man, and also a good and righteous man, had not consented to what the chief priests and rulers of Israel had done. He was also looking for the kingdom of God, and was a secret disciple of Jesus, fearing the Jews.

He boldly went to Pilate and asked for the body of Jesus.

Pilate was amazed that Jesus was already dead and called the centurion in charge to ask how long Jesus had been dead.

The centurion verified that Jesus was dead, and told Pilate the details of his death. Pilate then gave the body of Jesus to Joseph of Arimathaea.

Nicodemus, who had come to Jesus by night, had also come to help with the dead body of Jesus. He brought with him about

† Further reading available at the end of this chapter.

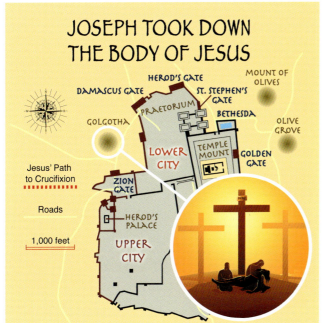

a hundred pounds of myrrh and aloes. Joseph brought linen cloth.

Joseph took down the body of Jesus and wrapped him in linen cloth with **spices**†, which was the burial custom of the Jews.

Now, near the place where Jesus was crucified, there was a garden, and in the garden there was a new tomb that had been carved out of the rock. No one had been buried in this tomb before.

They laid Jesus in the tomb and rolled a great stone up against the door of the tomb, and left.

The women who had come from Galilee followed after Joseph and his party and saw the place where Jesus' body was laid. Mary Magdalene was there, and the other Mary.

They returned to where they were staying to prepare spices and ointments for burial. But they rested on the Sabbath day.

The chief priests and Pharisees gathered together and came to Pilate. They said to Pilate:

Sir, we remember that this deceiver said while he was still alive that he would rise again after three days.

Command that the tomb be guarded until the third day, so that one of his disciples does not come and steal the body and say to the people that Jesus is risen from the dead, which would make matters worse.

Pilate said to them:

I will give you a squadron of guards so that you can go and make the tomb as secure.

So they went and secured the tomb where Jesus had been laid, sealing the stone and posting guards around it.

END OF CHAPTER SEVEN

† Further reading available at the end of this chapter.

CHAPTER SEVEN
COMPANION

BREAKING THE LEGS (page 278)
Since the cross stood upright, victims were in a position where the only way they could exhale was to push on their feet to try to raise themselves up. Eventually they would suffocate. In order to speed up the process, the soldiers would break the victim's legs so they couldn't push themselves up to breathe.

This was done to the two thieves on either side of Jesus, but when the soldiers came to Jesus, they didn't break his legs because they saw he was already dead.

CROSS (page 273)
A vertical beam with a horizontal piece attached to it. In crucifixion, a victim's arms were stretched out and attached, usually nailed, to the horizontal piece, and the feet were overlapped and nailed to the vertical part.

Since the cross stood upright, victims were in a position where the only way they could exhale was to push on their feet to try to raise themselves up.

MONEYCHANGERS (page 220)
Moneychangers were Jews who charged other Jews to change their currency into special temple currency. Many Jews traveled long distances to come to the temple in Jerusalem to sacrifice an animal as a symbol of the penalty for the sins they have committed. If it was too far to bring an animal, they had to buy an animal at the temple, but the people who sold the animals would only take temple currency.

PRAETORIUM (page 266)
The Roman military headquarters in a city where the Roman governor also resided. When the soldiers took Jesus into the praetorium, it was a room or a courtyard in complex from where Pilate ruled and probably lived.

THE STORY OF JESUS

SPICES AND OINTMENT FOR BURIAL (page 266)

Under Jewish burial custom, the body was washed, then wrapped tightly using strips of cloth with a combination of powdered and gummy spices in the folds to hold the cloth in place and make it smell nice out of respect for the person who died.

The body was wrapped from the ankles to the shoulders with a separate cloth for the head.

Aloes was probably a gum or perfume extracted from a fragrant wood. The head was often anointed and covered separately.

The women were in a hurry to bury Jesus before the Sabbath, and they probably wrapped his body and planned to come back later to add more spices and perfume.

This is another confirmation of the resurrection, because the burial cloths were wrapped tightly with what essentially was glue. It would have been like a body cast from Jesus' ankles to his shoulders. And yet on the third day he was walking around with no grave cloths.

TALENTS (page 240)

A significant amount of money. Possibly about a month's wages.

TIBERIUS CAESAR (page 267)

Jesus was crucified in the fifteenth year of the reign of Tiberius Caesar, the emperor of Rome. Tiberius had distinguished himself as a citizen for his oratory skills, as a soldier and a public official. As emperor of Rome he was slothful, self indulgent, licentious, vindictive and cruel. He was a master at lying and he was very cunning.

Roman coin with image of Tiberius Caesar

CHAPTER EIGHT

RESURRECTION OF JESUS

ANGELS ANNOUNCE THE RESURRECTION

When the Sabbath was past, on the first day of the week, early in the morning, they came to anoint the body of Jesus.

Mary Magdalene and the other Mary had prepared spices and were coming to prepare the dead body of Jesus for final burial.

Before they approached the tomb, there was a great earthquake and an angel of the Lord descended from heaven and came and rolled away the stone and sat upon it.

The angel's appearance was like lightning and his clothing was white as snow. The Roman guards were paralyzed with fear, and became like dead men.

Later, Mary Magdalene and the other Mary and others came to the place where Jesus had been buried. It was early Sunday morning.

The stone was rolled away and the Roman guards were gone. When they entered the tomb, the Lord's body was not there.

Mary Magdalene ran to find Simon Peter and the other disciple whom Jesus loved, and when she found them she said:

They have taken the Lord out of the tomb, and we do not know where they have laid him.

THE STORY OF JESUS

While Mary was going to get Peter and John, two angels appearing as young men in dazzling apparel appeared to those who were still at the tomb.

They were very frightened and bowed down their faces to the earth.

The angel said to the women:

Don't be afraid. We know that you are looking for Jesus, the Nazarene, who has been crucified.

Why are you looking for the living among the dead? He is not here, but he is risen, just like he said he would.

Don't you remember what he told you when he was in Galilee? The Son of man was going to be delivered up into the hands of sinful men and be crucified and rise again on the third day.

They remembered the words of Jesus.

The angel said:

Come, look at the place where they laid him! See the place where the Lord lay.

Now, go quickly and tell his disciples and Peter:

He is risen from the dead and he is going to meet you into Galilee. You will see him there.

They departed quickly and fled from the tomb with fear and with great joy. They ran to bring word to the disciples. They did not tell anyone they met on the way about what had happened, because they were trembling and astonished.

After Mary found them, Peter and John ran to the tomb. John outran Peter and arrived first. He stooped down and looked at the linen cloth that was lying in place.

Peter ran right into the tomb and saw the linen cloths lying by themselves and the napkin that had been upon Jesus' head. It was rolled up in a place by itself.

Then the other disciples entered the tomb and saw and believed that Jesus had risen from the dead.

The disciples went home wondering about all that had happened.

APPEARANCES OF THE RISEN CHRIST

After Peter and John had gone home to ponder what they had seen, Mary Magdalene returned to the garden where Jesus had been buried.

Mary was standing outside the tomb weeping. As she wept, she stooped down and looked into the tomb. She saw two angels in white, one at the head and the other at the foot of where Jesus had been laid.

Jesus then came up to Mary and said to her:

Garden Tomb

Woman, why are you weeping?

Mary did not recognize him because of her sorrow. She thought he was the gardener. She said:

They have taken away my Lord and I do not know where they have laid him.

She then turned back to Jesus and saw him plainly and recognized him. She said in Hebrew:

Rabboni (Teacher).

Jesus said to her:

Do not touch me, for I have not yet ascended to the Father. Go to my brothers and tell them I am ascending to my Father and your Father, and my God and your God.

Mary Magdalene went and told some of the disciples:

I have seen the Lord, he is alive.

But they disbelieved her.

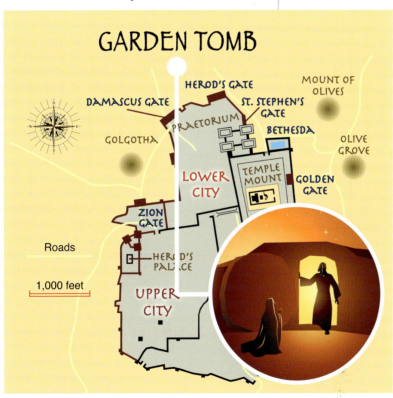

THE STORY OF JESUS

Later Jesus met Mary Magdalene and the others who had come to anoint his body. He said:

Rejoice!

They came and took hold of his feet and worshipped him.

Jesus said to them:

Do not fear, go tell my brothers who are going to Galilee that they will soon see me.

The ones who had seen Jesus were Mary Magdalene, and Joanna, and Mary, the mother of James and the other women who were with them.

They told the disciples, but they did not believe. The disciples thought it was idle talk.

GUARDS REPORT TO THE JEWISH RULERS

While the group of women were gone to tell the disciples, some of the soldiers who had been guarding the tomb went to the chief priest and told them all the things that had happened.

After they were assembled and had considered the matter, the officials gave money to the soldiers and told them to report that the disciples of Jesus had stolen the body of Jesus while they slept. The said:

If news of this gets to the governor's ear, we will persuade him to overlook the offense.

They took the money and did as they were told. The report spread among the Jews and is still reported to this day.

THIRD AND FOURTH APPEARANCES OF JESUS

After this, Jesus appeared to two disciples as they walked toward Emmaus, a village near Jerusalem.

As these two were talking to each other, Jesus walked up to them. Jesus hid who he was.

Jesus said to them:

Inside the Garden Tomb

What are you talking about as you walk?

They stood still, looking sad.

One of them, whose name was Cleopas, answered:

Are you the only one in Jerusalem who does not know what has happened in the past couple of days?

Jesus said:

What things?

They answered:

The things concerning Jesus the Nazarene, who was a prophet, mighty in word and deed before God and all the people.

And how the chief priests and our rulers delivered him up to be condemned to death, and crucified him. But we hoped that he was the one that was going to redeem Israel.

Besides all this, it is now the third day since these things came to pass. And some women of our company amazed us, having gone to the tomb and finding it empty. They saw a vision of angels who said that Jesus was alive.

Some of those who were with us went to the tomb and found it empty like the women said.

Jesus said to them:

O foolish men, and slow of heart to believe in all that the prophets have spoken. Wasn't it written that the Christ should suffer all these things, and enter into his glory?

And then, beginning from Moses and including all the prophets, he interpreted to them all the scriptures and all the things concerning himself.

As they came to their village, Jesus began to walk further. The disciples stopped him and said:

Stay with us, for it is getting dark and the day is almost over.

Jesus went with them and stayed with them. When it came time for the meal, he sat down to eat with them and he took bread and blessed it and gave it to them. At that moment, their eyes were opened, and they saw it was Jesus, and Jesus instantly vanished from their sight.

The disciples said to one another:

Didn't our hearts burn within us, while he spoke to us on the road and opened the scriptures to us?

They got up that very hour and returned to Jerusalem and found the 11 together and those who were with them *(about one hundred and twenty).*

They told the disciples and the others how Jesus had made himself known to them, but the disciples did not believe.

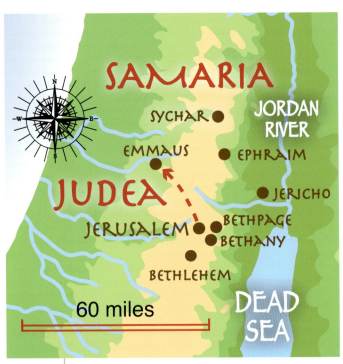

FIFTH APPEARANCE OF JESUS

While the disciples from Emmaus were still speaking, Jesus appeared to the disciples as they sat eating together.

The disciples were in fear of the Jews and had locked the doors where they were staying. So when they saw Jesus

they became terrified and afraid, thinking that he was a spirit.

Jesus scolded them for their unbelief and hardness of heart for not believing the eyewitnesses who had already reported his resurrection:

Why are you troubled and why do you have questions come up in your minds? See my hands and my feet. It is me.

Touch me for yourselves and convince yourselves that I am not a spirit. Does a spirit have flesh and bones, as you see that I have?

Then Jesus showed them the wounds in his hands and his feet and his side.

While they were still in shock and suffering from a combination of fear and joy, Jesus asked them:

Do you have anything to eat?

They gave Jesus a piece of boiled fish, and he took it and ate it in front of them.

The disciples were glad when they saw the Lord.

Jesus said to them:

Peace be with you. Just as the Father has sent me, in the same way, I send you.

When he had said this, he breathed on them and said to them:

Receive the Holy Spirit. Whoever's sins you forgive, they are forgiven, and whoever you withhold forgiveness from is not forgiven.

But Thomas, one of the twelve, called *Didymus*, was not with them when Jesus came.

When the other disciples told Thomas that they had seen the Lord, he did not believe it. He said:

Unless I see the nail prints on his hands and put my hand into the wound in his side, I will not believe.

SIXTH APPEARANCE OF JESUS

After eight days, the disciples were together again in a room that had been bolted from the inside for fear of the Jews. This time, Thomas was with them.

Peace be with you.

Then he said to Thomas:
Look at my hands and touch my wounds, take your hand and put it into my side. Don't be faithless but believe.

Thomas answered and said to Jesus:

My Lord and my God.

Jesus said to him:

Because you have seen me, you believe. Blessed are those who have not seen me and yet have believed.

Jesus made many other signs in their presence, which are not written in this book.

But these things are written that you might believe that Jesus is the Christ, the Son of God; and that by believing you may have life in his name.

SEVENTH APPEARANCE OF JESUS

After this, Jesus appeared to them again at the sea of Tiberias.

Peter had decided to go fishing and the other disciples followed along. They went into a boat and fished all night, but caught nothing.

When the morning came, they saw a man standing on the beach. The disciples did not immediately recognize that it was Jesus. Jesus said to them:

Children do you have anything to eat?

Almond tree blossoms in spring

They answered:

No.

Jesus said to them:

Cast your net on the right side of the boat and you will find some.

They did as Jesus said, and the nets were so full that they could not lift them into the boat.

John said to Peter:

It is the Lord!

When Peter knew it was Jesus, he wrapped his coat around himself and jumped from the boat and swam for shore.

The other disciples stayed in the boat and made their way to shore dragging the nets full of fish.

When they got to land, they saw that Jesus had started a fire and the coals were burning, and fish was cooking and there was bread.

Jesus said to them:

Bring some of the fish you have caught.

Peter pulled the nets full of fish onto the shore. They had caught one hundred and fifty three large fish, but the nets had not broken.

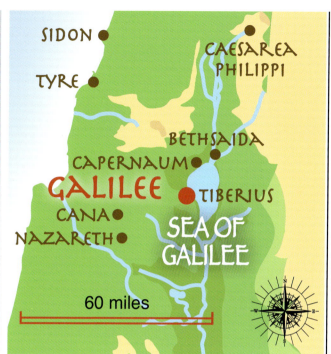

Jesus said:

Come and have breakfast.

Jesus gave them bread and fish.

This was the third time Jesus appeared to the disciples after he had risen from the dead.

After eating breakfast, Jesus said to Simon Peter:

Simon, son of John, do you love me better than fishing?

He answered:

You know that I love you.

Jesus said to him:

Feed my lambs.

Again the second time, Jesus asked Peter:

Peter, do you love me more than this fishing business?

Peter answered:

Yes, Lord, you know that I love you.

Then Jesus said to him:

Take care of my sheep.

Then Jesus said to Peter the third time:

Peter, son of John, Do you love me?

Peter replied:

Lord, you know all things, you know that I love you.

Jesus said to him:

Feed my sheep.

Truly, truly I tell you, when you were young, you walked where you wanted to walk. But

when you are old, you will stretch out your hands and someone else will carry you where you do not want to go.

Jesus was telling Peter ahead of time how his death would glorify God.

And after Jesus said this, he said to Peter:

Follow me.

Peter, turning around and seeing John, asked Jesus:

And what will happen to John?

Jesus said to Peter:

If I willed that John live until I come again, what business is that of yours?

Even though Jesus did not say that John would not die, the rumor got started among the other disciples that he would not die.

There are many other things that Jesus did, which if they should all be written would fill the world with books.

EIGHTH APPEARANCE OF JESUS

The eleven disciples went into Galilee, up on the mountain where the Lord had said that he would meet them. And they were joined by five hundred other friends and relatives of Jesus.

Jesus appeared to them all, and they worshipped him, but a few doubted.

Mount of Olives

THE GREAT COMMISSION

Jesus came to them and spoke to them:

All authority has been given to me in heaven and on earth.

Go into the world and preach the gospel to the whole creation. And make disciples of all the nations, baptizing them into the name of the Father and the Son and the Holy Spirit, teaching them to observe all the things I have commanded you.

He who believes and is baptized will be saved, but he who disbelieves will be condemned.

This it is written that the Christ should suffer and rise again from the dead on the third day, and that repentance and remission of sins should be preached in his name to all the nations, starting in Jerusalem.

And these signs will accompany those who believe: In my name they will cast out demons, they will speak with new tongues, they will take up serpents, and drink deadly things, and it will not hurt them. They will lay hands on the sick and they will be healed.

I am with you always, even to the end of the world.

THE STORY OF JESUS

NINTH AND TENTH APPEARANCES OF JESUS

Jesus also appeared to James. He showed himself to be alive to the apostles over the space of forty days and with many proofs. He spoke to them about the kingdom of God.

He told them not to leave Jerusalem, but to wait for the promise of the Father, who he said, he had heard from him.

Jesus reminded them:

John baptized with water. But you will be baptized in the Holy Spirit not many days from now.

These are my words which I spoke to you while I was with you, that all things written in the law of Moses and the prophets and the psalms concerning me needed to be fulfilled.

Then he opened their minds so that they would understand the scriptures.

He showed them where it was written that Christ should suffer and rise again from the dead on the third day, and that repentance and remission of sins would be preached in his name to all the nations, starting with Jerusalem.

Then Jesus told them:

I send you out with the promises of my Father. But stay in the city until you are clothed with power from on high.

They asked the Lord:

Is this the time you are going to restore the kingdom of Israel?

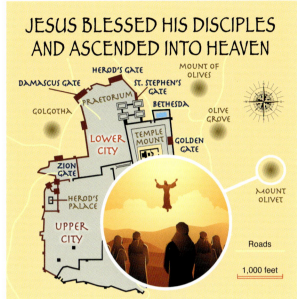

Jesus said to them:

It is not for you to know the time or seasons that the Father has set within his own authority.

But you will receive power, when the Holy Spirit is come upon you, and you will be my witnesses in Jerusalem, and in Judea and Samaria, and to the uttermost part of the earth.

THE ASCENSION

After the Lord had spoken to them, he led them out to the mount called Olivet. And he blessed them, and then he was carried into heaven.

They watched him ascend into a cloud and sit at the right hand of God. And they worshipped him.

And while they were still looking into heaven, two angels in human form, stood by them in white apparel.

And they said to them:

You men of Galilee, why are you standing here looking into heaven? Jesus, who was received up into heaven will come again in the same way that you saw him go.

Then they returned to Jerusalem from the mount called Olivet, with great joy.

And they were constantly in the temple, blessing God. And they went out and preached everywhere, the Lord working with them and confirming the word by the signs that followed.

Praise God!

OUR LORD APPEARS AFTER HIS ASCENSION

And the apostle Paul said:

And last of all, as to a child born late, he appeared to me also.

END OF CHAPTER EIGHT

OUR INVITATION

RESPONSE TO THE PROCLAMATION

Jesus began his ministry here on earth by choosing twelve disciples.

Jesus is still calling disciples. He wants you to know the story of his life so you will believe it, and put your trust in him as savior.

It is not an accident that you may at this very moment be considering claims he made to be the Son of God.

Can you see yourself as one of the characters in the story of Jesus?

Jesus wants you to realize that just as Lazarus was physically dead, so you also are spiritually dead in your sins.

He wants you to know that he stands ready to call you out of that place of death and give your real life.

Jesus wants you to see yourself as the man born blind. He stands ready to give you true sight.

Jesus wants you to see the deeper meaning of why he miraculously fed the five thousand people - that is, that he is the true bread of life.

He wants you to believe in him so that you will never be hungry or thirsty again.

Jesus wants you to look at the cross on which he was crucified and ask the question. "Was it for me, Jesus, that you hung there and died? Was it my sins that caused you all that pain?"

Jesus wants you to consider the empty tomb and ask yourself another simple question: "Who but God has the power to rise from the dead?"

The same God who came to earth and lived the sinless life that you could never live, and die the death that you deserved to die, wants more from you than just to consider his story. He has arranged this encounter so that you might believe in him and have eternal life.

If you would like to know more, please contact us — we'd love to hear from you.

Visit **www.thestoryofjesus.com** and select the contact us link.

CHECK OUT OUR WEBSITE FOR OTHER TITLES!

www.lighthouse.pub

Author and editor C.J. Lovik spins a spectacular story of a family at the turn of the 20th century, full of adventure, mystery, life lessons, and solid biblical teachings. The mysteries surrounding Heaven are carefully revealed in both the plain text of Scripture and then amplified by the skillful unfolding of allegories. Those who read this book will understand more about Heaven.

Are you trapped in a prison of addiction or an unhealthy relationship? Have you been a victim of an empty religious experience that promised you rest? If so, you have found yourself in a snare set by Satan that promised rest but ended in a darkness that has robbed you of hope. Call on the name of Jesus and ask for freedom from your prison, and you will find rest.

This wonderful three-book box set is a must-have for any new believer, or for anyone desiring to grow deeper in the faith. The series explores three of the major works in the life of a follower of Jesus—Justification, Sanctification, and Glorification.

From the editor of the critically acclaimed and recently republished Pilgrim's Progress, author and editor C.J. Lovik brings a unique contribution to the retelling of this classic tale. Lovik brings a fresh and unique view, allowing for a modern audience to read and understand, yet preserving the deep and beloved truths of Bunyan's timeless tale.

www.lighthouse.pub
Visit our website to purchase books, DVDs, and otherChrist-centered media, and to preview upcoming titles.

Check out these amazing resources, and begin your journey to a closer relationship with our **Lord and Savior!**

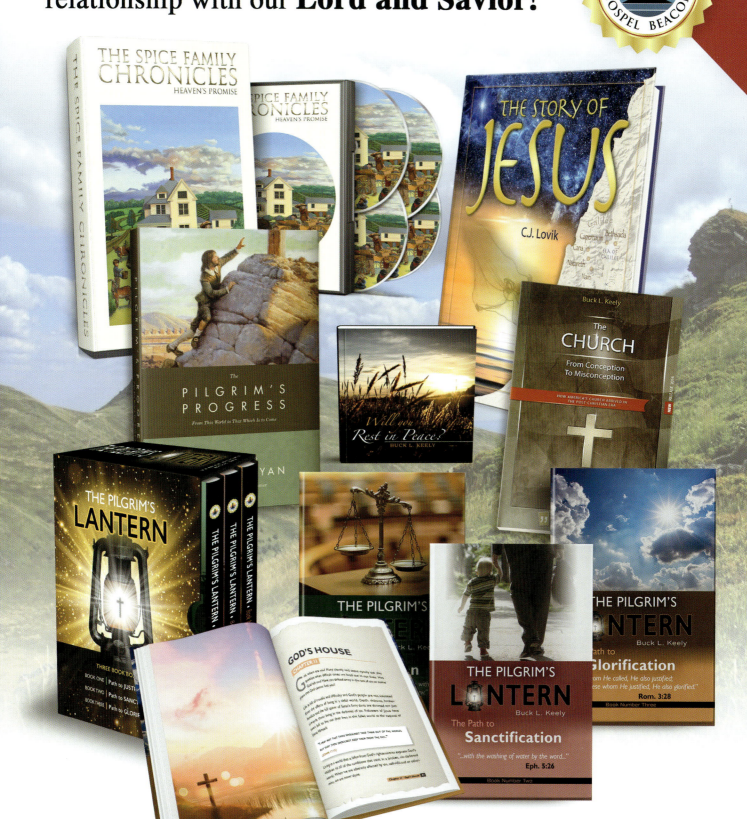

www.lighthouse.pub